T0133452

Accelerating Process Improvement Using Agile Techniques

Other Auerbach Publications in Software Development, Software Engineering, and Project Management

The Complete Project Management Office Handbook
Gerard M. Hill
0-8493-2173-5

Complex IT Project Management: 16 Steps to Success
Peter Schulte
0-8493-1932-3

Creating Components: Object Oriented, Concurrent, and Distributed Computing in Java
Charles W. Kann
0-8493-1499-2

The Hands-On Project Office: Guaranteeing ROI and On-Time Delivery
Richard M. Kesner
0-8493-1991-9

Interpreting the CMMI®: A Process Improvement Approach
Margaret Kulpa and Kent Johnson
0-8493-1654-5

ISO 9001:2000 for Software and Systems Providers: An Engineering Approach
Robert Bamford and William John Deibler II
0-8493-2063-1

The Laws of Software Process: A New Model for the Production and Management of Software
Phillip G. Armour
0-8493-1489-5

Real Process Improvement Using the CMMI®
Michael West
0-8493-2109-3

Six Sigma Software Development
Christine Tayntor
0-8493-1193-4

Software Architecture Design Patterns in Java
Partha Kuchana
0-8493-2142-5

Software Configuration Management
Jessica Keyes
0-8493-1976-5

Software Engineering for Image Processing
Phillip A. Laplante
0-8493-1376-7

Software Engineering Handbook
Jessica Keyes
0-8493-1479-8

Software Engineering Measurement
John C. Munson
0-8493-1503-4

Software Metrics: A Guide to Planning, Analysis, and Application
C.R. Pandian
0-8493-1661-8

Software Testing: A Craftsman's Approach, Second Edition
Paul C. Jorgensen
0-8493-0809-7

Software Testing and Continuous Quality Improvement, Second Edition
William E. Lewis
0-8493-2524-2

IS Management Handbook, 8th Edition
Carol V. Brown and Heikki Topi, Editors
0-8493-1595-9

Lightweight Enterprise Architectures
Fenix Theuerkorn
0-8493-2114-X

Outsourcing Software Development Offshore: Making It Work
Tandy Gold
0-8493-1943-9

Maximizing ROI on Software Development
Vijay Sikka
0-8493-2312-6

Implementing the IT Balanced Scorecard
Jessica Keyes
0-8493-2621-4

AUERBACH PUBLICATIONS

www.auerbach-publications.com
To Order Call: 1-800-272-7737 • Fax: 1-800-374-3401
E-mail: orders@crcpress.com

Accelerating Process Improvement Using Agile Techniques

Deb Jacobs

Auerbach Publications
Taylor & Francis Group
Boca Raton   New York

Published in 2006 by
Auerbach Publications
Taylor & Francis Group
6000 Broken Sound Parkway NW, Suite 300
Boca Raton, FL 33487-2742

© 2006 by Taylor & Francis Group, LLC
Auerbach is an imprint of Taylor & Francis Group

No claim to original U.S. Government works
Printed in the United States of America on acid-free paper
10 9 8 7 6 5 4 3 2 1

International Standard Book Number-10: 0-8493-3796-8 (Hardcover)
International Standard Book Number-13: 978-0-8493-3796-3 (Hardcover)

Library of Congress Cataloging-in-Publication Data

Catalog record is available from the Library of Congress

Taylor & Francis Group
is the Academic Division of Informa plc.

Visit the Taylor & Francis Web site at
http://www.taylorandfrancis.com

and the Auerbach Publications Web site at
http://www.auerbach-publications.com

Dedication

This book is dedicated to all the people I have had the opportunity to work with throughout my career. We all learn from each other and that is what makes us who we are today and who we will become in the future. Regardless of the experiences we have with each other, good or bad, we learn from each one of those people that touch our lives. Even in the bad experiences, we come away with important lessons to apply to our future endeavors. I want to thank each and every one of those people.

I especially want to thank my family who, as always, came to the rescue when I needed it and pitched in to help me get the book finalized. An extra thanks to my children and grandchildren for their patience when I told them to "Hold on," I have a sentence in my head! which was often. I can't leave out my pal, Angel, the dachshund, who came into my office when I was burning the midnight oil fussing at me to go to bed. Finally, to my friends, who were always there wanting to help whenever I needed it.

Contents

Preface

The purpose of the *Accelerating Process Improvement Using Agile Techniques* proposed in this book is to act as a tool to assist organizations in gaining process improvement. Process improvement will enhance their probability for successful IT projects. Scenarios described about Mark and Joe are prevalent throughout IT organizations, no matter what primary business a company may be engaged in. The result for companies includes loss of good people, money, reputations, and, ultimately, clients. This book describes a proven method for accelerating process improvement that will help set the direction and goals for organizations. This method will help get organizations started on the road to accelerated process improvement and to continue the journey to success.

In keeping with this book's goal to serve as a tool, a collection of templates, checklists, sample meeting agendas, and other materials are available for downloading from: http://www.crcpress.com/e_products/downloads/download.asp?cat_no=AU3796.

About The Author

Deb Jacobs is a Professional Consultant with Focal Point Associates specializing in process improvement and project management. She currently provides support to organizations in training, process improvement consulting, project management consulting, software engineering consulting, and proposal development. Ms. Jacobs has over 25 years' in project management, process improvement management, system/software engineering, and proposal development with a BS in Computer Science.

Ms. Jacobs's notable successes include leading successful CMM® Level 3 effort in one year, successfully reorganizing struggling projects, mentoring new managers, and gaining new business for companies through winning proposal development. She is former Software Process Improvement Network (SPIN) newsletter, SPINOUT, editor/originator; SES Process Focus newsletter editor/originator; IT magazine author; former CERT® Conference Chairperson; infotec Conference Deputy Software Tracks Chair; and SEI CMMI contributor.

About The Author

INTRODUCTION

Mark slugged down one more beer and figured it was about time to go home. This after-work party was getting boring. As he was getting ready to leave, Mark eyes a coworker that he has not seen in a long time.

"Hey, Joe!" Mark yelled across the crowded room.

"Mark, my man, long time," Joe answers, coming over to sit by Mark at the bar.

"How's life treatin' ya?" Mark asks, wondering why Joe, who's usually such a fun-loving guy, seemed so miserable.

"Oh, okay I guess," Joe said, unconvincingly, ordering another beer for himself and Mark.

"So, how's that high-profile project you were telling me about going?" Mark pressed.

"Hey between you, me, and the bartender, I've about had it!" Joe exclaimed.

"So, what happened?" Mark asked, "You said this was the opportunity of a lifetime last time we talked. The promotion to software project lead is what you've been working for since college."

"This has definitely turned out to be the project from hell! I thought the last project was bad but this one beats them all!" Joe complains. "We're always behind schedule and the costs are skyrocketing! We had to add three more engineers and you know what that's like, between training them and trying to get the real work done, we end up even farther behind."

"Yeah, I know what you mean," Mark empathized, "the project I'm on makes it hard to get out of bed in the morning, too."

"It just keeps going on and on with this company, all talk and no action," Joe says, "They tell us that they're working on it but nothing ever changes, same old thing every time. Get a new project, make unreasonable promises, and who suffers? We do."

"Yeah, I know what you mean!" Mark answers.

"Well I'm not going to take it any more; my resumé was out the door a week ago. I'm just fed up now. They can't all be this bad," Joe says hesitantly and adds, "Can they?"

"I hope not, I may be right behind you, Joe. Put in a good word for me when you find something," Mark says, commiserating as he orders another beer to wash down the gloom that is starting to overcome him, too.

Remind you of a project you've been on?

Chapter 1

Why Accelerate Process Improvement?

Mark and Joe represent many people in the IT industry today. This scenario is played out in organizations all over the country every day. Good people are lost, money is lost, reputations are lost, and, ultimately, clients are lost as a result of immature organizations. Companies can't afford to wait while bureaucracy plays itself out. The consequences can be overwhelming with projects over cost, over schedule, extensive overtime, loss of staff, misdirection, distrust, frustration, and confusion. Nobody likes to get caught with their pants down, which is typical of immature organizations. By accelerating the process improvement effort and getting processes in place quickly, an organization can concentrate on improving their processes over time and still remain competitive in an agile business environment.

Staying Ahead of the Competition

Process Maturity has proven to heighten the probability of success for IT projects. The problem with Process Maturity is that the majority of the time it costs companies a good deal of time and money that they cannot afford. By accelerating process improvement, they will be able to see their "bang for the buck" much quicker.

Many times the problems organizations encounter are due to excessive bureaucracy and lack of understanding. By using the Accelerated Process Improvement Methodology (APIM) organizations can overcome many of the bureaucratic obstacles that slow progress, hence achieving success quicker with less associated costs. APIM will be discussed in detail in later chapters.

IT projects have a distinct history of problems. Some of these problems have been curtailed by the trend toward process improvement and institutionalization of processes. The Standish Group[9,10,33] started researching projects and publishing their study results in 1994. They continue researching the success of projects on a larger and larger scale every other year, with the number of information technology projects up to 13,522 for the 2002 study, as reported in the 2003 CHAOS Report.

An initial look at the latest results published in 2003 makes it look as though projects are more successful; however, they actually point to more deep-seated problems. Figure 1-1, Standish Group Results Précis, summarizes the results of the

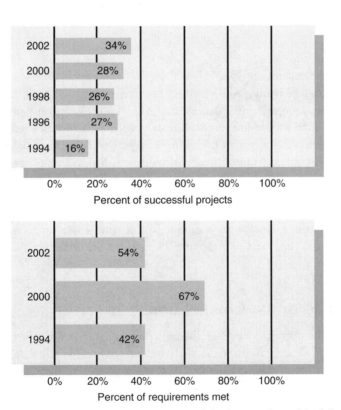

Note: Charts indicate year survey accomplished, reports issued the following year.

Source: The Standish Report

Figure 1-1   Standish Group Results Précis

CHAOS Reports.[9,10,33] These charts show that the success of projects has increased from only 16–34 percent. Success is defined as on schedule, within budget, and all original requirements (features and functions) are in place. Based on the current (2003) report, that leaves 66 percent of projects that are challenged or never delivered at all. In summary the 2003 CHAOS Report[9,10,33] shows:

- 66 percent of all software projects fail
- 82 percent of projects experience time overruns
- 48 percent of projects do not have the required features on product release
- $55 billion in US project waste (schedule, budget, scope).

One astonishing statistic that comes out of the CHAOS Reports[9,10,33] is that the majority of systems are delivered with only about 42–67 percent of requirements. This becomes even more critical when combined with findings that show 54 percent of system downtimes are caused by software and application errors, with another 19 percent caused by hardware and network errors, as shown in 2002 Monthly CENTS Survey based on over 97,000 entries. Hence, even though projects are being delivered on time and within budget, the statistics for delivering requirements and meeting customer expectations is decreasing significantly. Clearly, successfully making the schedule and cost at the expense of the product is not success.

The reality is that projects fail. In fact, they fail more often than they succeed according to the many surveys and studies conducted each year by leading independent groups and organizations. The studies agree that:

- Projects very often fail
- They are late
- They are over-budget
- They fail to deliver the product they were designed to produce
- Some projects don't produce any product at all.

The good news is that, sometimes, by examining our failures we can gain insight into what it takes to be successful. Many of the studies and surveys list why they have found that projects fail based on interviews with various project staff and managers. Consequently, many surveys and information technology experts have found there are many aspects of a project that have proven successful. Table 1-1, Success and Failure, lists some of these results.

Process Improvement offers a method of making the probability of success significantly higher for an organization's projects. It creates a smooth working environment where the wheel does not have to be reinvented for every project and projects reap the benefits of lessons learned from previous projects.

There have been a lot of changes and innovations that advertised that they would save development projects. Some of these include case tools, automated testing, agile development, and object oriented design and development. Each of

Table 1-1 Success and Failure

Reasons for Project Failures		
Standish Group Top Reasons for Project Failures	*Information Week Surveyed IT Managers*	*KPMG's Three Most Common Project Failure Reasons*
1. User involvement 2. Executive support 3. Experienced project manager 4. Clear business objectives 5. Minimized scope 6. Agile requirements process 7. Standard infrastructure 8. Formal methodology 9. Reliable estimates 10. Skilled staff	1. Poor planning or poor project management (77 percent) 2. Change in business goals during project (75 percent) 3. Lack of business management support (73 percent)	1. Poor project planning 2. Weak business cause 3. Lack of top management involvement and support

Essence of Success		
Standish Group Top Reasons for Project Success	*C. Jones Essential Attributes for Successful Software*	*S. McConnell's Software's Ten Essentials*

1. Most successful projects:
  • 6 month timeframe
  • Six people
  • $750,000 cost
2. User involvement
3. Executive support
4. Experienced project management
5. Clear business objectives
6. Good communications
	1. Effective project planning
	2. Effective project cost estimating
	3. Effective project measurements
	4. Effective project milestone tracking
	5. Effective project quality control
	6. Effective project change management
	7. Effective development processes
	8. Effective communications
	9. Capable project managers
	10. Capable technical personnel
	11. Significant use of specialists
	12. Substantial volumes of reusable material
		1. Product specification
		2. Detailed user interface prototype
		3. Realistic schedule
		4. Explicit priorities
		5. Active risk management
		6. Quality assurance plan
		7. Detailed activity lists
		8. Software configuration management
		9. Software architecture
		10. Integration plan

these has made things a little easier and has been successful in its own way to varying degrees with some making significant strides. However, the difference that the right application of process improvement can make to an organization far outweighs those benefits, not just in smooth operation but in a more satisfied staff and that's a major key to the success of any project.

What is Process Improvement?

Process Improvement puts the focus on the process in order to make the product better. It gives project staff and organizational staff members a consistent method of getting the same work done in the same general way, not technically but administratively, thus not reinventing the wheel each time a new effort is started and utilizing the valuable lessons learned from previous efforts.

Process Improvement came about as a result of the high failure rate and unpredictability of information technology projects. Various organizations jumped on the bandwagon to save information technology projects. There are many models and methodologies available for improving an organization's failure or success quota; a few of the more common ones include:

- Software Engineering Institute's (SEI) Capability Maturity Model® (CMM®), both the Software CMM® (SW-CMM®) and CMM® Integration (CMMI®);
- International Organization for Standardization (ISO) 9000 series;
- Software Process Improvement and Capability dEtermination (SPICE);
- Total Quality Management (TQM);
- Software Process Improvement in Regions of Europe (SPIRE);
- Project Management Institute's (PMI) Project Management Body of Knowledge (PMBOK®);
- Microsoft Operations Framework (MOF);
- Bootstrap;
- Business Process Reengineering (BPR) and Business Process Management (BPM);
- Knowledge Management;
- System Engineering Capability Model (SECM), also called Electronic Industries Alliance/Interim Standard (EIA/IS) 731;
- Six Sigma.

To date both the SW-CMM® and CMMI® have proven the most successful at providing viable process improvement thus maturing organizations. When used in combination with some of the other models and methodologies, such as the PMI PMBOK®, ISO 9001, and Six Sigma, organizations get the best of all worlds in process improvement to create a smooth working environment. It all depends upon your ultimate goals with the Process Improvement effort being undertaken.

In essence, Process Improvement provides a way of defining, documenting and continually improving processes for information technology organizations and projects.

What is a Process?

Organizations have a way of accomplishing business whether it's manual or automated. A process, in the context of Information Technology Process Improvement, is simply a means of documenting, organizing, and controlling the ways organizations accomplish business. When a particular model is used, an organization's processes should match the required elements of the selected model or methodology.

In general, a process is defined as:

- Webster's Dictionary: "A large or major undertaking, especially one involving considerable money, personnel, and equipment."
- CMMI®[3,4]: "Consists of activities that can be recognized as implementations of practices in a CMMI® model."
- IEEE: "A sequence of steps performed for a given purpose."
- SEI[5]: "...set of activities, methods, practices, and transformations that people use to develop and maintain software and the associated products."
- PMBOK®[30]: "A series of actions bringing about a result."

The key with processes is to remember that their primary purpose is to enable information technology staff to do their job more effectively by allowing them to concentrate on technical issues as opposed to administrative issues. If these primary goals are kept in mind throughout development of processes, it is more likely that the processes will be acceptable and used by organizational and project staff, which is the ultimate goal of any process improvement effort. In essence, processes give information technology staff the tools they need to benefit from lessons learned by others.

Process Maturity

Spencer Johnson, M.D., in his book *Who Moved My Cheese?*, said "Movement in a new direction helps you find new cheese."[21] This is especially appropriate for Process Maturity. Process Maturity is a constant change and evolution in a new direction and with that comes a new adjustment to the way things are done, in other words finding new cheese.

Immature organizations tend to rely on current staff knowledge. By doing so they tend to be constantly fighting fires and working in a reactive mode, as opposed to a proactive mode which is where the real work gets accomplished.

Process Maturity brings numerous benefits to an organization. The best way to illustrate that is by sharing comments from one of the successful Process Maturity efforts I conducted a few years ago. At the end of appraisal sessions, participants are asked "What is the one thing you feel has improved during the last year at your organization?" The participants included software and hardware engineers, business analysts, testers, Quality Assurance staff, Configuration Management staff, and Data Management staff, many of whom were naysayers at the beginning of the Process Maturity effort. They are reflective of the significantly positive changes that process maturity makes for an organization's day-to-day activities:

- "Communication."
- "Communication, working together."
- "Inter-project communication. Like All-Hands, presentations."
- "Communication between disciplines."
- "Things are written down and documented now so I can find information."
- "Use of WEB to share information."
- "Organization focus—establishing goals and objectives and achieving them."
- "Management's perception of the role and value of QA and CM."
- "Establishment of a common process and the processes."
- "Processes getting under control."
- "Project agreement that the PIs were important and that everyone can be involved."
- "Focus on process."
- "Process focus."
- "Processes in place that tell us how and what to do."
- "Movement towards plans and policies. More uniformity."
- "Documentation is much better."
- "Structure of program and process focus."
- "Control of software and the CM process."
- "Engineers saying that they understand the process."
- "Process. The following of processes."
- "Process definition."
- "Process focus, some cycle times have been cut in half."
- "More of an effort to get measures and try to improve the process."
- "Process improvements by the engineers. Their participation in the process."
- "Process helped us when short staffed."
- "Processes and organization."
- "Senior management sponsorship of process deployment and application."
- "Maturity of the organization."
- "Accelerated maturity of the organization."
- "Process awareness and acceptance."

- "Training."
- "Training and training budget."
- "Training has significantly improved."
- "This years training plan."

Why all the focus on process? Why not simply focus on people or technology? Processes have been proven to result in consistent quality products that require a significant amount of less rework, which significantly saves both time and money. A focus on processes has been a long-established premise with manufacturing and services industries but for some reason system development professionals many times balk at the idea. But the writing is on the wall; good living processes have proven to make a system development project much more successful and easier.

As discussed previously, surveys have found that by making people work harder instead of smarter makes them less productive because they are unhappy. That tends to be an overused adage but appropriate. In summary, you need a roadmap to apply technology appropriately.

Process Maturity Effect on Day-to-Day Operations

An effective Process Improvement effort will create a significantly smoother working environment. In essence, Process Improvement:

- Allows organizational staff the opportunity to solve the technical problems that are most important to building a system instead of worrying about the mundane details of a specific effort
- Gives new projects a place to go to find similar products to tailor to their needs thus eliminating that perpetual reinvention of the wheel
- Helps staff avoid making the same mistakes as others, avoid known pitfalls and problems
- Clarifies staff roles on projects and within the organization
- Identifies responsibilities to avoid confusion and overlapping duties that can cause conflicts
- Allows organizations to spread appropriate expertise throughout the organization
- Gives an organization a method of improving upon the organization and continuing to make it better.

As I've already indicated, Process Improvement is NOT about engineering, it's about giving engineers and the support staff a way of doing engineering through aids, processes, methods, templates, guidelines for both the engineer and the managers.

Process Maturity Enhancers and Barriers

There are several elements that can help an organization be successful in maturing processes, these are typically called enhancers. Some of the enhancers identified that can help organizations include:

- *Executive monitoring*—Executive monitoring provides the critical oversight and resources needed to accomplish process improvement.
- *Clear authority*—Clear authority must be given to a process improvement team so that they are armed with the authority to make changes as needed to meet the process improvement goals.
- *Assigned responsibility*—Staff must be given the responsibility to see that the process improvement goals are met.
- *Respected Process Group*—It is important during a process improvement effort that the group of staff members selected for the Process Group are respected members of the organization so that other staff members listen to them and follow their lead.
- *Involvement of technical staff*—By involving technical staff they are much more likely to buy into the process improvement effort and make the processes their own, thereby processes are more likely to be used by all organizational staff members.
- *Adequate resources*—Without adequate resources the entire effort will take longer or may not get accomplished at all. Adequate resources are subjective and will depend upon the scope and size of the effort.
- *Clear established goals*—Any task must have clear, established goals in order to know what direction to take the effort.

There are also some things that can hinder the progress of a process improvement effort, these are typically called barriers. Some of the barriers identified that can slow or negate progress for organizations include:

- *Organizational politics*—when managers within organizations concentrate on building politically correct relationships as opposed to project results it can have a very negative impact on the organization and projects. Relationships are important but can be harmful when put ahead of the team/project needs.
- *Overly ambitious*—An overly ambitious expectation of a project or of a process improvement effort can thwart the effort since they rarely are achieved and only create frustration and disappointment by all staff members.
- *Major reorganizations*—When there are major reorganizations in an organization, there are already many changes that staff must accumulate that a process improvement effort can be slowed or halted altogether.

- *Previous failures*—Organizations that have previous failures in maturing processes will cause their staff to be reluctant to put in the effort required to try to accomplish the process improvement goals. This is one reason that the APIM can be very successful since it results in small successes creating a winning attitude for the organization.
- *Hinders "real work" attitude*—The attitude that process hinders the "real work" is a typical attitude seen in many organizations. This is primarily due to the fact that many process improvement professionals tend to overwhelm organizations with a great deal of paperwork that may not be fully understood or accepted. The APIM stresses the "Keep It Short and Simple" method of developing processes, thus avoiding much of the paperwork that can be typically seen in organizations pursuing process maturity.
- *Executive turnover*—Organizational executives tend to have various agendas that are important to them, hence when a new executive comes into an organization many of the efforts such as process improvement can change, which may or may not be a deterrent to the current effort.
- *Paperwork approvals*—When there is a great deal of red tape and approvals to put things in place, it can significantly hinder progress.
- *Declined market*—When the market is declining, organizations may not be able to put the needed resources into process improvement efforts.
- *Turf guarding*—One of the basic premises of process improvement is sharing among projects, but when managers tend to guard their turf and not share their vast resources it can have a negative effect on both the process improvement effort as well as the organization as a whole.

Evolution of Process Improvement

Nightmare projects are not new. In fact, they've been around since information technology projects started being developed. The problem with the system development industry is that we still haven't learned from the mistakes of the past, we just keep doing things the same way over and over, even though we've learned better and it has been well documented by many well-known software gurus. There are many significant events in our history that have impacted the way American companies do business. Figure 1-2 illustrates a few of the ones that have had a significant impact.

Frederick W. Taylor, Father of Scientific Management

In the late 1800s, Frederick W. Taylor changed the way companies treated their workers. He developed principles for management that included the "one best

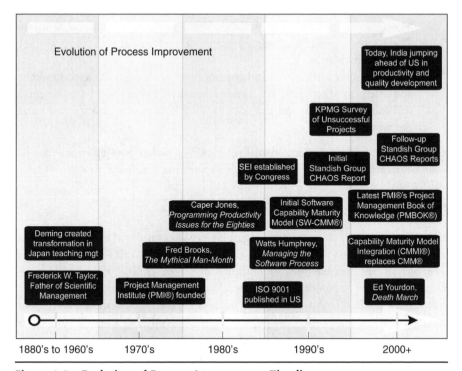

Figure 1-2 Evolution of Process Improvement Timeline

way"; he introduced the method of finding the "best way" to accomplish a task and then optimize it to get the greatest return in productivity. Frederick W. Taylor was a controversial character. To some he was seen as a "Workingman's Hero" and to others he was seen as a "soulless slave driver" but his principles are the basis for the way industry conducts business still today.

Frederick W. Taylor's primary goal was to increase efficiency in accomplishing tasks based upon time and motion studies of various production tasks. In 1911, he wrote a book called *The Principles of Scientific Management*[39] for which he became known as the father of Scientific Management. The principles set forth in this book became known as Taylorism. Some of these principles included:

- A "science" should be developed to find the "best way" to accomplish every job, including rules motion, standardized work implements, and proper working conditions.
- Workers should be selected carefully and scientifically based upon their abilities. They should then be trained to further develop their skills and given incentives to cooperate with the job science.

- Managements' relationship with workers should be one of cooperation. They must provide the needed planning and smooth the way as they accomplish their work.
- Finally, proportioning of tasks between management and workers should be addressed. In Frederick W. Taylor's words, "There is an almost equal division of the work and the responsibility between the management and the workmen."

Regardless of one's perception of Frederick W. Taylor, it is apparent that he started the momentum that led to today's Process Improvement efforts.

Dr. W. Edwards Deming

A significant individual in our more recent history who impacted the way American companies do business was Dr. W. Edwards Deming (1900–1993).[13] Dr. Deming's teachings of his management philosophy in Japan from 1950 created total transformation in Japanese business, resulting in what is known as "Japanese Industrial Miracle." Unfortunately, his teachings were not substantially accepted in America until the 1980s. The popular Plan-Do-Study-Act Cycle is sometimes attributed to Dr. Deming and is many times called the Deming Cycle. We will discuss this cycle in later chapters since it has formed the foundation for many of the current process improvement methodologies. Other contributions that Dr. Deming made to Process Improvement include the System of Profound Knowledge with the 14 Points for Management as shown in Figure 1-3. Finally, one of his most famous sayings is "In God we trust, all others bring data."

Project Management Institute Founded

The PMI has quickly become the "leading professional association in project management." It was founded in 1969 in the Commonwealth of Pennsylvania by five volunteers on the premise that management practices were common to various industries and crossed the typical boundaries of other practices. The founders felt that, regardless of the industry, most project management practices were the same.

Of note is that their first seminar and symposium in Atlanta, Georgia had 83 people in attendance so it's obvious that many were looking for a better, more common method of managing projects. The PMI has grown steadily since that first seminar to more than 100,000 members worldwide today. Members are from varying industries such as aerospace, automotive, business management, construction, engineering, financial services, information technology, pharmaceuticals and telecommunications.

The PMI's standards document is called the PMBOK®. It "includes proven, traditional practices which are widely applied as well as innovative and advanced

---

14 Points for Management
W. Edwards Deming

1. Create constancy of purpose toward improvement of product and service, with the aim to become competitive and to stay in business, and to provide jobs.
2. Adopt the new philosophy.
3. Cease dependence on mass inspection to achieve quality.
4. End the practice of awarding business on the basis of price tag.
5. Improve constantly and forever the system of production and service, to improve quality and productivity, and thus constantly decrease costs.
6. Institute training on the job.
7. Institute leadership.
8. Drive out fear, so that everyone may work effectively for the company.
9. Break down barriers between departments.
10. Eliminate slogans, exhortations, and targets for the work force asking for zero defects and new levels of productivity.
11. Remove barriers that rob the hourly worker of his right to pride of workmanship.
12. Remove barriers that rob people in management and in engineering of their right to pride of workmanship.
13. Institute a vigorous program of education and self-improvement.
14. Put everybody in the company to work to accomplish the transformation.

Figure 1-3   Dr. Deming's 14 Points for Management

ones which have seen more limited use."[30] By studying the PMBOK® as well as other PMI resources, members can become certified as a Project Management Professional (PMP®).

Fred Brooks, "The Mythical Man-Month"

More than 30 years ago, Fred Brooks wrote the infamous and, unfortunately, still applicable book, *The Mythical Man-Month.*[2] The book is based on the problems encountered when he was involved in two of the most influential computer projects of all time between the 1950s and 1970s. The projects were development of a Stretch interrupt system for IBM Stretch computer in 1957 that was patented by Brooks & Sweeney that introduced most of the features of today's interrupt systems and the IBM 360 Series that performed innovative at the time multi-tasking and introduced software compatibility between machines. Unfortunately, we are still making the same mistakes and having the same failures that he documented in his book. Based on books like this one we know what not to do and what to do to make projects successful but we don't seem to do them, thus costing companies billions of dollars each and every year. Some of his more famous and still applicable statements include:

- "... the man-month as a unit for measuring the size of a job is a dangerous and deceptive myth. It implies that men and months are interchangeable."[2]

- "... software managers often lack the courteous stubbornness of Antoine's chef."[2]
  - — "Good cooking takes time. If you are made to wait, it is to serve you better, and to please you." Menu of Restaurant Antoine, New Orleans[2]
- "Schedule progress is poorly monitored. Techniques proven and routine in other engineering disciplines are considered radical innovations in software engineering."

Capers Jones, "Programming Productivity for the Eighties"

Capers Jones is an international consultant who has written several books and thousands of articles on software management topics. He is the inventor of the first commercial software estimating tool to use function points and has been described as "an amazing source of metrics and data about every conceivable aspect of the software industry and the software engineering profession."

In the 1980s, Capers Jones wrote *Programming Productivity for the Eighties*[22] that consisted of 40 articles from the 1970s through 1986 era. This book discussed software productivity and quality and many of the common problems and major issues seen on software projects during that period of time. Some of the major issues discussed included measurements, requirements and design, life cycles, programming environments, and what he then called the "New Science of Software" in which reusability was a major topic. One of his most famous quotes is "If you can prevent defects or detect and remove them early, you can realize a significant schedule benefit. Studies have found that reworking defective requirements, design, and code typically consumes 40 to 50 percent of the total cost of software development."[22] Again, we are still making the same mistakes he described in his, unfortunately, still applicable book and the major issues and problems he discussed are still being discussed today.

SEI Established by Congress

In the early eighties, the Government was searching for ways to fix the problems they found that were inherent in the majority of projects. Congress established the SEI in 1984 at Carnegie Mellon University in Pittsburgh, Pennsylvania. The SEI found that there was a lack of shared vision in how to manage a project. They saw that there were some projects that had proven there were various processes that did not guarantee success but that gave projects a fighting chance. Some of the problems they encountered were that the development activities and the resulting products were unpredictable. They found that the development staff was the key to the success or failure of a project. They spent the next few years searching for a better way and continue improving upon those results.

Watts Humphrey, "Managing the Software Process"

About this same time, along came Watts Humphrey who is called the "Father of the Capability Maturity Model". In his book, *Managing the Software Process*[19], he introduced a framework of processes that would show the maturity of an organization based on best practices that were collected throughout industry. This framework eventually became what we know today as the Capability Maturity Model.

ISO 9001 Published in United States

International Organization for Standardization was established in 1947 by delegates from 25 countries "to facilitate the international coordination and unification of industrial standards." Currently, 147 countries are involved with headquarters in Geneva, Switzerland. ISO is primarily involved in setting technical standards for development, manufacturing and supply of products and services. Primarily, they are concerned with making products and services more efficient, safer, and cleaner, as well as making trade between countries easier and fairer.

ISO 9001 is part of the ISO 9000 family of international quality management standards and guidelines. It provides the requirements for certification by ISO as being a developer of quality products which refers to "services, processed material, hardware and software intended for, or required by, your customer." ISO 9001, Model for Quality Assurance in Design, Development, Production, Installation, and Servicing, focuses on anything that can affect the quality of products or services.

Initial Capability Maturity Model: SW-CMM®

The SW-CMM® is based on the "vision" of Watts Humphrey. Watts Humphrey was the original SEI director for development of this successful process improvement model. The model has been used by numerous Government and commercial organizations to mature their software development processes.

The original draft of the SW-CMM® was produced in 1990 with subsequent revisions until the final revision, Version 1.1, that's been widely used was produced in 1993. In 2000, the SEI upgraded the SW-CMM® to the CMMI® by integrating it with several other models and making it applicable to system development as opposed to just software development.

The SW-CMM® is based upon what the SEI found were best practices of many successful organizations as well as process management concepts of well-known software engineering and management gurus like Walter Shewart, Philip Crosby, W. Edwards Deming, and Joseph Juran. It provides a framework for generating and maturing software processes for organizations.

Initial Standish Group CHAOS Report

Several surveys have been accomplished in the quest to correct the success rate of software projects. The CHAOS Report[9,10,33] is the most popularized of these surveys with the initial CHAOS report being published in 1995. The CHAOS research was inspired by what bridge builders learned from the myriad of mistakes they made over time. They found that failures and mistakes made in the computer industry were "covered up, ignored, and/or rationalized. As a result, we keep making the same mistakes over and over again."[9,10,33] The moral of this story, we need to acknowledge our mistakes and learn from them.

KPMG Survey of Unsuccessful Projects

In 1997 an organization in Canada called KPMG published the results of surveys and research they did in failure of projects. The results of this survey are:

- Failure Project Statistics
  — 87% of failed projects exceeded schedule >30%
  — 56% of failed projects exceed budget >30%
  — 45% of failed projects failed to produce expected benefits.

These statistics are similar to the ones found by the Standish Group as well as other surveys.

Ed Yourdon, "Death March"[38]

Anyone who's been around software development for very long has heard of Ed Yourdon. He's a widely known consultant, commentator, advisor, writer, and practitioner. He's written 19 books and his articles have appeared in virtually all of the major computer journals. Computer developers may recognize him most as the innovator of the Yourdon Structured Method and co-developer of Coad–Yourdon Method for Object Oriented Analysis and Design. His most recent book is called *Death March: The Complete Software Developer's Guide to Surviving "Mission Impossible"*.[38] This book draws on his vast knowledge of software development. He tries, as many before and after him, to help projects learn from the vast failures or, in his words, "How to survive a programming project that seems doomed to failure, and how to tell when to bail out."[38]

Latest PMI PMBOK®

The PMBOK® consists of standards and practices that are widely accepted project management practices. They have been proven over time and include the more traditional methods used throughout industries as well as some more innovative ones. The PMBOK® has been approved as an American National Standard (ANS) by the American National Standards Institute (ANSI) with the ANSI standards number 99-001-2000. It is also recognized as a standard by the Institute of Electrical and Electronics Engineers (IEEE). Additionally, ISO has used it as a reference for managing software projects.

CMMI® Replaces SW-CMM®

The SEI found that organizations were using several models and methodologies in an effort to mature their organizations. Many of these models and methodologies were very much like the SW-CMM®. They saw a need for a coherent model that incorporated as many other like models as possible. From that need, the CMMI® was born. The following models were used as a basis:

- Software Engineering Institute's (SEI) Capability Maturity Model for Software Version 2.0 Draft C (SW-CMM®);
- Electronic Industries Association's Interim Standard 731 (EIA/IS 731), Systems Engineering Capability Model (SECM);
- Integrated Product Development Capability Maturity Model, draft V 0.98 (IPD-CMM®);
- ISO was considered; and
- Consistency and compatibility with ISO/IEC 15504 was considered.

In order to evolve organizations to the updated model, the SEI has no plans to continue maintaining the SW-CMM®. They have set up a program to "sunset" the successful model over time.

Follow-up Standish Group CHAOS Reports

The Standish Group continues to publish its study of the computer industry with even more extensive research. Unfortunately, the studies still show similar issues and similar problems being encountered. Figure 1-4 compares the top ten problems found on projects from the original CHAOS report in 1995 to the most current 2003 CHAOS report.[9,10,33] Similar problems on computer system development projects happen over and over and over again; this is the very

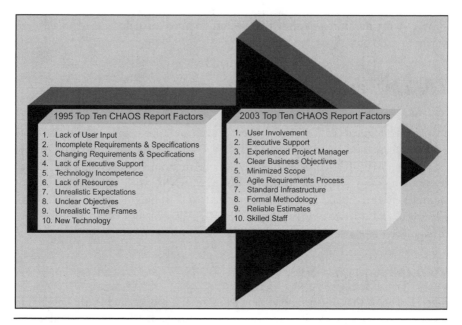

Figure 1-4   CHAOS Top 10

reason that process improvement models and methodologies have been so successful.

India Jumping Ahead of US

Did you know that India invented the zero and some actually credit them with making the first calculations of pi? Additionally, they developed complex astronomical observatories centuries ago. Today, they are making major strides in many diverse areas, including atomic energy, space remote sensing, biotechnology, electronics and oceanography. Oh Déjà vu! This does sound similar to Japan in the '50s and '60s; India is jumping ahead of America by leaps and bounds. Let this be our wake up call!

To what does India owe its success? Let's look at some of things that they value: quality and process. Top CMM® Appraisers indicate that they have never seen organizations embrace process improvement and project management improvement like India. They are making application of process and quality an integral part of their management philosophy. Models they tend to be embracing include both the SEIs CMM® and Six Sigma.

In order to keep up in the current fast moving international business environment, America needs to figure out how to keep up. A great start is by maturing organizational processes.

Summary

The consequences of immature organizations can be overwhelming. They can result in many adverse conditions such as projects over cost, over schedule, extensive overtime, loss of staff, misdirection, distrust, frustration, and confusion. By accelerating the process improvement effort and getting processes in place quickly, an organization can concentrate on improving its processes over time and still remain competitive in an agile business environment. We need to be able to keep up with countries like India that have had great success in producing quality software through use of process improvement.

Chapter Key Points

- By using the Accelerated Process Improvement Methodology (APIM) organizations can overcome many of the bureaucratic obstacles that slow progress, hence achieving success quicker with less associated costs.
- Studies show that, even though projects are being delivered on time and within budget, the statistics for delivering requirements and meeting customer expectations is decreasing significantly.
- Process Improvement gives project staff and organizational staff members a consistent method of getting the same work done in the same general way, not technically but administratively, thus not reinventing the wheel each time a new effort is started and utilizing the valuable lessons learned from previous efforts.
- To date both the SW-CMM® and CMMI® have proven the most successful at providing viable process improvement, thus maturing organizations.
- When used in combination with some of the other models and methodologies such as the PMI PMBOK®, ISO 9001, and Six Sigma, organizations get the best of all worlds in process improvement to create a smooth working environment
- A Process is a means of documenting, organizing, and controlling the ways organizations accomplish business.
- An effective Process Improvement effort will create a significantly smoother working environment.
- Nightmare Projects are not new. They've been around since information technology projects started being developed; the problem with the system development industry is that we still haven't learned from the mistakes of the past, we just keep doing things the same way over and over even though we've learned better and it has been well documented by many well-known software gurus.

Tips for Success

- Accelerating process improvement helps organizations get their "bang for the buck" much quicker.
- Remember, "Movement in a new direction helps you find new cheese." (Spencer Johnson, M.D., *Who Moved My Cheese?*)
- Executive monitoring provides the critical oversight and resources.
- Arm Process Improvement team with clear authority.
- Assign responsibilities.
- Select respected organization staff for Process Improvement team.
- Involve technical staff.

Chapter 2

How to Accelerate Process Improvement?

Process Improvement is difficult whether you accelerate the process improvement effort or take it slow and easy. It means changing the way an organization's staff operate and people don't take to changes easily. By accelerating the process improvement effort staff begin to see changes quickly so that they can start to adapt to the changes.

Finding New Cheese

Spencer Johnson, M.D. wrote a very appropriate and entertaining book, *Who Moved My Cheese?*[21] The book describes the reactions of four mice, Scurry, Sniff, Haw, and Hem, when change occurs in their lives, symbolized by moving cheese in the maze. The cheese represents elements in life such as career, happiness, financial success, relationships, peace of mind, health, or whatever one may want in life. Figure 2-1 illustrates Spencer Johnson, M.D.'s handwriting on the wall.

One of the most appropriate sayings from this book is "The Quicker You Let Go Of Old Cheese, The Sooner You Find New Cheese."[21] By accelerating the process improvement effort, the sooner the staff see the "new cheese" and realize that change is on its way. They also realize that it doesn't really hurt that much and in fact feels pretty good if accomplished properly. The further into the maze they scurry, the more confidence they start feeling about the end result.

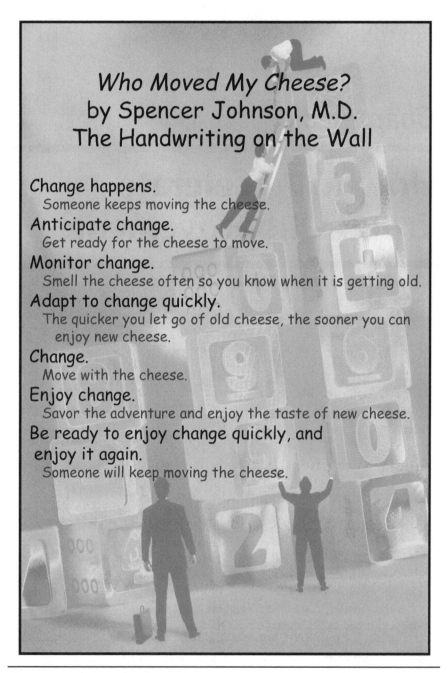

Figure 2-1 *Who Moved My Cheese?*

Questions, Questions, and More Questions

There are many questions organizations must address prior to undertaking an effort like Process Improvement. Some of the questions that should be considered include:

- Do you need help doing what you do best?
- Do you have "not enough" process or "too much" process?
- Are projects running smoothly?
- Are projects meeting budgets and schedules?
- Are your project managers reacting or planning and monitoring their projects proactively?
- Are your engineers concentrating on technical issues or wasting precious time on process details?
- Do you have projects in crisis?
- Are your projects meeting the contract requirements?
- Has your organization attempted process improvement efforts only to fail over and over again?
- Just how does your company stack up?

Once these questions have been addressed and an organization is committed to making changes to help them be more successful, you are ready to start maturing processes. The next decision should be how to accomplish maturing the organizational processes. An organization must weigh the importance of the advantages and disadvantages based on their unique environment to determine whether to take it slow and easy or accelerate process improvement. This will be discussed further later.

What You See Is Relative to Where You're Standing

We all see things in different ways based on where we are, our past experiences, and what we are responsible for. One of the keys to successful Process Maturity is to, as much as possible, focus on what's relative to the organization based on their perspectives. That means starting from where you are based on how you currently accomplish business, not on how another company does things, then improving upon that based on others' successes. Successful process improvement models, as well as organizations that assist in improving processes, give you that freedom to determine what works for your organization instead of using a one-size-fits-all solution.

Selecting the Right Model or Methodology

There is a multitude of models, methodologies, and techniques that have been developed to help correct the crisis seen in development of IT projects.

The following discusses a few of the more successful ones. We will discuss the CMMI® in further detail in a later chapter since that is the model that is recommended, but the other models, methodologies, and techniques can be very useful in combination with the CMMI®, especially the PMBOK® and ISO 9001.

Software Engineering Institute's (SEI) Capability Maturity Model® Integration (CMMI®)

The CMMI® provides an integration of the SW-CMM® with other popular, successful process models. The biggest difference is that the CMMI® takes a systems-level approach rather than a software-specific approach to processes needed to make projects successful. Many of the same practices were retained or enhanced in this updated Capability Maturity Model. These practices will be discussed in further detail in later chapters.

Software Engineering Institute's (SEI) Capability Maturity Models for Software (SW-CMM®)

The SW-CMM® consists of a collection of common sense practices for developing software that have been collected over time from numerous successful projects. It is the precursor of CMMI® and has proven to be a very successful process improvement model in its time. The SEI no longer supports this model.

Software Engineering Institute's (SEI) Personal Software Process (PSP^SM)

The PSP^SM is a methodology for engineers based upon the practices set forth in the CMMI®. It helps them make more accurate and realistic estimates and develop products with the needed quality, within budget, while meeting all customer commitments. As the name indicates, the PSP^SM is intended for individual engineers to create a more disciplined approach to development of software where the CMMI® is for an organization.

The SEI recommends using the PSP^SM in conjunction with the Team Software Process.

According to the SEI, these two tools in combination help "the high-performance engineer to:

- Ensure quality software products
- Create secure software products
- Improve process management within an organization."

Software Engineering Institute's (SEI) Team Software Process (TSP^{SM})

The TSP^{SM} methodology is also based on the practices set forth by the CMMI$^®$ but it is intended for use by teams. Team members must be PSP^{SM}-trained engineers prior to being part of a TSP^{SM} because TSP^{SM} is built upon the foundation of the CMM$^®$ and PSP^{SM}. The TSP^{SM} acts as "a guide in forming and managing high-performance integrated product teams." It is intended for software teams of three to twenty engineers with the proper training in PSP^{SM} and TSP^{SM}.

Software Engineering Institute's (SEI) People Capability Maturity Model (P-CMM$^®$)

The P-CMM$^®$ concentrates on the people side of process improvement. It focuses on "improving the management and development of human assets." This includes knowledge development, skill development, and staff motivation. This tool is especially useful for companies that have adopted either the SW-CMM$^®$ or CMMI$^®$ because people management changes as a result of improved processes put in place by these models.

There are five process areas of maturity for the P-CMM$^®$ which are:

- Level 5 ⇒ Optimizing ⇒ Change Management focus;
- Level 4 ⇒ Predictable ⇒ Capability Management focus;
- Level 3 ⇒ Defined ⇒ Competency Management focus;
- Level 2 ⇒ Managed ⇒ People Management focus;
- Level 1 ⇒ Initial ⇒ Inconsistent Management.

International Organization for Standardization (ISO) 9001

ISO 9001 is part of the ISO 9000 family of international quality management standards and guidelines. The quality management is concerned with the customer's quality requirements and applicable regulatory requirements as applicable to enhancement of customer satisfaction and continual improvement. These standards and guidelines provide some key administrative elements important to ensuring process conformance. It has proven a very good, successful tool for improving organizations in combination with the CMMI$^®$.

ISO 9001 "requires an organization to design, implement, and maintain a Business Management System" (BMS). The BMS consists of five main elements:

- Product/Service Lifecycle
- Supporting Activities
- Environment

- Management
- Continuous Improvement.

The Product/Service Lifecycle refers to the design, build and delivery of a product or service. The Supporting Activities are what the lifecycle depends upon to enable the design and development of a product. The Environment is the operating environment with emphasis on information and knowledge accessibility, particularly it's control and communication. Management is the management of the BMS as opposed to the information. Continuous Improvement provides for measurement and improvement of the BMS, completing what ISO calls a "closed-loop system."

ISO 9001 consists of 20 elements that must be met. Table 2-1 lists these elements.

Software Process Improvement and Capability dEtermination (SPICE)

SPICE is a major initiative to support institution of an international standard to be used to assess a software process. The need for an international standard

Table 2-1   ISO 9001 Elements

Identifier	Element
4.1	Management responsibility
4.2	Quality system
4.3	Contract review
4.4	Design control
4.5	Document and data control
4.6	Purchasing
4.7	Control of customer-supplied equipment
4.8	Product identification and traceability
4.9	Process control
4.10	Inspection and testing
4.11	Control of inspection, measuring, and test equipment
4.12	Inspection and test status
4.13	Control of nonconforming product
4.14	Corrective and preventive action
4.15	Handling, storage, packaging, preservation and delivery
4.16	Control of quality records
4.17	Internal quality audits
4.18	Training
4.19	Servicing
4.20	Statistical techniques

resulted from the concerns of the acquirers of large, critical software systems, especially defense and telecommunications organizations. A major mandate of the SPICE Initiative is to accomplish the SPICE Trials which are "empirical trials of ISO/IEC 15504." ISO/IEC 15504 defines a set of requirements for an Assessment Model in order to be ISO/IEC 15504-conformant and an Assessment and a two-dimensional Reference Model.

SPICE consists of five levels of process maturity similar to the CMMI® but SPICE is more software oriented. The five levels are as shown in Table 2-2.

Table 2-2 SPICE Levels of Maturity

Level	Title	Brief Description
0	Not-performed	No common features—a general failure to perform the base practices in the process—no easily identifiable work products or outputs of the process.
1	Performed-informally	Base practices generally performed. Individual knowledge and effort is driver.
2	Planned and tracked	Performance of the base practices is planned and tracked. Moving toward well-defined process.
3	Well defined	Base practices are performed. Well-defined processes using approved, tailored versions of organizational standard.
4	Quantitatively controlled	Detailed measures of performance. Ability to predict performance.
5	Continuously improving	Quantitative process effectiveness and efficiency. Continuous process improvement against goals.

Total Quality Management (TQM)

TQM is a process for managing quality as well as a philosophy of perpetual improvement. It was a very popular philosophy in the 1980s. The following defines the steps and principles of TQM.

Ten steps to TQM:

1. Pursue New Strategic Thinking
2. Know your Customers
3. Set True Customer Requirements
4. Concentrate on Prevention, Not Correction
5. Reduce Chronic Waste

6. Pursue a Continuous Improvement Strategy
7. Use Structured Methodology for Process Improvement
8. Reduce Variation
9. Use a Balanced Approach
10. Apply to All Functions.

Principles of TQM:

1. Quality can and must be managed.
2. Everyone has a customer and is a supplier.
3. Processes, not people, are the problem.
4. Every employee is responsible for quality.
5. Problems must be prevented, not just fixed.
6. Quality must be measured.
7. Quality improvements must be continuous.
8. The quality standard is defect free.
9. Goals are based on requirements, not negotiated.
10. Life cycle costs, not front end costs.
11. Management must be involved and lead.
12. Plan and organize for quality improvement.

Software Process Improvement in Regions of Europe (SPIRE)

The SPIRE project concentrates on process improvement projects for small software developers. SPIRE funds software developers in Austria, Ireland, Italy and Sweden to conduct software process improvement projects with a mentor. SPIRE is a European Systems and Software Initiative (ESSI) project funded by the European Commission. The project was taken up by the Centre for Software Engineering in Dublin, Ireland, where activities were coordinated with partners in Austria, Italy, and Sweden.

The primary aim for the SPIRE project is to provide smaller companies with a tool to mature processes and avoid the inherent overhead that comes with other models. Some areas they seek to avoid include needed model training, the very costly certification, and the process improvement effort required which can result in lost productivity, hence lost income during training and early implementation.

Project Management Institute's (PMI) Project Management Body of Knowledge (PMBOK®)

The PMBOK®[30] is intended to describe the "sum of knowledge" for project management. It includes proven traditional practices as well as more innovative and advanced practices. It breaks project management into Knowledge Areas including:

- Project Integration Management
- Project Scope Management
- Project Time Management
- Project Cost Management
- Project Quality Management
- Project Human Resources Management
- Project Communications Management
- Project Risk Management
- Project Procurement Management.

It further defines five Process Groups:

1. Initiating Processes
2. Planning Processes
3. Controlling Processes
4. Executing Processes
5. Closing Processes.

Processes within a Knowledge Area are designated to a specific Process Group and linked by their inputs and outputs.

The processes defined by the PMBOK® are well-suited for combination with the Capability Maturity Models. Many organizations have had great success combining these two powerful tools.

Microsoft® Operations Framework (MOF)

The MOF is a set of processes developed by Microsoft® for management of distributed IT systems. It is separated into four basic operational functions:

1. Changing
2. Operating
3. Supporting
4. Optimizing.

The processes include a team model, process model, risk discipline, and an extensive set of:

- Operations guides
- Assessment tools
- Operations kits
- Best practices
- Case studies

- Templates
- Support tools
- Services.

The MOF team model consists of five guiding principles:

1. To provide timely, efficient, and accurate customer service.
2. To understand the business priorities and enable IT to add business value.
3. To build strong, synergistic virtual teams.
4. To leverage IT automation and knowledge management tools.
5. To attract, develop, and retain strong IT operations staff.

The MOF process model consists of four guiding principles:

1. *Structured architecture*—operational activities organized for mission-critical computing.
2. *Rapid life cycle, iterative improvement*—supports iterative, flexible IT life cycle.
3. *Review-driven management*—operations management reviews required at key points.
4. *Embedded risk management*—proactively managed risk.

The MOF Risk Management Discipline consists of five principles:

1. Assess risks continuously.
2. Integrate risk management into every role and every function.
3. Treat risk identification positively.
4. Use risk-based scheduling.
5. Establish an acceptable level of formality.

Control OBjectives for Information and related Technology (COBIT)

COBIT provides a Management Guideline and Maturity Model that identifies critical success factors, key goal indicators, key performance indicators, and a maturity model for governing IT projects. COBIT has defined several levels of maturity based upon the governance of information technology and associated processes balancing risk over return as follows:

0. *Non-existent*—lack of recognizable IT process governance.
1. *Initial/Ad-hoc*—evidence that IT governance issues are recognized but on a case-by-case or ad-hoc basis.
2. *Repeatable but intuitive*—awareness of IT governance issues.
3. *Defined Process*—need to act on IT governance issues is understood and accepted.

4. *Managed and Measurable*—full understanding of IT governance issues supported by training.
5. *Optimized*—advanced and forward-looking understanding of IT governance issues and solutions.

Business Process Reengineering (BPR) and Business Process Management (BPM)

In an effort to improve the way a company does business, BPR/BPM was adapted by many companies in the 1990s. Unfortunately, due to the way it was used, it has been perceived negatively since the result of BPR/BPM many times resulted in massive layoffs and reorganizations. BPR/BPM is a key methodology for restructuring business operations to give them that needed competitive advantage which does not necessarily include staff restructuring and layoffs.

The main premise of BPR/BPM is elimination of waste in business processes. The proponents of BPR/BPM contended that much effort was wasted passing tasks between departments and proposed that it would be much more efficient to appoint a team responsible for specific tasks within a process. Many extended this to suppliers, distributors, and other business associations.

The results of numerous BPR/BPM efforts are very successful since they result in improved customer satisfaction, particularly in manufacturing. As long as the people aspects of the BPR/BPM efforts are appreciated, this method can be applied successfully.

System Engineering Capability Model (SECM) also called Electronic Industries Association/Interim Standard (EIA/IS) 731

The SECM, sometimes called the SE-CMM®, is a model for improving and appraising systems engineering processes. It was a major model used in the CMMI® project. It provides the systems engineering aspect to the CMMI® with focus on "plateaus of performance" that organizations must achieve to improve their system engineering processes. It discusses maturity in terms of capability levels as opposed to maturity levels. As part of the CMMI®, this will be discussed in later chapters.

Six Sigma

Six Sigma is a quality improvement methodology focused on reduction of product and services failure rate. The term refers to 3.4 defects per million opportunities or 99.99966 percent accuracy. The emphasis is on identifying and avoiding defects or variation by using data collection and analysis to uncover sources of errors and discover ways of eliminating them. This results in a high level of quality products with as close to zero defects as possible. This methodology has proven to be very successful in combination with the CMM® models.

Knowledge Management

Harnessing information within an organization for use when it's needed, by whom it's needed, and where it's needed, is the primary purpose of knowledge management. It focuses on making good use of data collected and investments in data by organizations. As knowledge is collected by an organization's staff, inroads are being made into the capture, combination, and wide distribution of such knowledge whether it's documented or undocumented. This is a growing area that continues to show promise for improving an organization's way of achieving and maintaining a competitive edge. The military talks about having "information superiority" but the same concept of achieving "information superiority" can be shifted to the business industry.

Keeping It Short and Simple

Regardless of the model or methodology selected, by using the keep it short and simple (KISS) principle, many basic elements can be put in place quickly to kick things off, thus building a foundation for continued improvement. Sometimes we tend to concentrate on the gory details and forget the big picture. Mountains of paperwork only tend to confuse things but, by keeping things simple, staff tend to understand it much easier and feel less intimidated.

Sometimes several levels of simplicity may be needed to provide the depth of detail needed for some of the more difficult processes. In later chapters, various methods for defining processes will be discussed. Many times we tend to concentrate on the details and forget the big picture, but, by making simplicity a goal, we can minimize the unneeded details or layer our processes in such a way that they are easily understood and thus followed.

Summary

Process improvement means changing the way an organization's staff operates and people don't take to changes easily. In order to ease this process, accelerating the process improvement effort helps the staff begin to see changes quickly. When they start seeing these positive changes taking place they can start to adapt to the changes. There are numerous models to select, depending upon an organization's ultimate process improvement goals.

Chapter Key Points

- There are many questions organizations must address prior to undertaking an effort like Process Improvement.
- There are a multitude of models, methodologies, and techniques that have been developed to help correct the crisis seen in development of IT projects.
- Start from where you are, how you currently accomplish business.
- Successful process improvement models, as well as organizations that assist in improving processes, give you that freedom to determine what works for your organization instead of using a one-size-fits-all solution.

Tips for Success

- "The Quicker You Let Go Of Old Cheese, The Sooner You Find New Cheese." Spencer Johnson, M.D.'s, *Who Moved My Cheese?*
- By accelerating the process improvement effort, the sooner the staff sees "new cheese."
- Focus on what's relative to the organization based on their perspectives.
- Use the keep it short and simple (KISS) principle.

Chapter 3

Key Success Criteria

There are several key success criteria that organizations should meet prior to attempting to accelerate a process improvement effort. If these criteria are not a part of the organizational culture, they should be worked on prior to attempting to attain process maturity or should be an integral part of the maturity effort. Each organization is different so it is incumbent upon the organization to determine if they meet these criteria and the degree to which they are met or need to be met for success.

Key Success Criteria

The following nine key success criteria are important for an organization to possess or attain prior to undertaking a process improvement effort.

1. Executive Management Commitment

Executive Management has been quoted by many as the key to process improvement success. Where executive management commitment is a very important key, there are other levels of management that are also the key to success, depending upon the size of an organization. For smaller organizations, executive management becomes increasingly more the key to success. The size of the organization is not linear, it is exponential in character; the larger an organization gets, the executive management's role becomes much less the key to process improvement success. This is not to imply that executive management is not critical to the success of any effort undertaken within an organization but to show that other levels of management become more important as an organization's size increases.

Executive Management commitment will ensure that the appropriate resources are made available for the effort as well as ensuring proper enforcement of the processes that are put in place during the process improvement effort. Without executive buy-in, it will be virtually impossible to move ahead in any process improvement effort; however, for an accelerated process improvement effort it becomes even more critical to success since the appropriate resources must be available.

2. Mid-Level Management Commitment

Anyone in business for very long realizes that mid-level management is where things actually get done in larger organizations. Without mid-level management driving efforts they tend to fall through the cracks even with executive management support. There must be a level of staff that actually drives the key efforts within an organization depending upon the size of the organization. Mid-level management will ensure that things get done and they will ensure that they get done in a certain way, such as using the processes developed by the process team. Processes can be and are written over and over again in organizations but if they are not used they are a waste of time; however, with commitment from mid-level manager they tend to be used as opposed to shelved.

3. Organizational Adaptability → Flexible

An organization must be able to adapt to all changing circumstances or it will die. This has been proven over and over again in industry; giant companies have gone bankrupt when they don't keep pace with the changing world. They must be ready to adapt to new, different, or changing requirements. Flexibility should always be the main purpose for any organization, especially when preparing for a process improvement effort. Even though an organization should always start where they are they also need to be willing to institute elements into their organization that differ from the way they have been doing business, hence flexibility becomes even more key to success.

4. Project Management Style → Proactive

Process Improvement fosters proactive management but it is important to have a proactive outlook to project management in order to accomplish process improvement. It has been proven that poor Project Management easily destroys even the strongest projects. It can lead to budget overruns, schedule slippage, and general customer and staff dissatisfaction. Proactive decision making enables managers to make fact-based decisions rather than the more reactive firefighting that is typically seen on information technology projects. It enables project managers to be prepared to handle unexpected circumstances.

Many times projects value the heros and firefighters of the organization. Managers rely upon them to make a project successful. The staff members who use systematic, proven, common sense methods for managing projects should be more relied upon to ensure that a project is brought in successfully. If they had not used this method of managing a project, they may be the hero or firefighter instead and all the organization's projects would be in jeopardy.

There are many reasons why projects fail but project planning has been named by many experts and in many surveys as key to project success. Additionally, project planning has been defined by many models and methodologies as a key process for achieving project success. Planning provides for employment of a forward-looking philosophy to ensure that an organization and a project are prepared for each task while ensuring enough flexibility to accommodate changing task priorities. Ultimately, it minimizes the impact of any surprises.

Up front planning, done properly, can:

- Significantly reduce and even eliminate costly and risky replanning
- Improve the quality of the products and processes
- Reduce risk by providing better understanding and potential impacts
- Result in fewer instances of scrap and rework
- Lower costs
- Ultimately culminates in a better quality product.

Planning should always be an iterative process. As things change on an effort or as further insight is attained, planning should be revisited and further refined as needed.

5. Training Style → Proactive

Training ensures that all staff members know how to accomplish their assigned activities the way the organization wants them accomplished. By proactively training staff there will be little room for misunderstandings and misinterpretations. Training includes both needed technical training as well as administrative training of processes so that staff understand how the organization wants activities accomplished. It is important that staff get the knowledge they need to succeed and proactive training and mentoring-type programs provide the most advantageous method of accomplishing the knowledge transfer.

Process training will also provide a way of getting buy-in into the processes developed as well as ensuring understanding. Training should be provided by appropriate training staff who promote overall staff involvement with group discussions and acceptance of recommendations to improve processes. Appropriate training staff will ensure that open communications take place during training as opposed to "shoving it down their throats." Training staff must form a partnership with the students to ensure that they get what they need when they walk out the door to do their job.

Training must be aligned to the appropriate staff members so that they don't all get inundated with useless training. It should always be based on the staff member's position as well as their skill level. There are several methods of evaluating training needs organizationally and per staff member. An assessment of existing training and training methods will help determine the training needs, training effectiveness, where training needs improvement, and any hidden training needs and training gaps in the organization's training program. As long as the organization considers training a critical activity for the organization, the rest comes easy. They understand that, by building staff skills, they become more competitive with decreased time to market, increased productivity, and higher staff satisfaction.

6. Communications Style → Open and Non-Inhibitive

Communications and cooperation ensure that there are no misunderstandings or misconceptions on either side. Clear, concise communication throughout all projects is critical to success and ensures that all stakeholders understand what is expected.

Stakeholders include anyone that is affected by the project and the resulting products, such as managers, including executive, mid-level, and project managers; all staff members; all customers and end-users. In other words nearly everyone. That does not mean that all information needs to be passed to all stakeholders, it means that all stakeholders get appropriate information needed for them to do their job. A communications plan developed for the organization, or for a project early that identifies each stakeholder's needs, can help manage information flow. It should include the project organization, responsibilities, project disciplines, logistics, information sharing/distribution including the appropriate media, and a detailed reporting approach.

Open, non-inhibitive communication with all stakeholders helps to identify and mitigate problems before they can get out of hand. All managers should promote delivery of bad news as soon as possible and get away from the "kill the messenger" mentality. By promoting bad news, it allows them to plan and react proactively as opposed to firefighting.

7. Delegation of Authority

Micromanagement has proven unsuccessful. Organizations must hire staff that they can trust to get the job done. Then provide the appropriate level of oversight to ensure that efforts are progressing as needed. By delegating authority, it enables managers to react appropriately to issues without having to go through red-tape and multiple levels of unneeded bureaucracy. Managers at all levels should be empowered to make decisions for their teams to rapidly and effectively resolve any issues as they arise.

8. Process Improvement Model Familiarity

Process Improvement models can be difficult to understand. Some experience working with the selected Process Improvement model will enhance an organization's probability for success in using the model.

Familiarity with the model selected, along with organizational needs, existing potential processes, and resources needed, help build a solid productive process improvement effort. Lessons learned from previous experience provide great fodder for future efforts. These lessons help you avoid the common mistakes made in many typical Process Improvement efforts. They can help select and implement various strategies that fit the organizational needs based on their familiarity and potentially experience with the selected model. Additionally, they can advise an organization of the implications of the selected strategy and work with the organization based on decisions made. They can help identify any potential risks or obstacles to help you mitigate those and be ready to combat them when and if they arise. Ultimately, they can help steer you toward success.

9. Process Acceptance Factor → Positive

One of the most difficult parts of Process Improvement is getting the processes used. When an organization starts with a positive process acceptance factor, they are 100 steps ahead of one that is negative or even marginal. Many technical staff believe that processes get in the way of the real work. At times this is because of the methods used to implement the Process Improvement effort. When mountains of bureaucracy are imposed, staff resist the effort since they see this as a negative impact to their work. There are many ways to promote the process acceptance factor that will be discussed throughout this book but the key factor is use of the KISS principle.

Change Management Challenges

Peter F. Drucker, sometimes called the father of modern management, states "It is not true, as a good many industrial psychologists assert, that human nature resists change. On the contrary, no being in heaven or earth is greedier for new things. But there are conditions for man's readiness for change.

The change must appear rational to him . . ."[15] Appearing rational—this is the key to promoting Process Improvement in an organization. You must appeal to a staff's rational side. There will be resistance to change but, if it is promoted properly by the Process Improvement team and management, the resistance will be minimal.

By studying marketing trends, we can determine some methods of marketing Process Improvement and resulting processes developed as part of that effort. Several key methods, which have proven successful, can be adapted for marketing the Process Improvement effort. Additionally, by studying some of the scientific theories, organizational change can be further understood. Some key methods that can help Process Engineers focus on the appropriate areas include Everett Roger's Adoption Curve for dissemination of ideas, as well as the detractors of this theory, Roger Chiocchi's Inductive Marketing theory, the Perspective Factor, to ensure that each stakeholder's perspective is considered, some of the varied Sociotechnical theories, and the Science of Organizational Change. Change management is discussed at length in Chapter 19.

Summary

The defined Key Success Criteria can make a difference between the success or failure of a Process Improvement effort. If these criteria are not a part of the organizational culture, the organization should take some time prior to the Process Improvement kick-off to instill these into the organizational culture. Each organization is unique so each one needs to determine the degree to which each of these criteria should be met prior to initiating the Process Improvement effort. People want change but it must always be a rational change or it will not be accepted easily.

Chapter Key Points

- Executive management has been quoted by many as the key to Process Improvement success. Where executive management commitment is a very important key, there are other levels of management that are also key to success depending upon the size of an organization.
- Without mid-level management driving efforts they tend to fall through the cracks even with executive management support.
- Organizations must be able to adapt to all changing circumstances or they will die.
- Proactive decision making enables managers to make fact-based decisions rather than the more reactive firefighting that is typically seen on information technology projects.

- Training ensures that all staff members know how to accomplish their assigned activities the way the organization wants them accomplished.
- Communications and cooperation ensure that there are no misunderstandings or misconceptions on either side. Clear, concise communication throughout all projects is critical to success and ensures that all stakeholders understand what is expected.
- Some experience working with the selected Process Improvement model will enhance an organization's probability for success in using the model.
- Change must appear rational for people to accept it. By studying some of the scientific theories, organizational change can be further understood.

Tips for Success

- Rely on staff who use systematic, proven, common sense methods for managing projects.
- Use process training to facilitate buy-in for processes.
- Managers should promote delivery of bad news.
- Don't micromanage.

Chapter 4

CMMI® Basic Training

The Capability Maturity Model (CMM®) is a model not a methodology. Many mistake it for a methodology which tells you how to accomplish something but the CMM® is a model which only tells you what needs to be accomplished. It is only a framework and does not tell an organization how to implement processes, hence it can work well in many system development environments, including the growingly popular Agile Methodologies.

Put simply, the CMM® provides a framework for developing processes that have proven to make projects and organizations more successful. For example, it tells you that each project must plan, it does not tell you how to plan but that you must plan and some of the attributes of a successful plan. The idea is that processes will be developed and improved to work with that industry's unique characteristics. The best practices are an accumulation of proven practices from both industry and government.

The Capability Maturity Model®—Integrated (CMMI®),[3,4] the latest CMM®, is the focus of this chapter. It provides the best tool for maturing an organization based on the results of numerous successful CMMI® endeavors. This model was first published in 2000 in order to merge several popular, successful models together into one coherent model. It was a collaborative effort undertaken by the SEI, government representatives, and industry representatives. The main objective was to "develop an integrated model that is consistent with as many other well-known models as possible."

Flavors of CMMI®

The CMMI® comes in two flavors: staged and continuous. The use of which flavor to select will depend upon your organization's process improvement goals. Both models have significant advantages and disadvantages. The staged model has specific levels, with associated process areas which must be met to achieve a certain level of maturity, each building upon the next. Figure 4-1 illustrates the staged model. The continuous model allows an organization to select the order in which they wish to improve their organization with the level referring to the degree in which each Process Area is met. Figure 4-2 illustrates the continuous model.

The staged model has shown significant success since the initial SW-CMM® model was developed. Figure 4-3 illustrates the CMMI® staged levels much like a staircase which allows organizations to climb their way to success. Each Maturity Level is composed of various Process Areas which contain the practices key for the success of organizations and associated projects.

The continuous model was brought over from the System Engineering-CMM® (SE-CMM®) or EIA/IS 731. Figure 4.4 illustrates the CMMI® continuous levels

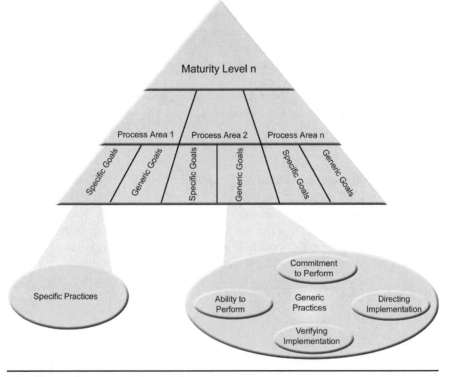

Figure 4-1   CMMI Staged Model

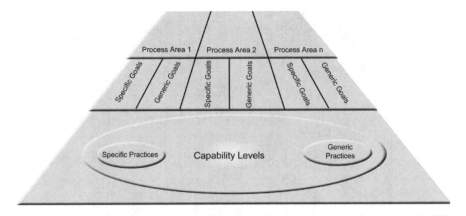

Figure 4-2   CMMI Continuous Model

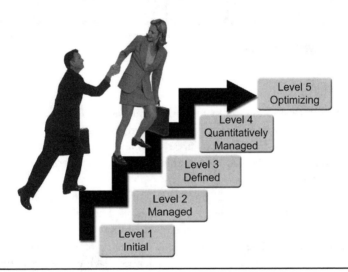

Figure 4-3   Staged CMMI Stairs to Success

which allow organizations to choose a Process Area to concentrate upon. Each Capability Level is composed of a set of practices relating to a single Process Area.

The information and process areas for maturing an organization are virtually identical so we will concentrate on the staged model for the purposes of this book.

CMMI® Terminology

- *Maturity Levels*—These levels show where an organization is in developing processes based on the best practices defined by the CMMI®. Each level is

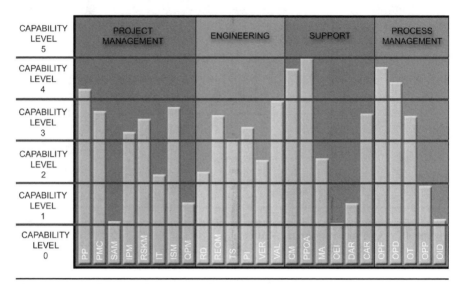

Figure 4-4 CMMI Continuous Levels

a layer in the foundation to a mature organization. The five levels are initial, managed, defined, quantitatively managed, and optimizing.

- *Process Areas*—The process areas define the activities that must be performed in order to meet that maturity level. These are all based on best industry practices.
- *Specific Goals*—The goals provide a summary of the practices with the specific goals related to the specific practices. Each of these specific goals is considered key to enhancing process capability.
- *Generic Goals*—The goals provide a summary of the practices with the generic goals related to the generic practices. Each of these generic goals is considered key to enhancing process capability. The same generic goals are included in multiple process areas.
- *Specific Practices*—These practices are the activities designated as important to achieving the associated goals. They describe processes that organizations will typically implement.
- *Generic Practices*—These practices are the activities that ensure the processes developed to meet the specific process areas will be effective, repeatable, and lasting.
- *Commitment to Perform*—One of the common features used to indicate whether the implementation and institutionalization of a Process Area is effective, repeatable, and lasting. Commitment to Perform is the organizational expectations for processes. The key is organizational direction from senior management.

- *Ability to Perform*—One of the common features used to indicate whether the implementation and institutionalization of a Process Area is effective, repeatable, and lasting. Ability to Perform is what is needed to perform the process and achieve established objectives. The key is the plan, resources, assigned responsibility, training, process definition.
- *Directing Implementation*—One of the common features used to indicate whether the implementation and institutionalization of a Process Area is effective, repeatable, and lasting. Directing Implementation is the establishment of product integrity. The key is managing products through configuration, stakeholder involvement, process monitor and control, and measures.
- *Verifying Implementation*—One of the common features used to indicate whether the implementation and institutionalization of a Process Area is effective, repeatable, and lasting. Verifying Implementation is the credible assurance that the established processes are being followed. The key is to evaluate adherence and management review.

CMMI® Maturity Levels

As shown in Figure 4-3, the CMMI® staged model consists of five levels: Initial, Managed, Defined, Quantitatively Managed, and Optimizing. Each of these levels indicates the level of maturity that the organization has achieved.

Maturity Level 1—Initial

The features of a Level 1 or Initial organization are that the processes are chaotic or non-existent, the organizational environment is unstable where a successful project is based on the staff assigned to the project. Many times they rely on heros that put in long hours in order to get a task accomplished. Even when resulting products work, most of the time, the project has exceeded both the budget and the schedule. One of the keys to identifying a Level 1 organization is to watch them during a crisis when, typically, they simply abandon the processes for more firefighting-related reaction.

Maturity Level 2—Managed

At level 2 organizations, typically, are starting to get some order to things. They're managing requirements, processes are planned, used, and measured to ensure they are working the way they were intended, and processes are being controlled just as a software baseline is controlled. When a crisis does occur the process is used, not thrown out, because they don't have time to use them. They understand that when a process is thrown out they are asking for more problems. The projects are managed by a well-thought out and documented plan. Management is kept up-to-date via statusing so that the products and services are visible to them. Finally, work products are reviewed with appropriate stakeholders and that products meet the requirements.

Maturity Level 3—Defined

Level 3 is a typical that organizations strive for because this is where you really start to see a difference in an organization. The processes are understood by all staff as a result of training, the processes are established and improved over time as lessons are learned or as things change. The processes used on one project are similar to the ones used on another project so when staff goes from one project to another they are understood. Reassigned staff doesn't have to relearn all the mundane administrative stuff and they can get on with their real job since the processes are held organizationally and tailored for each project. This is a key distinction between Level 2 and 3—processes are held organizationally as opposed to for a specific project. The processes tend to be a bit more detailed and adhered to more rigorously by all organizational staff. The organization proactively manages the processes at the organizational level.

Maturity Level 4—Quantitatively Managed

More metrics are the key to Level 4. This is where they come into play at a more stringent level. Statistical and quantitative processes are used to control sub processes. The quality and performance criteria are established and managed. Any process variations are identified and corrected. These are incorporated in the measurement repository. The key to Level 4 is predictability—you can predict what will happen on a project or tasks as you plan it.

Maturity Level 5—Optimizing

Level 5 is sometimes called NIRVANA—this is where processes are continually improved based on measure or metrics. There is a focus on incremental and innovative improvements. Process Improvement objectives are established for the organization and business objectives are revised to reflect changes. The key to Level 5 is the identification of common causes of variations and resolution of them.

CMMI® Continuous Capability Levels

As shown in Figure 4-4, the CMMI® continuous model consists of six levels: Incomplete, Performed Informally, Planned and Tracked, Well-Defined, Quantitatively Controlled, and Continuously Improving.

Capability Level 0—Incomplete

The features of a Capability Level 0 or Incomplete indicate that a process is not performed or that it is only partially performed.

Capability Level 1—Performed Informally

The features of a Capability Level 1 or Performed Informally indicate that specific goals of a process area are satisfied. These are sometimes called the base practices.

Capability Level 2—Planned and Tracked

The features of a Capability Level 2 or Planned and Tracked indicate that a process satisfies Capability Level 2 but is planned and executed in accordance to a policy. It also indicates that resources are adequate and staff have the appropriate skills to accomplish the process. Further, it involves monitoring, controlling, and reviewing.

Capability Level 3—Well-Defined

The features of a Capability Level 3 or Well-Defined indicate that a process is tailored from the organization's set of standard processes. It also indicates that a set of tailoring guidelines are in place and used to accomplish the tailoring. Further, it indicates that the organization maintains a process asset library.

Capability Level 4—Quantitatively Controlled

The features of a Capability Level 4 or Quantitatively Controlled indicate that a process is statistically and quantitatively controlled. Measurable quality goals are established and performance is objectively managed.

Capability Level 5—Continuously Improving

The features of a Capability Level 5 or Continuously Improving indicate that quantitative process is established and that Process Improvement performance is continuously improved. Common causes are addressed for variations.

CMMI® Categories

The process areas can be separated into four areas or categories: Project Management, Process Management, Engineering, and Support. The Project Management process areas are primarily concerned with planning, monitoring, and controlling. Figure 4-5 maps the four areas or categories to the corresponding

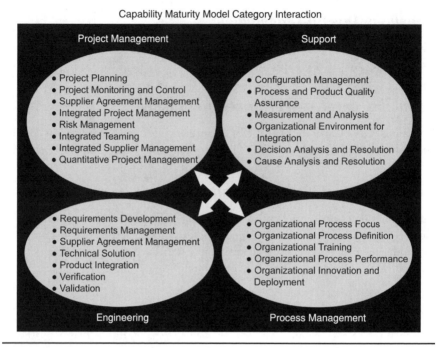

Figure 4-5   CMMI Category Interaction

Process Areas. The Process Management Processes are concerned with defining, planning, resourcing, deploying, implementing, monitoring, controlling, appraising, measuring, and improving processes. The Engineering processes are concerned with development and maintenance activities shared across engineering disciplines. Finally, the Support processes are the processes used in the context of performing other processes, they are targeted toward projects but can also include some organizational support.

CMMI® Process Areas

The process areas separate the practices into succinct areas for concentration. Each Maturity Level is composed of Process Areas that define the activities needed to meet the needs to the success of attaining a particular level. Table 4-1 shows the Process Areas associated with each Maturity Level.

CMMI® Specific Goals and Practices

The goals and practices are the key elements of the CMMI®. They are what the CMMI® is all about; in other words, they provide the essence of the

Table 4-1   CMMI Process Areas

Capability Maturity Model—Integrated (CMMI) Process Areas (PA)

Level	Level Name	Process Areas	Acronym
1	Initial		
2	Managed	Requirements Management	REQM
		Project Planning	PP
		Project Monitoring and Control	PMC
		Supplier Agreement Management	SAM
		Measurement and Analysis	MA
		Process and Product Quality Assurance	PPQA
		Configuration Management	CM
3	Defined	Requirements Development	RD
		Technical Solution	TS
		Product Integration	PI
		Verification	VER
		Validation	VAL
		Organizational Process Focus	OPF
		Organizational Process Definition	OPD
		Organizational Training	OT
		Integrated Project Management (partially IPPD)	IPM
		Risk Management	RSKM
		Integrated Teaming (IPPD)	IT
		Integrated Supplier Management	ISM
		Decision Analysis and Resolution	DAR
		Organizational Environment for Integration (IPPD)	OEI
4	Quantitatively Managed	Organizational Process Performance	OPP
		Quantitative Project Management	QPM
5	Optimizing	Organizational Innovation and Deployment	OID
		Causal Analysis and Resolution	CAR

model. The rest of the model is to provide structure and organization to these practices.

The goals are absolute, they are what needs to be done for implementation of that Process Area. The specific and generic goals are required to meet the requirements of the associated Maturity Level. These are what are used during appraisals to determine where an organization falls in terms of process maturity.

Specific practices are for implementation to satisfy the goals where the generic practices provide for institutionalization to satisfy the goals. The specific and generic practices are expected to meet the requirements of the associated Maturity Level. They are used to describe what organizations typically do to implement a particular goal. They are used as a guide for appraisals with viable alternative practices that meet the goal acceptable. There is a one-to-one mapping of goals to practices.

Level 2 Requirements Management (REQM)

Requirements Management provides a method of managing requirements to ensure that resulting products meet customer needs and contractual requirements. Table 4-2 lists the goals and practices associated with the Requirements Management Process Area. Figure 4-6 illustrates how the goals interact and some of the external interfaces for the Requirements Management Process Area.

Level 2 Project Planning (PP)

Project Planning defines the plan for performing the work. It provides the basic blueprint for the project. Table 4-2 lists the goals and practices associated with the Project Planning Process Area. Figure 4-7 illustrates how the goals interact and some of the external interfaces for the Project Planning Process Area.

Level 2 Project Monitoring and Control (PMC)

Project Monitoring and Control provides for proactive management in order to identify and avert events that potentially cause undesirable consequences. Table 4.2 lists the goals and practices associated with the Project Monitoring and Control Process Area. Figure 4-8 illustrates how the goals interact and some of the external interfaces for the Project Monitoring and Control Process Area.

Level 2 Supplier Agreement Management (SAM)

Supplier Agreement Management provides a method of selecting suppliers based on organizationally established criteria. Table 4-2 lists the goals and practices associated with the Supplier Agreement Management Process Area. Figure 4-9 illustrates how the goals interact and some of the external interfaces for the Supplier Agreement Management Process Area.

Level 2 Measurement and Analysis (MA)

Measurement and Analysis provides a method for maintaining and development of measurements in order to provide management with the means of monitoring a project's progress. Table 4-2 lists the goals and practices associated with the Measurement and Analysis Process Area. Figure 4-10 illustrates how the goals interact and some of the external interfaces for the Measurement and Analysis Process Area.

Table 4-2 Specific Goals to Specific Practices

One-to-One Mapping of Specific Goals to Specific Practices

Goal	Practice
Requirements management Manage requirements	• Obtain an understanding of requirements • Obtain commitment to requirements • Manage requirements changes • Maintain bidirectional traceability of requirements • Identify inconsistencies between project work and requirements
Project planning Establish estimates	• Estimate the scope of the project • Establish estimates of work products and task attributes • Define Project Life Cycle • Determine estimates of effort and cost
Develop a project plan	• Establish the budget and schedule • Identify project risks • Plan for data management • Plan for needed knowledge and skills • Plan stakeholder involvement • Establish the project plan
Obtain commitment to the plan	• Reviews plans that effect the project • Reconcile work and resource levels • Obtain plan commitment
Project monitoring and control Monitor project against plan	• Monitor project planning parameters • Monitor commitments • Monitor project risks • Monitor data management • Monitor stakeholder involvement • Conduct progress reviews • Conduct milestone reviews
Manage corrective action to closure	• Analyze issues • Take correction action • Manage corrective action
Supplier agreement management Establish supplier agreements	• Determine acquisition type • Select suppliers • Establish supplier agreements
Satisfy supplier agreements	• Review COTS products • Execute the supplier agreement • Accept the acquired product • Transition products

(continued)

Table 4-2   Continued

One-to-One Mapping of Specific Goals to Specific Practices

Goal	Practice
Measurement and analysis	
Align measurement and analysis activities	• Establish measurement objectives • Specify measures • Specify data collection and storage procedures • Specify analysis procedures
Provide measurement results	• Collect measurement data • Analyze measurement data • Store data and results • Communicate results
Process and product quality assurance	
Objectively evaluate processes and work products	• Objectively evaluate processes • Objectively evaluate work products and services
Provide objective insight	• Communicate and ensure resolution of noncompliance issue • Establish records
Configuration management	
Establish baselines	• Identify configuration items • Establish a configuration management system • Create or release baselines
Establish integrity	• Establish configuration management records • Perform configuration audits
Track and control changes	• Track change requests • Control configuration items
Requirements development	
Develop customer requirements	• Elicit needs • Develop the customer requirements
Develop product requirements	• Establish product and product-component requirements • Allocate product-component requirements • Identify interface requirements
Analyze and validate requirements	• Establish operational concepts and scenarios • Establish a definition of required functionality • Analyze requirements • Analyze requirements to achieve balance • Validate requirements with comprehensive methods

(*continued*)

Table 4-2 Continued

One-to-One Mapping of Specific Goals to Specific Practices

Goal	Practice
Technical solution	
Select product-component solutions	• Develop detailed alternative solutions and selection criteria • Evolve operational concepts and scenarios • Select product-component solutions
Develop the design	• Design the product or product component • Establish a technical data package • Design interfaces using criteria • Perform make, buy, or reuse analyses
Implement the product design	• Implement the design • Develop product support documentation
Product integration	
Prepare for product integration	• Determine integration sequence • Establish the product integration environment • Establish product integration procedures and criteria
Ensure interface compatibility	• Review interface descriptions for completeness • Manage interfaces
Assemble product components and deliver the product	• Confirm readiness of product components for integration • Assemble product components • Evaluate assembled product components • Package and deliver the product or product component
Verification	
Prepare for verification	• Select work products for verification • Establish the verification environment • Establish verification procedures and criteria
Perform peer reviews	• Prepare for peer reviews • Conduct peer reviews • Analyze peer review data
Verify selected work products	• Perform verification • Analyze verification results and identify corrective action
Validation	
Prepare for validation	• Select products for validation • Establish the validation environment • Establish validation procedures and criteria
Validate product or product components	• Perform validation • Analyze validation results

(continued)

Table 4-2   Continued

One-to-One Mapping of Specific Goals to Specific Practices

Goal	Practice
Organizational process focus	
Determine process-improvement opportunities	• Establish organizational process needs • Appraise the organization's processes • Identify the organization's process improvements
Plan and implement process-improvement activities	• Establish process action plans • Implement process action plans • Deploy organizational process assets • Incorporate process-related experiences into the organizational process assets
Organizational process definition	
Establish organizational process assets	• Establish standard processes • Establish life-cycle model descriptions • Establish tailoring criteria and guidelines • Establish the organization's measurement repository • Establish the organization's process asset library
Organizational training	
Establish an organizational training capability	• Establish the strategic training needs • Determine which training needs are the responsibility of the organization • Establish an organizational training tactical plan • Establish training capability
Provide necessary training	• Deliver training • Establish training records • Assess training effectiveness
Integrated project management (partially IPPD)	
Use the project's defined process	• Establish the project's defined process • Use organizational process assets for planning project activities • Integrate plans • Manage the project using the integrated plans • Contribute to the organizational process assets
Coordinate and collaborate with relevant stakeholders	• Manage stakeholder involvement • Manage dependencies • Resolve coordination issues

(continued)

Table 4-2 Continued

One-to-One Mapping of Specific Goals to Specific Practices

Goal	Practice
Risk management	
Prepare for risk management	• Determine risk sources and categories • Define risk parameters • Establish a risk management strategy
Identify and analyze risks	• Identify risks • Evaluate, classify, and prioritize risks
Mitigate risks	• Develop risk mitigation plans • Implement risk mitigation plans
Integrated teaming (IPD)	
Establish team composition	• Identify team tasks • Identify needed knowledge and skills • Assign appropriate team members
Govern team operation	• Establish a shared vision • Establish a team charter • Define roles and responsibilities • Establish operating procedures • Collaborate among interfacing teams
Integrated supplier management	
Analyze and select sources of products	• Analyze potential sources of products • Evaluate and determine sources of products
Coordinate work with suppliers	• Monitor selected supplier processes • Evaluate selected supplier work products • Revise the supplier agreement or relationship
Decision analysis and resolution	
Evaluate alternatives	• Establish guidelines for decision analysis • Establish evaluation criteria • Identify alternative solutions • Select evaluation methods • Evaluate alternatives • Select solutions
Organizational environment for integration (IPPD)	
Provide IPPD infrastructure	• Establish the organization's shared vision • Establish an integrated work environment • Identify IPPD-unique skill requirements
Manage people for integration	• Establish leadership mechanisms • Establish incentives for integration • Establish mechanisms to balance team and home organization responsibilities

(continued)

Table 4-2   Continued

One-to-One Mapping of Specific Goals to Specific Practices

Goal	Practice
Organizational process performance	
Establish performance baselines and models	• Select processes
	• Establish process performance measures
	• Establish quality and process-performance objectives
	• Establish process performance baselines
	• Establish process performance models
Quantitative project management	
Quantitatively manage the project	• Establish the project's objectives
	• Compose the defined process
	• Select the subprocesses that will be statistically managed
	• Manage project performance
Statistically manage subprocess performance	• Select measures and analytic techniques
	• Apply statistical methods to understand variation
	• Monitor performance of the selected subprocesses
	• Record statistical management data
Organizational innovation and deployment	
Select improvements	• Collect and analyze improvement proposals
	• Identify and analyze innovations
	• Pilot improvements
	• Select improvements for deployment
Deploy improvements	• Plan the deployment
	• Manage the deployment
	• Measure improvement effects
Causal analysis and resolution	
Determine causes of defects	• Select defect data for analysis
	• Analyze causes
Address causes of defects	• Implement the action proposals
	• Evaluate the effect of changes
	• Record data

Level 2 Process and Product Quality Assurance (PPQA)

Process and Product Quality Assurance provides for work product and process evaluations, work product and process audits, and corrective action monitoring and assist. Table 4-2 lists the goals and practices associated with the Process and

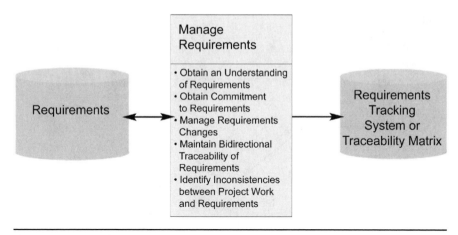

Figure 4-6   Requirements Management Process Area

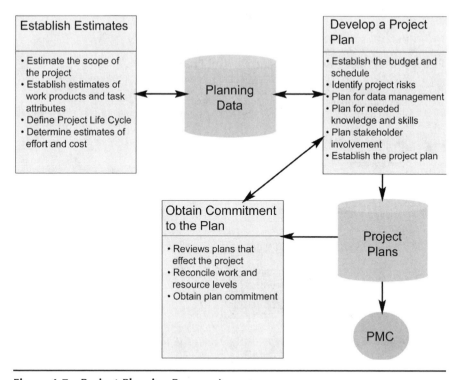

Figure 4-7   Project Planning Process Area

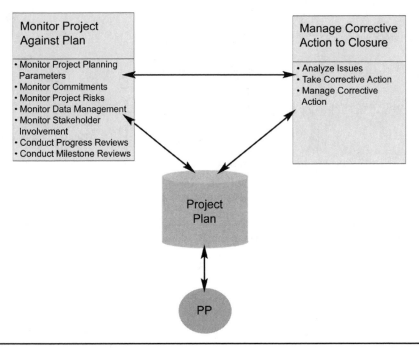

Figure 4-8   Project Monitoring and Control Process Area

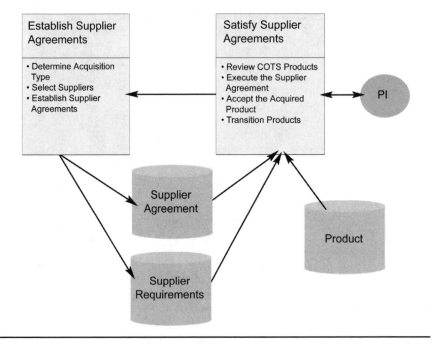

Figure 4-9   Supplier Agreement Management Process Area

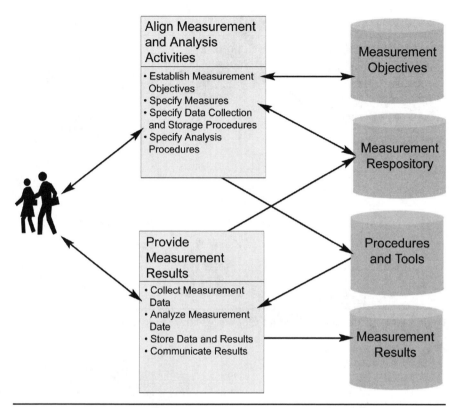

Figure 4-10   Measurement and Analysis Process Area

Product Quality Assurance Process Area. Figure 4-11 illustrates how the goals interact and some of the external interfaces for the Process and Product Quality Assurance Process Area.

Level 2 Configuration Management (CM)

Configuration Management provides for proactive management of product with version control to ensure the proper version of the product is available. Table 4-2 lists the goals and practices associated with the Configuration Management Process Area. Figure 4-12 illustrates how the goals interact and some of the external interfaces for the Configuration Management Process Area.

Level 3 Requirements Development (RD)

Requirements Development provides a method for fully developing the customer requirements to ensure a complete understanding using techniques to elicit

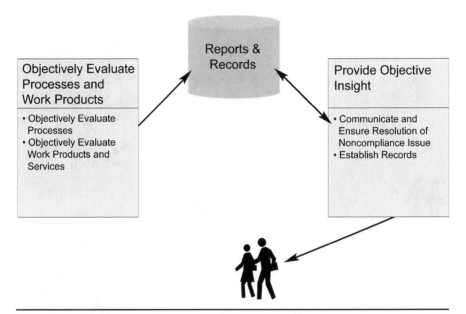

Figure 4-11   Process and Product Quality Assurance Process Area

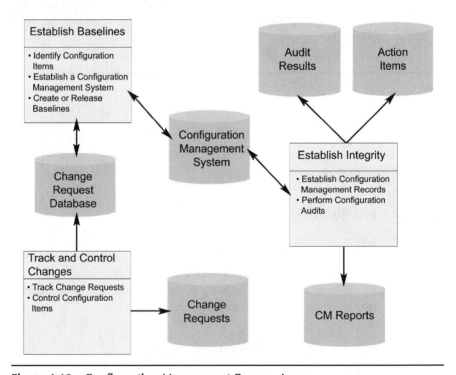

Figure 4-12   Configuration Management Process Area

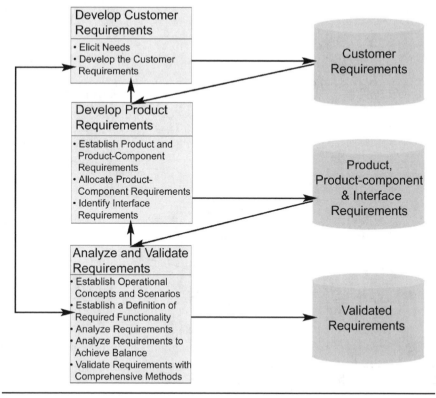

Figure 4-13   Requirements Development Process Area

requirements from users. Table 4-2 lists the goals and practices associated with the Requirements Development Process Area. Figure 4-13 illustrates how the goals interact and some of the external interfaces for the Requirements Development Process Area.

Level 3 Technical Solution (TS)

Technical Solution provides for product and product-component design and implementation such as coding as applicable. Table 4-2 lists the goals and practices associated with the Technical Solution Process Area. Figure 4-14 illustrates how the goals interact and some of the external interfaces for the Technical Solution Process Area.

Level 3 Product Integration (PI)

Product Integration provides for integration of the system in a controlled, smooth manner. Table 4-2 lists the goals and practices associated with the Product

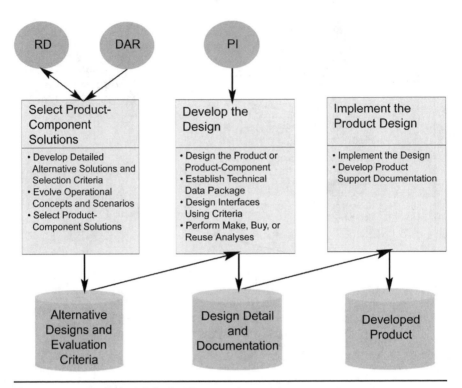

Figure 4-14   Technical Solution Process Area

Integration Process Area. Figure 4-15 illustrates how the goals interact and some of the external interfaces for the Product Integration Process Area.

Level 3 Verification (VER)

Verification provides for ensuring that the resulting products meet requirements and work in the operational environment properly. Table 4-2 lists the goals and practices associated with the Verification Process Area. Figure 4-16 illustrates how the goals interact and some of the external interfaces for the Verification Process Area.

Level 3 Validation (VAL)

Validation provides for ensuring that resulting product and product components operate properly in their ultimate final operational environment, sometimes called operational testing. Table 4-2 lists the goals and practices associated with the Validation Process Area. Figure 4-17 illustrates how the goals interact and some of the external interfaces for the Validation Process Area.

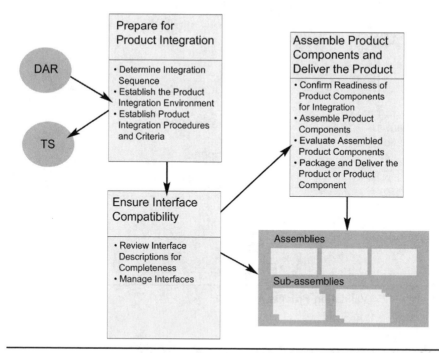

Figure 4-15   Product Integration Process Area

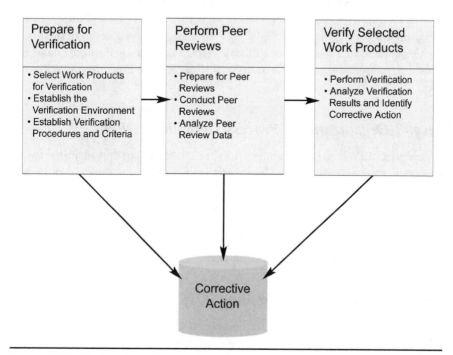

Figure 4-16   Verification Process Area

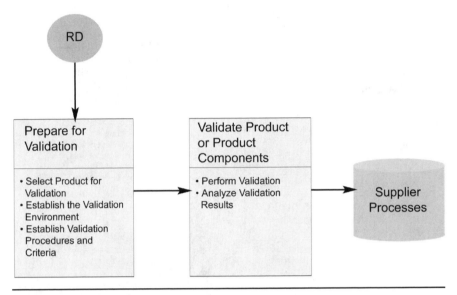

Figure 4-17   Validation Process Area

Level 3 Organizational Process Focus (OPF)

Organizational Process Focus provides for the planning of an implementation of the process improvement effort. It stresses strengths, weaknesses, and improvement opportunities management. Table 4-2 lists the goals and practices associated with the Organizational Process Focus Process Area. Figure 4-18 illustrates how the goals interact and some of the external interfaces for the Organizational Process Focus Process Area.

Level 3 Organizational Process Definition (OPD)

Organizational Process Definition provides for establishment and management of the organization process assets. The Process assets include the standard processes, approved life-cycle models, tailoring criteria and guidelines, measurement repository, and other assets associated with processes and process implementation. Table 4-2 lists the goals and practices associated with the Organizational Process Definition Process Area. Figure 4-19 illustrates how the goals interact and some of the external interfaces for the Organizational Process Definition Process Area.

Level 3 Organizational Training (OT)

Organizational Training provides for training to ensure proficiency to accomplish tasks as needed on projects to meet requirements of products and to ensure

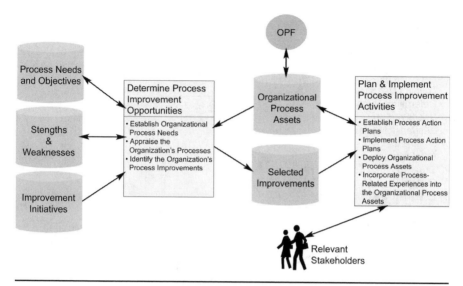

Figure 4-18   Organizational Process Focus Process Area

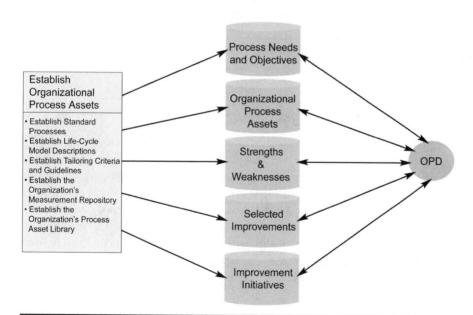

Figure 4-19   Organizational Process Definition Process Area

understanding of roles and responsibilities. Table 4-2 lists the goals and practices associated with the Organizational Training Process Area. Figure 4-20 illustrates how the goals interact and some of the external interfaces for the Organizational Training Process Area.

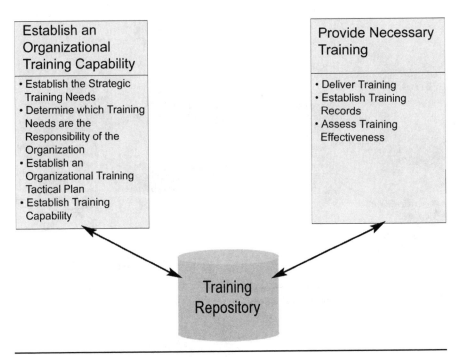

Figure 4-20   Organizational Training Process Area

Level 3 Integrated Project Management (IPM)

Integrated Project Management provides for the establishment and management of the organization's project processes that are a tailored version of the organizational processes. It stresses involvement of relevant stakeholders through collaboration and coordination. Part of this Process Area applies to organizations that use the Integrated Product and Process Development (IPPD) Methodology, which refers to a methodology that formalizes concurrent engineering. Table 4-2 lists the goals and practices associated with the Integrated Project Management Process Area. Figure 4-21 illustrates how the goals interact and some of the external interfaces for the Integrated Project Management Process Area.

Level 3 Risk Management (RSKM)

Risk Management provides for proactive management in order to identify and avert events that potentially cause undesirable consequences. Table 4-2 lists the goals and practices associated with the Risk Management Process Area. Figure 4-22 illustrates how the goals interact and some of the external interfaces for the Risk Management Process Area.

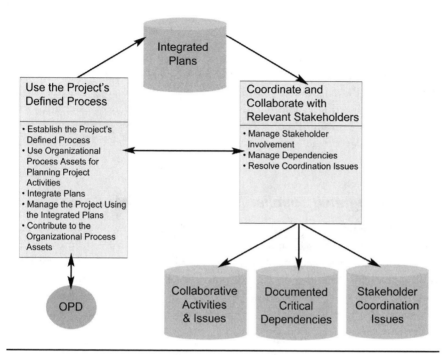

Figure 4-21   Integrated Project Management Process Area

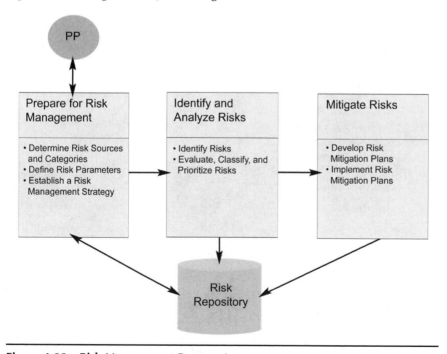

Figure 4-22   Risk Management Process Area

Level 3 Integrated Teaming (IT)

Integrated Teaming provides for forming and sustaining an integrated team for development of work products. This Process Area only applies to organizations that use the IPPD Methodology which refers to a methodology that formalizes concurrent engineering. Table 4-2 lists the goals and practices associated with the Integrated Teaming Process Area. Figure 4-23 illustrates how the goals interact and some of the external interfaces for the Integrated Teaming Process Area.

Level 3 Integrated Supplier Management (ISM)

Integrated Supplier Management provides for identity, analysis, and selection of sources of products based upon the "best fit." Additionally, it provides for coordination and management of suppliers, supplier agreements, and the assigned work. Table 4-2 lists the goals and practices associated with the Integrated Supplier Management Process Area. Figure 4-24 illustrates how the goals interact and some of the external interfaces for the Integrated Supplier Management Process Area.

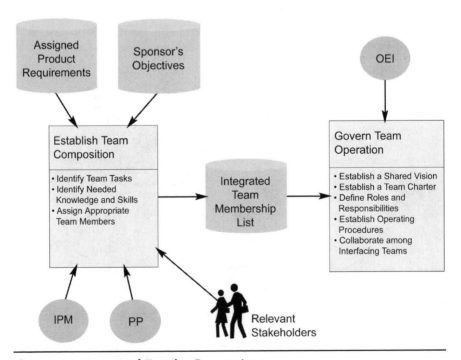

Figure 4-23   Integrated Teaming Process Area

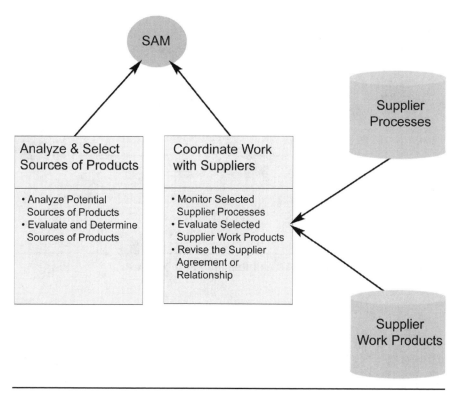

Figure 4-24   Integrated Supplier Management Process Area

Level 3 Decision Analysis and Resolution (DAR)

Decision Analysis and Resolution provides for analysis of decisions including a formal process to evaluate alternatives with specified criteria. It recommends documented guidelines for the evaluation, with issue management especially associated with high- and medium-risk items. Table 4-2 lists the goals and practices associated with the Decision Analysis and Resolution Process Area. Figure 4-25 illustrates how the goals interact and some of the external interfaces for the Decision Analysis and Resolution Process Area.

Level 3 Organizational Environment for Integration (OEI)

Organizational Environment for Integration provides for establishment of a "shared vision" for organizations as well as several other aspects associated with IPPD Methodology. This Process Area only applies to organizations that use the IPPD Methodology which refers to a methodology that formalizes concurrent engineering. Table 4-2 lists the goals and practices associated with the

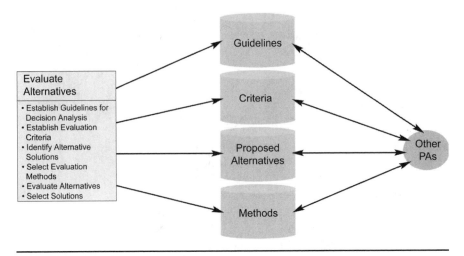

Figure 4-25   Decision Analysis and Resolution Process Area

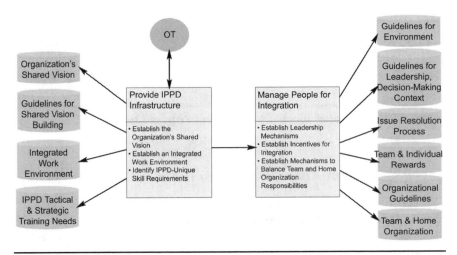

Figure 4-26   Organizational Environment for Integration Process Area

Organizational Environment for Integration Process Area. Figure 4-26 illustrates how the goals interact and some of the external interfaces for the Organizational Environment for Integration Process Area.

Level 4 Organizational Process Performance (OPP)

Organizational Process Performance provides for establishment and maintenance of the organizational process performance based upon quantitative data collected.

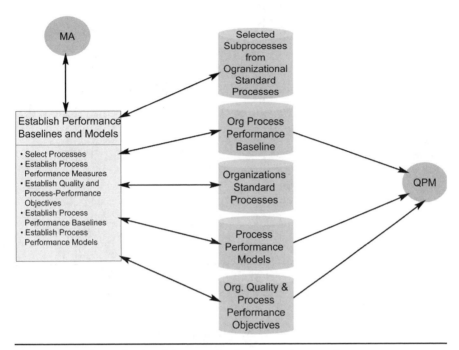

Figure 4-27   Organizational Process Performance Process Area

Table 4-2 lists the goals and practices associated with the Organizational Process Performance Process Area. Figure 4-27 illustrates how the goals interact and some of the external interfaces for the Organizational Process Performance Process Area.

Level 4 Quantitative Project Management (QPM)

Quantitative Project Management provides for establishment and maintenance of project performance based upon quantitative data collected and project objectives using analytical tools and techniques. Table 4-2 lists the goals and practices associated with the Quantitative Project Management Process Area. Figure 4-28 illustrates how the goals interact and some of the external interfaces for the Quantitative Project Management Process Area.

Level 5 Organizational Innovation and Deployment (OID)

Organizational Innovation and Deployment provides for improvement and maintenance of organizational processes and technologies. It revolves around looking for new things for improvement. Table 4-2 lists the goals and practices associated with the Organizational Innovation and Deployment Process Area.

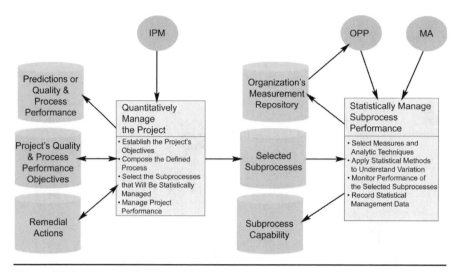

Figure 4-28   Quantitative Project Management Process Area

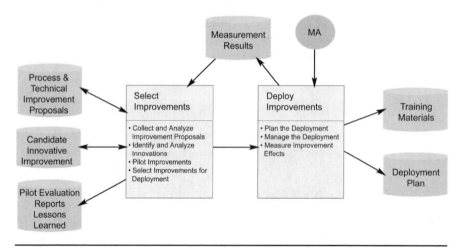

Figure 4-29   Organizational Innovation and Deployment Process Area

Figure 4-29 illustrates how the goals interact and some of the external interfaces for the Organizational Innovation and Deployment Process Area.

Level 5 Causal Analysis and Resolution (CAR)

Causal Analysis and Resolution provides for identification of the causes of defects and problems; and also taking action to prevent recurrence of defects and

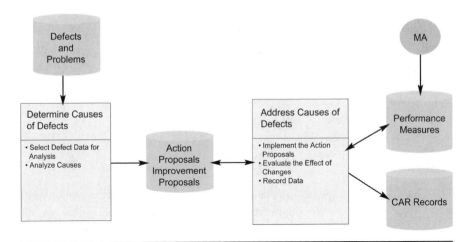

Figure 4-30   Causal Analysis and Resolution Process Area

problems. Table 4-2 lists the goals and practices associated with the Causal Analysis and Resolution Process Area. Figure 4-30 illustrates how the goals interact and some of the external interfaces for the Causal Analysis and Resolution Process Area.

CMMI® Generic Goals and Practices

Generic goals and practices are important to ensuring that the Process Improvement effort is institutionalized. The key is effective, repeatable, and lasting changes made by the introduction of the maturity level. Table 4-3 lists the maturity levels with their associated goals and practices.

Table 4-3   Generic Associated Goals and Practices

Level 2 Generic Goal: Institutionalize a managed process.

Associated practices:
- Establish organizational policy
- Plan the process
- Provide resources
- Assign responsibility
- Train people
- Manage configurations
- Identify and involve relevant stakeholders
- Monitor and control process
- Objectively evaluate adherence
- Review status with higher level management

Level 3–5 Generic Goal: Institutionalize a defined process.

Associated practices:
- Establish defined process
- Collect improvement information

SW-CMM® Mapping to CMMI®

As discussed in the previous chapter, the CMMI® is the replacement for the SW-CMM®. Figure 4-31 shows the mapping between the SW-CMM® Key Process Areas and the CMMI® Process Areas for Level 2. Figure 4-32 shows mapping for Level 3. Figure 4-33 shows mapping for Level 4. Finally, Figure 4-34 shows mapping for Level 5.

Summary

The CMM® is a model which tells an organization what needs to be accomplished. It is a framework for developing processes that is proven successful. It does not tell an organization how to implement processes. Many varying system development environments can successfully use the CMMI, including the growingly popular Agile Methodologies.

Chapter Key Points

- The Capability Maturity Model (CMM®) is a model not a methodology.
- CMM® is a framework and does not tell an organization how to implement processes, hence it can work well in many system development environments including the growingly popular Agile Methodologies.

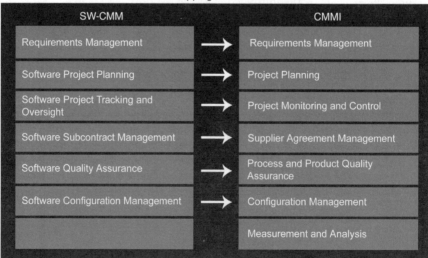

Figure 4-31   SW-CMM to CMMI Level 2 Mapping

SW-CMM Mapping to CMMI for Level 3

SW-CMM	CMMI
Organization Process Focus →	Organizational Process Focus
Organization Process Definition →	Organizational Process Definition
Training Program →	Organizational Training
Intergroup Coordination →	Integrated Project Management
Integrated Software Management →	Risk Management
	Technical Solution
	Verification
Software Product Engineering	Validation
	Product Integration
Peer Reviews	Requirements Development
	Decision Analysis and Resolution
	Integrated Supplier Management
	Integrated Teaming
	Organizational Environment for Integration

Figure 4-32   SW-CMM to CMMI Level 3 Mapping

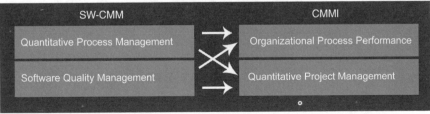

SW-CMM Mapping to CMMI for Level 4

SW-CMM	CMMI
Quantitative Process Management	Organizational Process Performance
Software Quality Management	Quantitative Project Management

Figure 4-33   SW-CMM to CMMI Level 4 Mapping

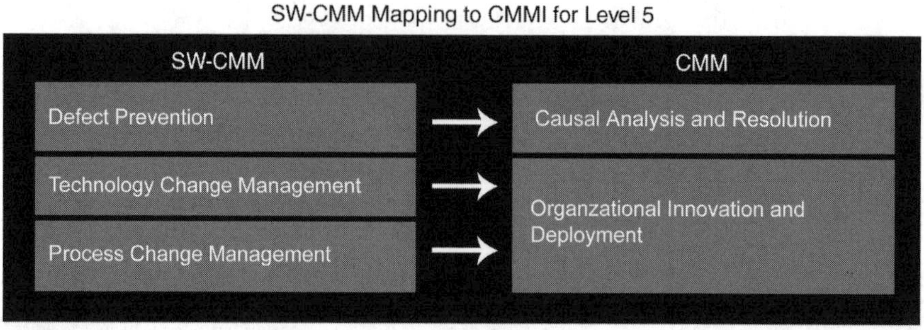

SW-CMM Mapping to CMMI for Level 5

SW-CMM	CMM
Defect Prevention	→ Causal Analysis and Resolution
Technology Change Management	→ Organzational Innovation and Deployment
Process Change Management	→

Figure 4-34 SW-CMM to CMMI Level 5 Mapping

- CMM® consists of best practices that are an accumulation of proven practices from both industry and government.
- The CMMI® comes in two flavors: staged and continuous. The use of which flavor to select will depend upon your organization's Process Improvement goals.
- The CMMI® staged model consists of five levels: Initial, Managed, Defined, Quantitatively Managed, and Optimizing.
- The CMMI® continuous model consists of six levels: Incomplete, Performed Informally, Planned and Tracked, Well-Defined, Quantitatively Controlled, and Continuously Improving.
- The process areas can be separated into four areas or categories: Project Management, Process Management, Engineering, and Support.
- The goals and practices are the key elements of the CMMI®. They are what the CMMI® is all about; in other words, they provide the essence of the model.

Tips for Success

- Understand the CMMI, especially the goals and practices.
- Weigh the advantages and disadvantages to select continuous or staged model.

Chapter 5

Implementing the CMMI®

Implementing a Process Improvement effort can be difficult but ultimately very rewarding. In summary, the CMMI®, like many other models and methodologies, requires:

- Numerous processes and procedures to be documented as well as followed by the entire or, at the very least, a large majority of the organization
- A set of organizational standard processes
- Appropriate training of the organizational standard processes
- A process architecture consisting of the numerous process elements, approved system development lifecycle approaches, and tailoring guidelines for adapting organizational standard processes for each program and project
- Development of project processes, tailored from the organization's standard processes
- Measurement, analysis, control, and continuous improvement.

Requiring that much detail and coordination takes a systematic approach to accomplish the model or methodology goals.

Plan-Do-Study-Act (PDSA) Cycle

The Plan-Do-Check (Study)-Act Cycle (aka PDSA Cycle or PDCA Cycle or Shewhart Cycle or Deming Cycle) is a basic approach that has been a very useful model as the basis of numerous approaches for improvement and analysis. It will be referred to as the PDSA Cycle in this publication. The PDSA Cycle was originally called the Shewhart Cycle in the 1930s, after its original creator Walter A. Shewhart, a Bell Laboratories scientist who was W. Edwards Deming's friend and mentor. The Shewhart Cycle later became known as the Deming Cycle in the 1950s when Deming popularized it.

The PDSA Cycle indicates an uphill progression of never-ending improvement; when you complete one cycle another is started on its heels as illustrated in Figure 5-1. The PDSA Cycle is a four-step process: Planning, Doing, Studying, and Acting. Some have added a secondary cycle within the DO to show that it may also cycle continuously.

The cycle starts with PLAN. At the planning stage, data is gathered and a plan developed. The DO or Doing stage is where the plan is tested, so to speak, on a small stage or trial basis so that impact is minimal. During the next stage, STUDY (sometimes called check), the effects of the implemented plan are analyzed. Finally, the appropriate actions are taken based upon the analysis during the ACT, which can involve adoption of the plan, abandonment of the plan, or modification. At this point the cycle is restarted based upon the changes or a new cycle to build upon the previous plan, thus continuous improvement begins.

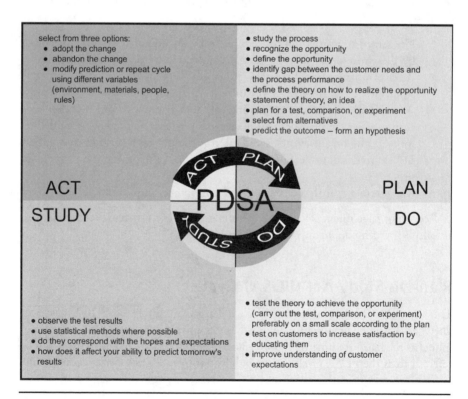

select from three options:
- adopt the change
- abandon the change
- modify prediction or repeat cycle using different variables (environment, materials, people, rules)

ACT
STUDY

- study the process
- recognize the opportunity
- define the opportunity
- identify gap between the customer needs and the process performance
- define the theory on how to realize the opportunity
- statement of theory, an idea
- plan for a test, comparison, or experiment
- select from alternatives
- predict the outcome – form an hypothesis

PLAN
DO

- observe the test results
- use statistical methods where possible
- do they correspond with the hopes and expectations
- how does it affect your ability to predict tomorrow's results

- test the theory to achieve the opportunity (carry out the test, comparison, or experiment) preferably on a small scale according to the plan
- test on customers to increase satisfaction by educating them
- improve understanding of customer expectations

Figure 5-1   PDSA Cycle

IDEAL^{SM} Model

All sorts of variations on the PDSA cycle improvement process are used with the key being its cyclical process. One popular model that used this as a basis is the IDEAL^{SM} Model[7] that was developed by the SEI for process improvement. This model defines five basic stages:

1. Initiating

    a. Stimulus for Improvement
    b. Set Context & Establish Sponsorship
    c. Establish Improvement Infrastructure

2. Diagnosing

    a. Appraise & Characterize Current Practice
    b. Develop Recommendations & Document Phase Results

3. Establishing

    a. Set Strategy and Priorities
    b. Establish Process Action Teams and Plan Actions

4. Acting

    a. Plan, Execute, and Track Installation
    b. Plan and Execute Pilots
    c. Define Processes and Measures

5. Leveraging

    a. Document and Analyze Methods
    b. Revise Organizational Approach.

The Initiating phase is where the stimulus, context, and goals of the change or improvement are defined. The sponsorship to making improvements is built and the infrastructure of the effort is developed. The resources are determined, organized and obtained including the process group. This sets the stage for continuing through the IDEAL^{SM} cycle.

The Diagnosing phase is for identification of the problems that have been found as needing improvement. An appraisement is accomplished in the form of an assessment, mini-assessment, or gap analysis in order to characterize the problem. Based upon the results of the appraisement, recommendations are made for correction or improvement. The results of this phase are documented, presented, and archived.

During the Establishing phase the strategies and priorities are set in order to set the stage for correction. The process action teams are built to tackle the assigned problem(s). The process action teams typically develop an action plan to document their strategy and improvement approach. The identified resources are collected and the actual improvement work is kicked off.

The Acting phase is where the solutions to the problem(s) are developed, piloted/tested, and refined as needed by the process action team. The support needs are identified and the solutions are turned over to the process group. At this time the action team is, typically, disbanded. The solution is implemented as approved and the process and process measures are defined.

Developing solutions during the Acting phase can take many forms based upon the problem being tackled. It has been broken down into six steps. The first step, Step 1, is to fully understand the problem and that can be accomplished by conducting a gap analysis or mini-assessment. There are several tools and techniques that are used during this step in the Acting phase, including impact analysis identifying the dependencies, risks, assumptions, brainstorming, multi-voting to prioritize, and development of a problem statement.

Step 2 is where ideas are generated to identify the potential solutions. Several tools and techniques have been identified to help that process, including brainstorming, surveys, and multi-voting to prioritize.

Step 3 requires a cost/benefit analysis. There are many methods available for performing this analysis that involve gathering data for analyzing and selecting a solution, evaluation of the potential solutions, and elimination of any solutions that are deemed impractical. Several tools and techniques have been identified for accomplishment of this step, including decision-making matrix, control charts, force field analysis, cost estimation, and Pareto charts.

Step 4 is selection of the best solution for the available options. This involves evaluation of solutions based on the defined business goals, business objectives, assumptions, risk, and any other defined criteria. Finally, selection of the most appropriate solution is accomplished. Several tools and techniques have been identified for accomplishment of this step, including decision-making matrix, cost estimates, and control charts.

Step 5 is where the effectiveness measurements are defined to determine how the organization will know if or when the solution has been successful. The process to define the data gathering for accomplishing measurements is defined by determining the how, what, frequency, and who. Several tools and techniques have been identified for accomplishment of this step, including check sheets, control charts, and run charts.

Step 6, the final step in the Acting phase, is completion of the implementation plan which includes determining a test or piloting strategy, training schedule, and the go/no go approval to start implementation. Several tools and techniques have been identified for accomplishment of this step, including capacity planning, implementation or action plan template, project plan templates.

The final phase of the IDEAL^{SM} Model is the Leveraging phase. The results of the implemented solution are analyzed in this phase, lessons learned are generated, and the approach is revised as needed based upon these results. Any future actions are recommended and the IDEAL^{SM} cycle begins again.

The IDEAL^{SM} model has been successful for many Process Improvement efforts. The APIM is based upon this model as well as the PDSA Cycle but has been significantly tailored to accelerate the process improvement effort. Once several successes have been seen, organizations may want to move to a more rigid, time-consuming process like the IDEAL^{SM} model to further improve their processes. It will depend upon their ultimate goals with process improvement. The APIM can be effectively used for continued process improvement.

Organizational Processes

Starting where you are is a key to developing processes for an organization. Build processes based upon how your organization does business. Reuse processes from your organization or from other organizations that may be available if, and only if, they fit the way you do business, but be careful that they really do meet the way you do business or they will end up hampering the process rather than aiding it.

Meeting the model is secondary since the ultimate goal is to improve the way an organization does business. The basic premises of the selected model should be met but alternative practices are acceptable if formal appraisal for a level is a goal. Processes are not judged on "goodness" but they can be judged on "effectiveness" which is the key to any process developed. The CMMI® does not tell you how to develop or how to accomplish a process but what process should be developed to meet the goals.

Processes will never be perfect, they will always need to be improved, which is a basic premise of all Process Improvement models. Processes should never inhibit the "Cowboy Coder" in any of us but instead should promote individuality and creativity. A key concept of any Process Improvement effort is to always keep it short and simple, use the KISS principle when developing processes. When processes are easily understood, they are more likely to be used.

Process Architecture

First let's talk about organization of processes. This is important because if a process can not be found or understood, it will not be used. There are several ways to organize processes but it depends upon how your organization is set up. This section will make some recommendations to consider.

Watts Humphrey defined three levels for process models for defining and organizing processes: Universal (U), Worldly (W), and Atomic (A).[19] The Universal level consists of the organizational policies, the Worldly level is the procedures and guidelines, and the Atomic level is the standards, templates,

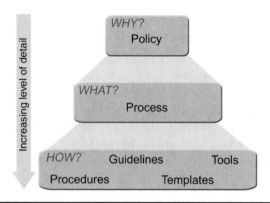

Figure 5-2 Organizational Process Library

and tools. This method will result in a cascading level of detail for processes as illustrated in Figure 5-2.

Tim Olsen, QIC, Inc., in a presentation at the Software Engineering Process Group Conference in 1999, *Defining Software Processes in Expert Mode*,[34] took this to another level and defined three process definition modes that work well for defining procedures and guidelines for organizations. The three modes are Beginner Mode, Intermediate Mode, and Expert Mode.

The Beginner mode is intended for the process user with little to no experience with that process. It will typically include very detailed information which can include training materials, process guidance, and lessons learned. On the other hand, the Intermediate mode is for the process user with some experience with that process. It will typically include less detailed information which can include process guidance, and lessons learned. Finally, the Expert mode is for users who are very experienced with that process. It will typically include a very high-level description of the process such as checklists, forms, or tables, as opposed to the step-by-step details in the other modes. They may contain pointers to the more detailed procedures in case they need to be referenced.

Developing Processes

There are many methods available for developing processes. This section will introduce a few of the popular, more successful ones.

When developing processes, there should be several layers to the processes including at least process flows, policies, procedures, forms, and templates. Checklists are great for the expert mode for each procedure. Blaise Pascal said "The present letter is a very long one, simply because I had no leisure to make it shorter."[40] Always remember KISS, keep it short and simple.

Processes should be a combination of pictures and text. Fred R. Bernard said, "One picture is worth a thousand words."[16] Being able to conceptualize a process is effective in clarifying the steps for the user and showing the relationships between processes. It enables users to visualize what needs to be accomplished and many times is more effective than text, especially pure text. The text should complement the graphical depiction of the process.

Some very effective methods of graphically and textually depicting a process are briefly discussed below.

Structured Analysis and Design Technique (SADT)

The SADT was developed in the early 1970s by Doug Ross, Softech/MIT. It is used extensively in modeling systems. Figure 5-3 illustrates the SADT method. The diagrams are arranged in a hierarchy to show increasingly more detail at lower levels. As the diagrams grow, they can become difficult to understand so care needs to be taken to keep them as simple as possible and still get the right message across.

Integrated Computer Aided Manufacturing (ICAM) Definition (IDEF)

The IDEF, sometimes referred to as simply Integrated DEFinition, is based on the SADT modeling technique. It was developed by the Air Force in the 1970s for the

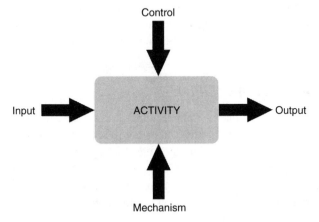

Inputs:	elements transformed by activity
Outputs:	elements inputs transformed into
Mechanism:	how activities are realized or external aids such as tools and techniques used for transformation
Control:	items that put constraints on the activity

Figure 5-3   SADT

Integrated Computer Aided Manufacturing (ICAM) project. The IDEF is a family of methods that supports modeling of an enterprise and business area. It was originally developed for systems engineering but has seen evolved to support other areas of modeling. The family/suite of models, each describing a different perspective, includes:

- IDEF0—Function Modeling
- IDEF1—Information Modeling
- IDEF1X—Data Modeling
- IDEF2—Simulation Model Design
- IDEF3—Process Description Capture
- IDEF4—Object-Oriented Design
- IDEF5—Ontology Description Capture
- IDEF6—Design Rationale Capture
- IDEF8—User Interface Modeling
- IDEF9—Scenario-Driven IS Design
- IDEF10—Implementation Architecture Modeling
- IDEF11—Information Artifact Modeling
- IDEF12—Organization Modeling
- IDEF13—Three Schema Mapping Design
- IDEF14—Network Design.

Figure 5-4 illustrates the basic IDEF0 model and Figure 5-5 provides a sample process using the IDEF method.

The other models in the IDEF suite are built upon this basic model. These models have proven increasingly successful in Process Improvement process definition; the one selected depends upon the level of detail selected.

Data Flow Diagrams (DFD)

DFDs identify the functional components and indicate the data that flows between the function components. They are used primarily for data discovery. It is based on the structured analysis and design methods for software development that was introduced and popularized by software experts like DeMarco, Sarson, Gane, and Yourdon in the late 1970s. These diagrams provide a useful tool for developing process diagrams as well as showing how data flows through the process. Figure 5-6 illustrates the structure of these diagrams.

Role Based Models

Role Based Models group activities into roles. Two of the more popular ones are the Role Activity Diagrams (RAD) and Petri Net.

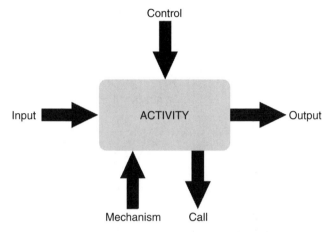

Inputs: elements transformed by activity
Outputs: elements inputs transformed into
Mechanism: how activities are realized or external aids
             such as tools and techniques used for
             transformation
Control: items that put contraints on the activity
Call: details shared linking models together;
             signifies there is not a child diagram to
             detail activity

Figure 5-4   IDEF

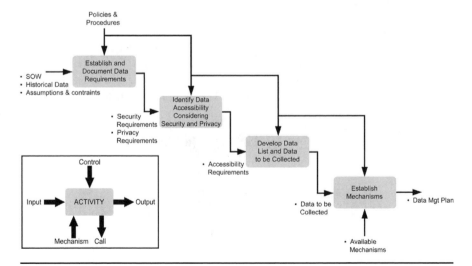

Figure 5-5   IDEF Sample

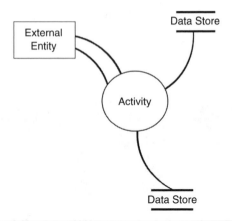

Figure 5-6   Data Flow Diagram

The RAD is a flowchart-type notation that depicts a business in terms of roles and their interactions. It was introduced in a paper by M.A. Ould and C. Roberts at the International Software Process Workshop in 1986.[24]

The Petri Net was developed by Carl Adam Petri in the early 1960s. This system modeling tool has been enhanced over time and is widely used in Denmark, Germany, and Norway. A key feature of this method is the depiction of concurrently occurring events.

The Role Based Models are worth looking into for a tool that depicted roles versus activities with concurrently occurring events.

Entry-Task-Validation-Exit (ETVX)

The ETVX is a popular process model that is expressed as a set of interconnected activities with attributes of entry, task, validation, and exit. It was developed in the 1980s by IBM to counter many problems they encounter in software development projects in terms of cost and estimation. Figure 5-7 illustrates this task based model where every cell is oriented around a task. The combined cells are combined to create processes.

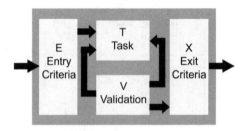

Figure 5-7   ETVX

The ETVX is made up of the following elements:

1. *Inputs or triggers*—a trigger/input invokes/initiates the process which usually comes from the preceding process. When the entry criteria are met, the process may be activated.
2. *Tasks or procedures*—the actions that the process will accomplish. This includes a validation step to ensure that the process does not terminate until the exit criteria are met.
3. *Controls*—limits deliberately placed on the process to avoid undesirable outcomes. These are usually audits, integrity checks, checkpoints, gated, or error detection and correction.
4. *Constraints*—limits imposed on the process to avoid undesirable outcomes. These usually include technical capabilities, time constraints, or resources.
5. *Outputs*—produced by the process when all exit criteria are met.

Entry-Task-Exit-Measure (ETXM)

The ETXM[18] takes the ETXV a step farther by adding measures. This model was defined by Watts Humphrey in 1989 and has since been used extensively for Process Improvement.

The ETXM model is made up of the following elements:

1. *Entry*—the conditions which must be met prior to entering into the task.
2. *Exit*—the results produced by the task including how they are the level of validation and other conditions.
3. *Feedback*—data from other stages of the process

    a. *In*—feedback from other stages
    b. *Out*—feedback to other stages

4. *Tasks*—the activities to be accomplished including what, who, how, and when. It is the standards, procedures, and responsibilities for the process.
5. *Measurements*—the task metrics and measures such as lines of code (LOC), requirements issues, or defects.

Flowcharting

Flowcharting has been used effectively for many years to visualize software but it is equally as effective in visualizing a process for Process Improvement. Figure 5-8 illustrates a typical flowchart. The method provides a graphical representation of a process, depicting inputs, outputs, decision points, and units of activity where the steps are represented in boxes and each arrow represents the sequence of steps.

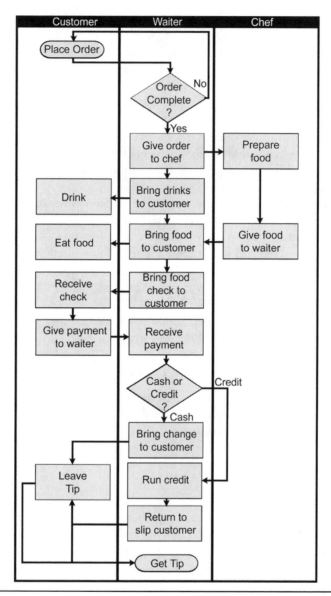

Figure 5-8   Flowcharting

It can be used with whatever level of detail is needed, allowing for analysis and optimization as needed.

Flowcharting is very effective in quickly identifying any bottlenecks or potential bottlenecks in the process, thus facilitating easy improvements as needed. There are numerous tools available for flowcharting.

Chunking

Chunking is a method used to organize and arrange information so that it is easier to read, understand, access, and retrieve. It is a method of subdividing and organizing into short "chunks" of information in a uniform format. The key is that, for certain types of information, the simpler the better with clutter being the villain. The premise is to group information and white space to break information into manageable components. This is sometimes called visual chunking and results in greater readability and accessibility. Chunking can be used extremely effectively in development of processes.

In writing, some of the components of chunking include:

- A chunk should be a manageable bit of information.
- Keep sentences to one or two points.
- Keep paragraphs short. A one sentence paragraph is OK.
- Use lists.
- Use fragments and phrases.
- Use pictures and other visual elements.
- Don't write prose.

Figure 5-9 illustrates the advantages of chunking. When you look at elements in logical groupings you are able to remember and understand them much easier.

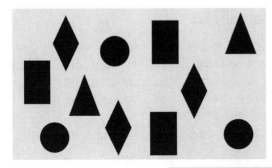

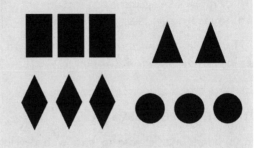

Figure 5-9   Chunking "which box makes it easier to understand"

There are things to avoid with chunking including over-generalization and being over-specific. Keep it simple but don't take away from content either so it is not fully understood.

Information Mapping®

Information Mapping® provides a method of organizing information in such a way as to make it more visual and thus more understandable. This method has evolved over time providing a structured method of visualizing information based on how the human brain reads, processes, remembers, and retrieves information. It was developed by Robert E. Horn while at Harvard and Columbia Universities in the 1960s.

Horn developed this method by conducting research on how a reader deals with large quantities of data. Based on this research he developed an approach for communicating information based upon learning theory, human factors engineering, and cognitive science. Some of the key principles include chunking, labeling, relevance, consistence, integrated graphics, and accessible detail. Horn was awarded a Lifetime Achievement Award for his work on the Information Mapping® method from the Association of Computing Machinery (ACM) in 2002.

Organizational Process Library

The organizational process library is typically where processes are stored. Several methods are very effective in organizing this library depending upon the organization's existing policies. A good method of organizing the processes is according to the function or primary role involved. The categories used in the CMMI® are very useful for organizing the processes:

- Project Management
- Engineering
- Process Management
- Support.

The next level of organization that works well is the Process Areas identified for each category as shown in Chapter 4.

Tailoring Processes

Organizations may choose to start with developing processes for one or more projects and use those projects as pilots. This is a plausible solution or they may choose to start with the organization as a whole. Whichever method is selected eventually, the processes will become part of an organizational process library. When a new project is started, this library will be used to develop processes to be implemented during the planning phase of the project.

Once the processes are part of the organizational process library, tailoring guidelines are used to tailor these processes for the project. The guidelines are important for the projects to understand so that precious upfront time is not spent doing this process. Again, the KISS principle is important. Keep the guidelines short and simple.

As a minimum the tailoring guideline should specify what can and what cannot be tailored out of a process. Many times a process will consist of parts that impact the project's effectiveness, based upon the Process Improvement model used such as the CMMI®. The guideline should specify how much of the process can be tailored and the impact when certain parts are tailored.

Some effective methods of accomplishing the tailoring is the use of tailoring workshops, sometimes called Project Kick-offs. These should have an agenda identified and tools specified for accomplishing this effort. A member of the process groups should act as the mentor and/or lead during this process and, depending upon the size of the organization or the project, the process group member will have varying levels of responsibility. Regardless of the name of the effort, or who leads the effort, it should be accomplished as early in the project as possible, with enough of the project staff involved as to get the appropriate processes identified and the highest level of buy-in as possible.

Enforcing Process Use

Finding a method for enforcing processes or a particular process can be difficult. Whether to use a hammer or a compliment can make a world of difference in how processes are accepted within an organization. The method will be determined based upon the organization's existing culture and their ultimate Process Improvement goals. The following lists a few methods that can be considered:

- Promote managers based on their use of processes.
- Reward staff based upon progress as compared to plan.
- Reward staff using processes, not the heroes.
- Dismiss staff not using processes.
- Reward teams, not just managers.
- Remember to walk the walk and talk the talk; if staff see upper management following processes they are more likely to follow suit.
- Advertise even the smallest successes in Process Improvement!

Summary

Process Improvement takes a systematic approach to implement properly. It requires numerous elements that must be managed and coordinated. Even though it can be difficult to achieve it is very rewarding for an organization as well as the people who work in the organization.

Chapter Key Points

- The Plan-Do-Check (Study)-Act Cycle (aka PDSA Cycle or PDCA Cycle or Shewhart Cycle or Deming Cycle) is a basic approach that has been a very useful model as the basis of numerous approaches for improvement and analysis.
- The IDEAL^{SM} Model was developed by the SEI for process improvement. This model defines five basic stages: Initiating, Diagnosing, Establishing, Acting, and Leveraging.
- The three modes Beginner Mode, Intermediate Mode, and Expert Mode are a good method for architecting processes.
- When developing processes, there should be several layers to the processes including at least process flows, policies, procedures, forms, and templates.
- Organizational process library is used to store processes. A good method of organizing the processes is according to the function or primary role involved.
- Tailoring guidelines are used to tailor these processes for the project.
- Reward staff using processes, not the heroes.
- There are a good many methods of enforcing processes; organizations can choose to use a hammer or a compliment in doing so, depending upon their existing culture and Process Improvement goals.

Tips for Success

- Always remember KISS, keep it short and simple.
- Processes should be a combination of pictures and text.
- Chunking can be used extremely effectively in development of processes.
- Use Information Mapping® techniques to organize information and make it more visual.
- Keep tailoring guidelines simple so they will be used.
- Walk the walk and talk the talk.

ACCELERATING PROCESS IMPROVEMENT METHODOLOGY (APIM) INTRODUCTION

It was just another day, not much unlike the other days and nights before it. While most people were at home with their families, Joe just sat at his desk with his head in his hands. He felt like pulling out all his hair, that is if he still had any left, he was down to his last nerve.

At 4:30 the project manager had walked into Joe's office and asked him to provide an estimate for some new work they were pursuing to revamp an old database on the POLMO system for a 10:00 meeting. As excited as Joe was to, finally, be able to bring this antiquated system into the 21st century, the task he had been assigned was impossible. He was trying to figure out what to do with the information he was given and how to compensate for the information he was not given.

"Hey, Joe, you're working late!" Mark called from the doorway as he walked into Joe's office.

"Hey Mark, I was looking for you earlier! I thought you might be able to help me out with some estimates. Bob came in about an hour ago and threw this on my desk," Joe says as he hands Mark the one page of vague information he had been given earlier.

As Mark reaches for the paper and sits down across from Joe, he explains, "I heard I was putting out yet another fire over on the KIDI project, they just can't seem to get it right. The latest version of the LBSystem files was lost. Can you believe it? They lost files again on that project and we go to test tomorrow. Weeks of work almost down the drain, the new version of files was just lost. If we hadn't spent the last 2 hours going through the developer's files and found his working files, we'd be completely lost. As it is, the developers have to spend the next few hours going through the files one by one and making sure that they are the correct ones and that the interfaces have not been impacted. Even after they finish that painstaking process, the rebuild itself is going to take another 5 hours and then we have to pray that it works. Just another day in paradise."

As Mark starts looking at the information Joe had handed him, Joe says, "So what's the answer here Mark, crisis after crisis and I don't think I can take much more, good thing the pays so good or I'd give it all up and open an antique shop."

"Didn't give you much to work from, did they? As usual!" Mark exclaimed after looking over the information Mark was working from for his estimates.

"I heard they were using some tool over on the ZIPA project called Momo, Mumu, Cococa, no, no, no, that's not right," Joe says as he tries to remember the name of that tool he'd heard about, "Cocomo, like the Beach Boys song" Joe remembers, "I called Jim but he'd gone home already."

"I did this on the PRAPM project, let me go over to my office and I'll show you how I handled it. It really came down to a SWAG," Mark says.

"Did you make the schedule and budget?" asked Joe.

"Are you kidding, why do you think they call it a SWAG, Scientific Wild Anatomical Guess," Mark laughed, "When was the last time this company met a schedule, we're lucky to get half the requirements into the systems."

"I know, I know," Joe said exasperated. "When's this going to change? They keep talking about this process improvement they're working on, what's it been, two years now?"

"I know, they sure have a lot of meetings but nothing changes, just takes people away from projects that I need them for. All talk but no action." Mark agrees, "I haven't seen one thing come out of that whole effort, have you?"

"No, but I keep hearing how it's going to help things run smoother," Joe says.

"I know there's a better way than this, at least I keep hearing there is, wish I could see something happening," Mark expresses.

"Well, if you don't mind, I'd love to see how you did your SWAG, anything's better than nothing," Joe says, getting more frustrated by the minute, "By the time I figure out how to really get this project estimated, we could have the work done. Seems like such a waste of time when we know we won't make the schedule anyway. Guess that's why we get paid the big bucks, huh, Mark?"

"Maybe you, not me," Mark laughs.

"By the time they get this process improvement thing going this company will be out of business because they can't keep up," Joe exclaims, as frustrated as ever but realizing it's just another day just like the rest.

Remind you of a project you've been on?

Chapter 6

Accelerating Process Improvement Methodology (APIM) Description

In order to avoid repeated scenarios like the one described for Mark and Joe, the APIM considers timing the key. For the majority of businesses "faster, better, cheaper" is the mantra of the day. Businesses know that they must keep up in order to stay in business and the only way to do that is to meet their schedules, budgets, and realize the requirements they have signed up to meet.

The APIM uses the IDEAL^{SM} Model, the Agile programming methodology, and lessons learned as a basis. This combination of successful models and methodologies provides the best method for ensuring that all the key aspects of Process Improvement are met in an agile fashion.

Agile Programming Methodology

Agile Programming Methodologies claim to have changed the way software is developed. In many ways they have but the jury is still out on how successful these methodologies will be over the long run. The key element they bring to the software development community is that they make software developers question the way they develop software. With the numbers, as discussed in an earlier chapter, so astoundingly abysmal for successful software projects, when the software community starts questioning what could be wrong, it sets the stage for things getting better and that is a positive thing. Perhaps a melding of the old software development principles and the more agile development principles will show even more promise since many of the old and many of the newer agile principles have proven successful.

What these agile methodologies offer are some very effective principles that work well in a good many situations. Applying the principles to areas such as a Process Improvement effort has proven successful.

Agile Programming Methodologies have been getting more and more attention since the early 1990s. Several agile methodologies have evolved during the last several years. Table 6-1 lists some of the more popular ones and provides a brief description of each.

There are several recurring themes in the agile methodologies. These include short iterations, close collaboration both with customers and within the development team, open communications, frequent deliveries, tight teaming, simplicity, refactoring, continuous testing, and proactive plan management.

Short Iterations

Development is partitioned into a series of logical pieces starting with a core set of capabilities/functions. Partitioning the development schedule into workable stages is a key aspect of the agile methodologies. This allows the developer the chance to measure success often and plan accordingly for the next iteration. This principle allows functions, or a group of functions, to be incrementally added as the system is built. This allows a strong foundation to be built and tested prior to adding more complex functionality. Even outside the realm of agile programming, this has been a successful method for building systems, especially when testing is accomplished at each iteration to ensure that the system continues to function properly and can be corrected prior to having to dig through a multitude of functionality to find where the real problems lie. This principle significantly reduces risks in a system development by weeding out problems and defects early.

Frequent Deliveries

Frequent deliveries allow the customer to ensure that they are getting what they really want. One of the most difficult things on any project is requirements for both the requirements giver and the requirements receiver. For the requirements giver, it is very hard to articulate requirements either in writing or verbally even if

Table 6-1 Agile Programming Methodologies

Methodology	Brief Description
Extreme Programming (XP)	XP was developed by Kent Beck and Ward Cunningham in the early 1990s. They were looking for a way to help a struggling project and came upon one that worked. Kent Beck popularized it in several books along with others who embraced the Extreme Programming Methodology. XP's four values are improved communication, seeking simplicity, getting feedback, and courage to proceed. There is a strong emphasis on testing where developers actually write the tests as they write the code.
Crystal Methodologies	The Crystal Methodologies is actually a family of methodologies that was developed by Alistair Cockburn. It is based around different kinds of projects which require different kinds of agile methodologies. The key is the human and communications aspects of a project. This approach is based on his own experiences as well as interviews with others in the development community.
Adaptive Software Development (ASD)	Jim Highsmith developed this methodology which evolves around the adaptive nature of new methodologies as opposed to predictive nature of older methodologies. His methodology consists of three overlapping phases: speculation, collaboration, and learning.
Scrum	Scrum is an iterative, incremental process based on 30 day iterations called sprints. A short meeting is held daily for the development team to plan the day with a scrum report going to management daily to status the project.
Feature Driven Development (FDD)	FDD was developed by Jeff De Luca and Peter Coad. It is based on short iterations of two weeks and consists of five processes: develop an overall model, build a features list, plan by feature, design by feature, and build by feature.
Dynamic System Development Method (DSDM)	This methodology started in Britain in 1994 as a consortium of UK companies. It started with 17 founders and has grown into a full-time organization with manuals, training courses, and accreditation programs. The DSDM principles include active user interaction, frequent deliveries, empowered teams, testing throughout the cycle. It uses short iterations of between two and six weeks.

you know exactly what you want. For the requirements receiver it is just as difficult understanding what others are trying to articulate. We tend to overlook seeing things from another point of view. When engineers and clients start working together and understanding the other point of view, we will truly be able to do effective Requirements Engineering. Frequent deliveries with constant feedback from the client is a great method of ensuring that the customer gets what they want and what they are paying for.

Open Communications

Open communications and respect for each other's position is crucial on any project. There's enough to panic about when developing a system without the added stress of misunderstandings or misconceptions. Communication ensures that all stakeholders understand what is expected and provide management and the customer with insight into progress to alleviate problems and issues as they occur.

Close Collaboration

Working closely with the customer throughout the development process can make the difference between success and failure. The key to close collaboration is for the customer to help ensure the system's desired functionality is realized and the developer to fully understand what the system's desired functionality is from the customer's point of view. Some of the terms used by the agile methodologies are "Active Stakeholder Participation" and "On-Site Customer."

Tight Teaming

There is never enough to say about how important teamwork is on any project. Managers, customers, and developers must be all part of the team dedicated to delivering software that meets the user needs. It is key to a project's success that development teams and customers work as one team to develop effective requirements, thus developing effective products. If we look at things from each other's vantage point, the chance of success grows by leaps and bounds. We all look at things differently based on our background, education, experience, and simply from where we are standing at the moment. Open communications and respect for each other's position is crucial.

Simplicity

Simple and clean design is a key concept in agile methodologies. Keeping the design as simple as possible enables programmers to easily evolve their code as requirements evolve or change, which, as anyone who's done software development for very long knows, happens regardless of the methodology used to develop the system.

Refactoring

"Do the simplest thing that will work" is a key phrase in agile methodologies. Refactoring is the process of reworking any written material to improve its readability or structure while keeping the meaning or behavior intact. For software development, previously developed complex software uses refactoring to make "the code clearer, cleaner, simpler, and elegant" and "avoid needless clutter and complexity." This does not mean changing the functionality or rewriting the software but simplifying it for easier use.

It can be used when adding new functionality or behavior as long as the developer is able to let go of their original design. A key aspect of refactoring is frequent testing even for the smallest change or "refactoring." This avoids serious impact to existing functionality as the refactoring is accomplished.

Continuous Testing

XP changed the name of their functional tests to acceptance tests to reflect the intent to "guarantee that a customer's requirements have been met and the system is acceptable." Meeting customer requirements is the ultimate goal of any system development project, thus getting feedback from the customer early so that any changes can be made with the least amount of impact. For agile programming methodologies, changing requirements is a way of life not an impediment. Systems are developed with that premise in mind as well as technology insertion as needed.

Proactive Plan Management

An overall plan is developed at the beginning of a project with inputs from all stakeholders. For XP, "user stories" are estimated in terms of an ideal week. The user stories are put on cards and moved around a table consisting of both the developers and the customers. By the end of the session, a set of stories based on priority and value to the system are created that make up the next release. Planning and replanning accomplished at the beginning of each iteration is called release planning. Learning is a continuous and important feature of agile programming methodologies and as such you start out by realizing that plans will change and evolve as development evolves. In the Agile Manifesto they put "responding to change over following a plan."

APIM

Indeed, Process Improvement can be quite complex, just as software development is. However, the key to Process Improvement is improving the way you do business; once a good foundation is built using an accelerated method and results are realized, the organizational staff are more likely to put their full weight behind the effort.

Many of the agile themes are good themes for accelerating a Process Improvement effort and in fact are good themes for any Process Improvement effort. Taking a page from the very successful Jack Welch, retired Chairman and CEO of General Electric, "You can't behave in a calm, rational manner. You've got to be out there on the lunatic fringe."

Figure 6-1 illustrates the APIM.

APIM Phases

The APIM has three phases: Pre Maturity, Maturity, and Post Maturity. Each phase consists of various steps required to develop an organization's maturity. This methodology takes an agile approach with simplicity and common sense the magic words. Many times organizations tend to over-process with multiple forms, plans,

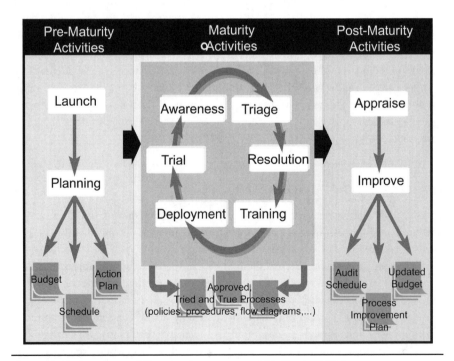

Figure 6-1   Accelerated Process Improvement Method (APIM)

and procedures that end up being meaningless. As is usually the case, the devil is in the details. Table 6-2 provides a quick overview of each step in the APIM.

Pre Maturity Phase

The Pre Maturity Phase consists of steps that need to be accomplished in preparation for the Process Improvement effort. This phase will set the stage for later phases. It is the key to getting early buy-in from key managers and the resources needed to get the effort off to a good start. It also is where the initial Action Plan will be developed.

Maturity Phase

As illustrated in Figure 6-1, the Maturity Phase is iterative. It is repeated until an organization is ready for a more formal appraisal or for continued Process Improvement. This is the most critical phase in the process since this is where most of the real work is accomplished.

A good timeline may help kick things off but an organization must be open to this timeline changing in much the same way as the agile programming methodology planning. Things will change no matter what great plans are put in place. These changes may be based on a good many factors, such as acceptance of the processes developed, capabilities of the process development team, where in the development cycle the system development teams are, the system development lifecycles being used on most projects, etc.

Post Maturity Phase

The Post Maturity Phase consists of steps that should be accomplished when the organization decides it is ready to move away from the APIM and into a formal appraisal or continuous improvement. An organization may or may not want to undergo a formal appraisal at this time. They may want to use the APIM to kick off the effort and then go to a less agile method once some of the processes that form a good foundation for further improvement are in place. This depends upon their ultimate Process Improvement goals. The APIM works well for kicking off an improvement effort and building a foundation as well as continued improvement, depending upon the organization's success using the model and the APIM.

Summary

The APIM considers timing the key to facilitate the "faster, better, cheaper" mantra of the day. APIM combines the more traditional Process Improvement method,

Table 6-2   APIM Quick Overview

Phase	Step	Objectives
Pre maturity	Launch	• Executive approvals • Set process improvement goals • Task authorization • Executive steering committee • Initial resources/appointments • Budget • Kickoff meeting(s)
Pre maturity	Planning	• Develop brief action plan • Communications planning • Data management planning • Issue resolution planning • Process peer review planning • Process format planning • Quality assurance liaison planning • Risk management planning • Tool planning: databases, techniques, methods, and models • Detail master schedule • Develop metrics and measures • Select projects • PAT action planning • Establish regular status meetings and reports • Process group meeting planning • Executive steering committee • Plan and conduct training: organizational and process group
Maturity	Awareness	• Conduct mini-assessment to identify strengths and weaknesses—initial and progress • Select mini-assessment methodology • Compose mini-assessment team • Conduct pre- mini-assessment activities • Conduct mini-assessment activities • Conduct post mini-assessment activities • Baseline mini-assessment results
Maturity	Triage	• Prioritize actions using triage approach • Develop key selection criteria • Conduct process group meeting to prioritize • Manage actions

(*continued*)

Table 6-2   Continued

Phase	Step	Objectives

Maturity	Resolution	• Establish process action teams
		• Develop action plan
		• Resolve process action or issue as assigned
		  — Develop processes (remember KISS)
		    ✓ process flows
		    ✓ policies
		    ✓ procedures
		    ✓ forms
		    ✓ templates
		• Conduct peer reviews
		• Report status and any issues
		• Propose a solution to the problem
		• Train staff involved in pilot
		• Pilot test the solution mentoring staff throughout
		• Manage actions

Maturity	Training	• Determine methods to be used for training • Prepare training materials • Conduct training • Accomplish post training assessment
Maturity	Deployment	• Pilot processes to selected project • Tweak processes, as needed • Mentor pilot project(s)
Maturity	Trial	• Assess effectiveness of processes • Determine outcome • Deploy processes • Collect and analyze lessons learned
Post maturity	Appraise	• Determine maturity level • Identify strengths and weakness for future improvement

Post maturity	Improve	• Keep the momentum going
		• Develop continuing process improvement plan
		  ✓ Improvement measures
		  ✓ Audit plans
		  ✓ Audit reports
		  ✓ Periodic progress assessments
		  ✓ Updated risks
		  ✓ Updated budget
		  ✓ Updated action plan
		  ✓ Task completion criteria
		• Audit processes
		• Training assessment

IDEAL[SM] Model, with the successful Agile programming methodology, along with many lessons learned to develop a method of quickly putting Process Improvement in place. This combination helps ensure that all the key aspects of Process Improvement are met in an agile manner.

Chapter Key Points

- Agile Programming Methodologies is making the software development community question the way they develop software.
- Several aspects of Agile Programming Methodologies can help accelerate Process Improvement such as: Short Iterations, Frequent Deliveries, Open Communications, Close Collaboration, Tight Teaming, Simplicity, Refactoring, Continuous Testing, and Proactive Plan Management.
- The APIM has three phases: Pre Maturity, Maturity, and Post Maturity. Each phase consists of various steps required to develop an organization's maturity.
- The Pre Maturity Phase consists of steps that need to be accomplished in preparation for the Process Improvement effort.
- The Maturity Phase is iterative; it is repeated until an organization is ready for a more formal appraisal or for continued Process Improvement.
- The Post Maturity Phase consists of steps that should be accomplished when the organization decides it is ready to move away from the APIM and into a formal appraisal or continuous improvement.

Tips for Success

- Partitioning significantly reduces risks by weeding out problems and defects early.
- Frequent deliveries allow the customer to ensure that they are getting what they really want.
- Open communications and respect for each other's position is crucial on any project.
- If we look at things from each other's vantage point, the chance of success grows by leaps and bounds.
- Keeping it as simple as possible enables easy evolution or change.
- "Do the simplest thing that will work" is a key phrase in agile methodologies.

Chapter 7

Pre Maturity Phase:
Step 1-Launch

The Launch step kicks off the Process Improvement effort. It is important to getting the support needed from the appropriate staff. This step should not be smoothed over since it can make the difference between being able to accelerate the effort or not.

Process Improvement Goals

This should have been accomplished prior to going into the Process Improvement effort. It is important for the organization to know what goals are targeted for completion of the effort. This may change as the Process Improvement effort progresses but going into the effort with a set of achievable goals needs to be determined.

Each organization is unique so the goals will vary significantly but some of the objectives that should be considered include:

- What model or models would help the organization gain the most advantage?
- What level of maturity is optimal?
- What practices are most important to achieve based on the organizational needs?
- Formal Appraisal vs Continued Process Improvement?
- What are customers' expectations concerning process maturity?

- Deployment of the processes to entire organization or subsets? What subsets?
- What level of technology can be allocated for the effort? Expertise needed to achieve?

There are numerous other areas to consider based on an organization's unique needs and available resources. There are always significant events that will drive the decisions made to even go into a Process Improvement effort that will hence drive the goals set for the effort.

Executive Management Buy-in

This is where you get buy-in from executive management if you don't already have it. Without executive buy-in it will be virtually impossible to move ahead in any Process Improvement effort; however, for an accelerated Process Improvement effort it becomes even more critical to success. Not having the right resources will significantly slow things down.

It's most likely that you already have executive buy-in prior to going into a Process Improvement effort. In fact, it is most likely that they kicked the Process Improvement off in the first place. Even in that case, there may be some executives that still need to be brought on board. Each and every one is critical to the success of the Process Improvement effort because they typically are responsible for providing the right resources to get the job done.

Another issue with executive buy-in is to maintain that buy-in past the honeymoon period of the effort. You have to be ever vigil of their support. It is important to maintain their confidence in the Process Improvement team to be able to get the job done and done right. Regular status meetings, just like any other project with the same status, measures, and risk discussions will help keep them on board. Status Meetings will be discussed in further detail in a later chapter. The key is not to give them false expectations since these will end up biting you later in the process and you could lose their support altogether or at the least slow support to a trickle.

Resources and Budget

The launch step is key to obtaining the appropriate resources and budget for execution of the APIM. The resources can be in terms of dollars, staff, training, equipment, work space, etc. This is again where the executive buy-in is important. Dollars for companies is a very precious commodity and is not given lightly, especially in our day and age of "Cash is King" mottos for organizations. What it ultimately comes down to for an organization is dollars, whether in the form of money, staff equipment, work space, supplies, or dollars for training.

In terms of resources staff must be allocated to ensure appropriate resources are available to accomplish essential tasks for Process Improvement. The lack of resources quoted by the Standish report has become a key problem over the years. The same estimation process should be accomplished for allocation of resources; this starts with a good Work Breakdown Structure (WBS). At this point a top-level work breakdown structure should be developed and refined during the Planning step. This is an iterative tool that should be used throughout the effort to replan, reassign, reallocate, and reapportion. Reference the toolkit for further discussion of this important method and samples for reference.

Each organization has their own method of handling a budget and resources but one thing to remember is justification. Regardless of the method used you should be able to justify every dollar allotted to the effort. Reference the toolkit for further discussion of budgeting and samples for reference.

Making estimates on the size of staff needed can be difficult. Some of the methods typically used on system development projects may be useful. Table 7-1 lists some of these methods. The most popular method of estimating, especially when little or no historical data is available, is the Wideband Delphi method. This method can be used effectively in a wide range of areas for estimating. It was developed by Rand in the 1940s and has been honed over time to make more

Table 7-1   Typical System Development Estimating Methods

Method	Brief Description
Historical data	Comparisons to similar work products estimates (actuals vs estimates)
Fuzzy logic method	Estimators assess planned product and roughly judge how its size compares to historical data
Standard component method	Comparisons to similar components from other projects to make progressively more refined estimates
Proxy-based estimating	Use of a proxy or stand-in with a close relationship to work product for visualizing functions
Function point methodology	Categorized according to relative development complexities
Wideband delphi	Several engineers produce individual estimates that are converged to get a consensus estimate
Prototyping	Develop prototype—more refined estimate

accurate estimates. It helps to filter out some of the more extreme early estimates and disregards politics that may impact the estimates. Wideband Delphi is described in further detail in the toolkit.

There are several methods of accomplishing cost estimating for system development including heuristics/rule of thumb, top down, bottom up, and parametric. These methods can be used effectively for estimating a Process Improvement effort as well with a few modifications. The SEI has estimated how much time it takes to accomplish a Process Improvement effort that can be used as a start. However, the APIM method can significantly accelerate that estimate.

The budget is the planned cost for the project for all "authorized" work. Three cost elements should be considered:

- Direct Cost
- Indirect Cost
- Management Reserve.

Direct cost is any cost that can be attributed to an activity or another cost objective such as labor, materials, or other direct cost (ODC). Indirect cost is any cost that cannot be specifically attributable to a task or specific cost objective such as administrative costs, supplies, facilities, interest, inflation adjustments, and other non-attributable costs. Management reserve is typically 10% of the budget and represents dollars set aside for unplanned or unanticipated activities. The toolkit includes a checklist that may be useful in developing or reviewing the budget.

Some organizations will already have a method of accomplishing the budgeting which should be used. They may have a financial department or executive management that has already determined the amount of available funds for the effort. Many use the Earned Value Management method which is very effective. Earned Value Management is based on the work that is accomplished; the value of that work is "earned."

Initial Master Schedule

The schedule provides a calendarization of the project plan. If a task-oriented WBS is developed, this can be used to develop the schedule. A schedule can serve many purposes including documenting the baseline schedule, documenting actual work-completed performance dates, documenting forecasted dates for work not yet begun, and tracking completed work as planned. The uses for any project schedule are invaluable including statusing, assigning staff, tracking, planning, and interfacing with other team members. For it to be effective, it should be used by the entire staff as well as being reviewed and updated as needed.

There are several elements that a good schedule should include as listed in Table 7-2.

Table 7-2   Key Elements of a Schedule

Method	Brief Description
Key milestones	These are essential elements for any schedule. They are significant, major, or intermediate events which mark progress. May include completion of a phase, major deliverable, or release or an event requiring management approvals. Typically, milestones have a zero duration.
Key events	Major events, the achievement of which are deemed critical to the execution of the project. This is where the activities take place between events.
Interfaces	Major activity, departmental, project, inter-organizational, and subcontractor interfaces.
Dependencies	A relation between activities, such that one requires input from the other called a logical relationship. The four types of logical relationships: – Finish-to-start: the "from" activity must finish before the "to" activity can start – Finish-to-finish: the "from" activity must finish before the "to" activity can finish – Start-to-start: the "from" activity must start before the "to" activity can start – Start-to-finish: the "from" activity must start before the "to" activity can finish
Predecessors	An activity that must be completed before a specified activity can begin.
Successors	An activity whose start or finish depends on the start or finish of a predecessor activity.
Critical path	The path (sequence) of activities which represent the longest total time required to complete the project. They are the series of tasks that must finish on time for the entire project to finish on schedule. There may be multiple critical paths. There also may be near critical paths, especially if risks are considered. Each task on the critical path is a critical task. The critical path may change as activities are completed ahead of or behind schedule or as the schedule changes due to replanning activities.

There are many ways of depicting the schedule besides just textually but the most popular ones today are the PERT and GANTT Charts.

The PERT Chart is a flowchart that shows all tasks and task dependencies. The tasks are represented by boxes and task dependencies are represented by lines connecting the boxes. On the light side, PERT means Problems Eventually Resolve Themselves! The PERT Chart provides a great method of showing dependencies but it can take a good deal of space to see the whole project.

The GANTT Chart provides a graphical representation of the schedule with horizontal bars. The activities are listed down one side and the other side provides the dates across the top with the horizontal bars showing the duration. This method was developed in 1917 by Henry L. Gantt as a production control tool. It has gained a good deal of popularity for use in Project Management.

Whichever method is selected for the schedule, there are many tools available to providing both of these formats as well as others.

At this point a high-level Master Schedule should be developed to show at least the major milestones and key events. These will be detailed during the next step and updated throughout the effort. The top-level Work Breakdown Structure should be used to build the initial Master Schedule. The toolkit includes a checklist that may be useful in developing the schedule, some of the items may be more appropriate for later, more detailed iterations of the schedule.

Any situation has both favorable and adverse conditions that must be considered that could potentially impact the schedule. These are called the critical success factors. Be sure to consider all critical success factors. These include conditions that currently exist or conditions which may occur or exist during the course of the effort. These conditions will impact the way that conflicts and risks are handled as well as the priority of the Process Improvement effort. Many conditions may impact the availability of staff or other critical resources needed to successfully see the effort through to success.

Authorization and Approvals

Each organization has their own method of authorizing tasks but you should get official executive approvals and task authorizations before proceeding. Approvals should be obtained from all levels of management even if they are simply verbal approvals even when not required. In doing so, you are able to build a rapport with the managers that you will need on your side later in the effort.

Executive Steering Committee

An executive steering committee should be formed during launch. Chapter 18 discusses the responsibilities of this important group which typically consists of key higher-management representatives. An executive steering committee can be very effective in providing leadership, overall direction, and needed resources as well as ensuring focus, and resolving major issues throughout the process.

Always remember to remain agile, do not let the bureaucracy typically associated with numerous committees bog you down. When you start putting in frequent, long-drawn-out review cycles and approvals, you get away from being agile.

Process Team Generation

Initial resources and appointments to the Process Team will be an important activity during launch. A good mix of skills and knowledge will ensure that the various areas associated with Process Improvement are dealt with properly. Chapter 18 discusses the responsibilities of this key group in detail.

It is recommended that the core Process Team be kept fairly small, depending upon the size of the organization, with enough hours assigned to the team to get the real work accomplished. Too many people can cause bottlenecks that prevent, or slow, real accomplishment. On the flip side, too few people, or too few hours for the people assigned, allows no room for accomplishing tasks. Additionally, the wrong people with a negative attitude assigned to the group can sabotage the effort.

The key will be to find the appropriate balance for the organization. It requires closely monitoring the group during start-up from the honeymoon stage (this is the time that people are most enthused) into the early start-up stages. It may take some trial and error to form the right group of people to accomplish the tasks required to accelerate Process Improvement.

In order to make a difference, the Process Team should be armed with the authority to make decisions and changes needed to meet the Process Improvement goals. Arming the Process Team, or at least the lead, with authority, levels the playing field for them by giving them an equal voice with Project Managers. By leveling the playing field within the organization, the Process Team will be better able to make reasonable changes. Even though there will, in all probability, be mistakes, the organization must be prepared to roll with the punches to ease a quick recovery. As Spencer Johnson said in *The Present*, "You cannot change the past, but you can learn from it. When the same situation arises, you can do things differently and become happier and more effective and successful today!"[20]

There's a wonderful story about the importance of teams that has circulated for years in emails and on many web sites. The author of this infamous story is unknown. It is called The Goose Story and is listed in the toolkit.

Kickoff Meetings

There should be at least two initial Kickoff Meetings for the organization during Launch.

1. Executive Management Kickoff Meeting

The initial Kickoff Meeting should be with the executive staff. This may have already been accomplished prior to launch but a follow-up meeting should be accomplished to present the early planning information and officially kick the effort off. A typical agenda will include: vision/measure of success statement (short description of successful end condition(s)), primary objectives, teams (including roles and responsibilities), budget, schedule (include discussion of critical success factors), risks, concerns, and issues. For follow-up meetings, or when an earlier executive meeting was held prior to actual kickoff, action items should be included. A sample agenda template is included in the toolkit.

Minutes should be taken and sent to each attendee to ensure that everyone is on the same sheet of music. In other words, ensure that there are no misunderstandings or misconceptions going into the effort. The minutes should include attendees, discussions, decisions, issues, action items, and any other items deemed necessary to ensure a full understanding and concurrence. A sample minutes template is included in the toolkit.

As with any meeting, a general set of meeting rules should be observed. Table 7-3 lists some of these meeting rules.

2. Process Team Kickoff Meeting

Once the initial resources and appointments have been determined, a Process Team Kickoff Meeting will be the first activity for bringing the process team together. A typical agenda will include: vision/measure of success statement (short description of successful end condition(s)), primary objectives, teams (including roles and responsibilities), schedule (include discussion of critical success factors), risks, concerns, and issues. The risks, concerns, and issues will vary from the executive management meeting. They may include lower-level risks, concerns, and issues that should be resolved at this level of the organization. The roles and responsibilities may be discussed in further detail so that each member understands their role.

This initial meeting will be the first chance to get a feel for how this key team will work together. Remember, this is still the honeymoon stage so it will be hard to really tell how the group will form until some time passes. The forming, storming, norming, and performing model concerning group development that was developed by Bruce Tuckerman in 1965 is worth considering in forming the team. Table 7-4 further briefly discusses these team-building terms. If all team members remember to bring solutions instead of excuses, the process team can be very effective in accomplishing the Process Improvement goals.

Table 7-3 General Meeting Rules

Always provide an agenda prior to the meeting so that participants are prepared for discussions.

Always provide minutes following a meeting so that there are no misunderstandings or misconceptions.

Only have meetings when absolutely necessary, use other means of communications for dispensing information as warranted.

Assign action items and expected completion dates during the meeting for resolution of issues or concerns.

Keep focus on meeting objectives and call for side meetings for discussion outside of the general group.

Ensure that all participants critical to discussions are available; if not reschedule meeting until all critical participants are available.

Keep all meetings as short as possible.

Discuss topics applicable to all participants or schedule multiple meetings with proper attendees based on meeting objectives.

Avoid conflicts during meeting. Remember: praise in public, criticize in private. Don't allow finger pointing. Take disagreements into another forum for discussion with only affected participants. A facilitator that is neutral can help facilitate a follow-up meeting.

Start meetings on time so that participants that are punctual are not impacted by those that are late.

Conduct meetings during normal work hours as much as possible.

Ask for suggestions during meetings to improve form, content, etc.

Marketing Process Improvement

Marketing the Process Improvement effort early in the process is important to ensure that everyone is aware of what's going on and to start getting buy-in from all organizational staff. Chapter 19 discusses methods of marketing the Process Improvement effort effectively.

Summary

Launch is the initial chance to kick the Process Improvement effort off to a good start. It can make the difference between success and failure. It is important that

Table 7-4 Tuckman's Forming, Storming, Norming, and Performing

Stage	Brief Description
Forming	This stage is characterized as getting to know each other. It is where discovery is occurring and people are determining who they like and what is expected of them. Team members are trying to determine what behaviors are appropriate and which ones are not. The vision, mission, and goals are being formed for the team.
Storming	This is when conflicts and confrontations start emerging. Many times this is due to members vying for positions or control. It is at this stage that members of a group can be lost or they lose interest when they become insecure. Treating each member fairly is key to helping get through this difficult stage.
Norming	Norms are generally accepted behaviors which is what starts happening at this stage. The group becomes more harmonized and starts to unify. Conflicts are reconciled and any resistances are overcome. Cooperation and communication begins to occur. People start feeling like they are part of a team.
Performing	This is where a team starts becoming effective in achieving its intended purpose. Small disagreements can erupt at this stage but with close attention paid to each member these can be alleviated before they "implode."

this step be taken seriously to ensure that staff get on board, appropriate staff are assigned to the effort, and the appropriate budget and other resources are in place.

Chapter Key Points

- Launch can make the difference between being able to accelerate the effort or not.
- Carefully consider and determine Process Improvement goals.
- Generate a WBS and Initial Master Schedule.
- Executive Management will ensure that budget and resources are available to accomplish the Process Improvement goals.
- Process Team should be generated ensuring good mix of staff with the right authority to make things happen in the organization.
- Plan carefully for Kickoff meetings, this is the first chance to start building support and buy-in.
- Marketing the Process Improvement effort is a key to success.

Tips for Success

- Goals are set in stone; be flexible enough to expect and accept changes smoothly.
- Maintain executive management confidence.
- WBS and schedule must be a "living schedule" to be effective.
- Don't let bureaucracy bog you down.
- Keep the Process Team fairly small.
- Arm the Process Team with authority to make a difference.
- Market the Process Improvement effort.

Chapter 8

Pre Maturity Phase:
Step 2-Planning

There are many reasons why projects fail but survey after survey has found that one of the top reasons for failure is lack of planning. Conversely, studies have found that a major reason for success is proper planning. Upfront planning is very important but, as with the very successful agile programming methodology, planning should remain as painless as possible and iterative.

A forward-looking philosophy should be employed to ensure that you are prepared for taskings but concurrently ensure enough flexibility to accommodate changing task priorities. In essence, the upfront planning should provide the basic strategy by which a Process Improvement effort operates. It's a matter of pay now or pay more later.

Managers can avoid the common mistakes made when a project is managed using reactive, firefighting methods of decision making rather than proactive. In a reactive environment, staff are frequently reacting with no time for fact-based planning, forecasting, decision making and improving. When planning takes a more proactive perspective, there is much less impact when things don't go as planned, thus it minimizes any surprises.

Iterative planning ensures that all aspects of activities are considered throughout the effort. As the effort evolves so should the plan. When an effort is in the early stages you don't fully understand all ramifications of the effort but, as it evolves, new things come to light so an iterative plan will enable the effort to take advantage of this additional information.

In the words of Lewis Carroll in *Alice in Wonderland*:

"Cheshire-Puss," she began, rather timidly,
"Would you tell me, please, which way I ought to go from here?"
"That depends a great deal on where you want to get to," said the cat.
"I don't much care where," said Alice.
"Then it doesn't matter which way you go," [8]

If you want to know which way to go, you must create a plan for how to get there.

Action Planning

The Action Plan will provide the detailed activities that are required to help an organization meet their Process Improvement goals. The action plan should be short and simple with only the necessary information, thus avoiding unneeded information that will be shelved. Don't spend too much time on this; it should be a fairly quick effort. The effort should include an overall action plan and an action plan for all major planned activities as deemed necessary. A sample Action Plan is included in the toolkit. The overall Process Improvement Action Plan should include the following:

- Objectives
- Goals (Short-Term and Long-Term Goals) with associated Success Measures
- Assumptions and Barriers
- Risks
- Organization For Process Improvement (Process Improvement Teams including their responsibilities)
- Process Improvement Roadmap
- Process Development Life Cycle
- Tracking and Reporting Process
- Schedule (major milestones and associated tasks)
- Measures for Success (remember KISS)
- Tools For Success
- Training Plans for Organization.

Key Planning Areas

There are several areas that need to be considered during the Planning Step. It is important to cover all areas that could impact the effort. To further quote Lewis Carroll in *Alice in Wonderland*, "It sounded an excellent plan, no doubt, and very neatly and simply arranged. The only difficulty was, she had not the smallest idea how to set about it." [8]

The following are some of the key areas to consider; they may be included in the Action Plan as needed but each area needs to be well thought-out and documented.

Short-Term and Long-Term Goals

The main element of the Action Plan is to define the goals for the Process Improvement effort. The short-term goals are typically those that are accomplished within six to twelve months. The long-term goals are the goals identified for being accomplished within one to three years. The long-term goals may actually follow the completion of the APIM or be part of the effort, depending upon the organization's Process Improvement overall goals.

Each goal, short and long term, should be associated with a success measure. They should be succinct elements that when achieved mean that the goal has been met. They represent the end result to be realized by the goal.

The Action Plan short- and long-term goals are different than the actions that are defined as part of the effort, in that they are overall goals defined by the Process Group that must be achieved in order to meet the overall organizational goals.

Communications Planning

Communications planning early in the effort that identifies each stakeholder's needs can help manage information flow, define lines of communication, and ensure that all stakeholders are considered. The planning should include:

- Responsibilities
- Project roles
- Logistics
- Information sharing/distribution including the appropriate media
- A reporting approach.

This will ensure that there are no misunderstandings and misconceptions. In short, the key is to know the who, what, when, where, and how.

There must be a clear understanding of who are the Decision Makers or Final Authorities. This includes who can:

- Add or approve a new process or requirements for a new process
- Change an existing process or requirements for a new process
- Accept changes to processes or requirements for a new process
- Direct the various teams
- Determine if a process needs have or have not been met
- Accept processes as met or not met.

A graphical depiction can help immensely in defining and keeping track of who's who. These should be approved by the appropriate managers and distributed to all stakeholders. These diagrams can be included in the Overall Process Improvement Action Plan.

Distribution lists for the various data elements being developed as part of the Process Improvement effort should be developed to ensure all stakeholders are included as needed. Distribution can be accomplished using many means; these are discussed in further detail in Chapter 19. Some of the mechanisms discussed include use of email, information portals, newsletters, etc., but the good old hardcopy may be feasible for many data items that need to be distributed. Some things to consider for data distribution include:

- Accessibility
- Security
- Quality required
- Size of distribution list.

Data Management Planning

Chapter 5 discussed the organizational process library which is typically where processes are stored. The organization of this key library is key but the management of this library is just as important to success. Additionally, other data items developed as part of the Process Improvement effort must be stored and managed. These data items may take the form of:

- Reports
- Manuals
- Charts
- Tapes
- Engineering drawings
- Specifications
- Photographs
- Films
- Electronic media
- Correspondence
- Any other data items produced as part of the effort.

The control of processes and other Process Improvement data items needs the same discipline as a software development project with version control, auditing, and other elements of configuration management to ensure that things are not lost, overwritten, misidentified, unverified, or distributed improperly. A change request process and formal acceptance process should be defined as part of this Process Improvement process.

The same provisions for configuration management of software should be considered for Process Improvement processes and other data items. These include:

- Planning
- Identifying
- Recording
- Controlling
- Storing
- Distributing
- Validating.

Figure 8-1 illustrates typical configuration management elements.

Issue Resolution Planning

Issues and problems can be initiated in many ways, including verbally from any staff member, at meetings, during peer reviews, or many other means of relaying issues can occur. A proactive approach should be used to handle issue/problem correction and prevention before they get out of hand. Corrective action is any action taken to eliminate an existing issue, nonconformance, deficiency, defect, or other undesirable conditions. Preventive action is any action taken to eliminate the cause of an existing issue, nonconformance, deficiency, defect, or other undesirable conditions in order to prevent recurrence. Wherever possible, organizations should strive to determine the root cause of a potential or existing deficiency, defect, or other undesirable situation to a level commensurate with the potential risks.

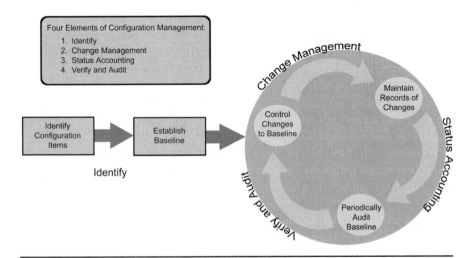

Figure 8-1   Configuration Management Elements

It is important to encourage regular contact with all organizational staff members by the Process Group. This enables them to discuss any complaints, issues, risks, problems, and opportunities when they arise. By doing so it helps enable proactive steps to be taken to resolve issues as quickly as possible and prevent them recurring. Key to this is ensuring that all issues are tracked to ensure non-recurrence and resolution.

Action Items should be initiated to track any issues and their associated activities. An Action Item process should be established to define, control, and track all actions. An Action Item Database is an effective method of managing issues and problems. There are many off-the-shelf databases available or a "homegrown" database can be developed for risk management.

Irresolvable action items should be reported to the executive steering committee during the regular status briefings for resolution, dissolution, or further elevation, as appropriate.

Process Peer Review Planning

Peer reviews, sometimes called quality reviews, walkthroughs, or inspections, are designed to investigate the correctness of work products. There are many ways of accomplishing peer reviews, some formal, and some less formal. Both work well but the key is to take the time to accomplish these reviews. To make them more accelerated, use the keep it short and simple (KISS) method and leave the bureaucracy usually associated with these reviews behind. Effective peer reviews are accomplished in a non-adversarial, investigatory manner. One significant side effect of peer reviews, outside of finding issues and problems, is that they tend to promote communications between team members.

The more formal peer reviews are meetings with the author, a moderator, quality assurance, and experts/stakeholders in the area being reviewed. Many organizations have tailored the *Fagan Inspection Technique*, developed by Michael Fagan at IBM in 1976, for peer reviews. It has proven to be a very powerful inspection method.

A less-formal peer review consists of determining a set of peers (one or more) that are qualified to evaluate the work and conducting a peer review using hardcopy or softcopy review of the product. Some sort of paper trail should be in place to track what has and has not undergone a peer review and maintain the actions that should be accomplished, since when things get hectic many times these can fall through the cracks.

One thing must always be kept in mind when doing a peer review; there's a right way and a wrong way to review someone else's work. Depending upon the manner conducted, a peer review can result in encouragement or resentment for the person whose work is being reviewed.

Process Format Planning

Chapter 5 discusses various process formats. This is the point where those decisions should be made. There are many formats that a process can use but there are a few elements that they should have which include:

- Purpose
- General Description
- Inputs
- Entry Criteria
- Outputs
- Exit Criteria
- Roles and Responsibilities
- Activities (Should Be Both Textual And Graphical Step By Step Procedures)
- Interfaces or References.

A sample procedure format is included in the toolkit.

Quality Assurance Liaison Planning

Just as the Quality Assurance staff should act as the eyes and ears for the Project Manager on a project as well as the Executive Management team, the Process Group needs to form a liaison with the Quality Assurance Group to provide that service for them as well. At least one quality assurance staff member should be an integral part of the process group. Many times the quality assurance group is the group responsible for Process Improvement but, as will be discussed in Chapter 18, The People Side of Process Improvement, the recommended staffing is a mix of disciplines with quality assurance staff an integral part of the team.

Risk Management Planning

All programs face some degree of risk. An effective Risk Management process will help identify and mitigate risks, avert events that have potential undesirable consequences and maximize a project's probability for success. Nothing completely eliminates all risks but a good Risk Management process limits the impact of risks. Every Process Improvement meeting that occurs should include some level of Risk Management discussions. Initially, the Risk Management should be accomplished as a separate activity so that the staff can concentrate on issues.

A risk is defined as the "possibility of loss or injury" but, as related to an organization, it is the probability of unwanted or unexpected consequences as measured against the expectations. These are the uncertainties, any cryptic project elements, the known unknowns, the unknown unknowns, or any possible or probable changes that could impact the organization or project.

Risk Management has been described as running up the down escalator since you are always trying to keep up with it. There are many good Risk Management processes but most of them include the following basic activities:

- Identify
- Analyze
- Plan
- Document
- Track
- Control
- Communicate.

There are many effective methods of identifying risks; the following ones can be used very effectively:

- Brainstorming
- Work groups
- Questionnaires
- Risk assessments
- Checklists
- Interviews (structured or unstructured)
- Performance models
- Cost models
- Network analysis
- Quality factor analysis.

Once risks have been identified they should be analyzed to clarify the risk, determine the seriousness of the risk, and determine any additional potential risks. Figure 8-2 illustrates a typical analysis process. Some risks may require rewording or combining, depending upon how they impact or interface with another risk. Risks can be categorized for easier management using categories that make sense for that effort. Categorization based on whether they are more administrative than technical can be very beneficial. There are a good many ways to categorize risks but these two categories keep it simple and easy to use. If a more complex method of risk categorization is required, there are numerous Risk Management methods that recommend categories.

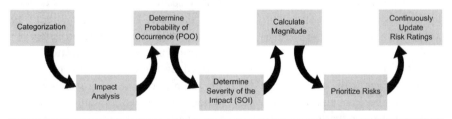

Figure 8-2   Risk Analysis

An impact analysis can simply consist of a statement discussing the impact of the risk occurring. Some areas to consider are any impact on the budget or the schedule as well as the timeframe that the risk may occur. Once this is accomplished, the Probability of Occurrence (POO) and Severity of Impact (SOI) can be determined so that the magnitude of the risk can be calculated. The POO is the likelihood of the risk occurring and the SOI is the effect that the risk will have if it does occur. The ranking can be anything that makes sense to the organization for ranking risks; typically three to five levels are identified such as:

- Probability Of Occurrence (POO)

  — Rank of 1 to 10:

    - 8–10 is very likely
    - 5–7 is probable
    - 1–4 is improbable.

  — Rank of 1 to 5:

    - 5 → very high → 95–100 percent
    - 4 → high → 75–95 percent
    - 3 → moderate → 25–75 percent
    - 2 → low → 5–25 percent
    - 1 → very low → 0–5 percent.

- Severity Of Impact (SOI)

  — Severity level from 1 to 10

    - 8–10 → critical
    - 5–7 → marginal
    - 1–4 → negligible.

  — Severity level from 1 to 5

    - 1 → no impact
    - 2 → relatively small impact
    - 3 → considerable impact
    - 4 → significant impact
    - 5 → catastrophic impact.

Once the POO and SOI are determined, the magnitude or priority can be calculated.

$$POO \times SOI = Magnitude$$

Figure 8-3 illustrates a typical graphic used to determine priority. This one is based on a 5-level system but can be used for any number of levels as needed.

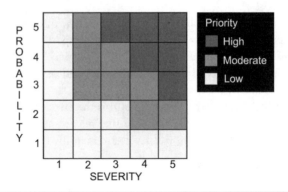

Figure 8-3   Determining Priority

Whichever method is used, the risks should be ranked from high to low. The risks can also be labeled as "Manage," "Monitor," or simply "Accept," where the "Accept" level risks are logged into the risk database but no immediate mitigation action is required.

All risks should be monitored throughout the effort until they no longer are applicable to ensure that the risk is mitigated if needed or at least the impact minimized. The priority ranking should be monitored and updated regularly to indicate the risks most likely to occur that have the biggest impact on the effort.

A Risk Management Database is an effective method of managing risks. There are many off-the-shelf databases available or a "homegrown" database can be developed for risk management.

Since the basis of Risk Management is to avert, control, or prevent the consequences of risks, a major goal of the process is to bring the level of acceptability to another level, be it elimination, reduction, or simply control. The planning stage is where a mitigation, aversion, or transference strategy is determined for the risks identified as high or manage. Several methods can be used for handling risks depending upon the risk:

- *Mitigation/Contingency or Intervention Plan*—set of tasks to reduce or eliminate risk.
- *Control*—acceptance of risk and monitoring risk to provide control.
- *Transference*—reallocation to another area.
- *Avoidance*—elimination of the risk by changing the effort in such a way that it will not occur.
- *Set Aside Resources*—set aside resource to reduce or eliminate risk.
- *Assumption*—assumptions can be made based on what is already known and a strategy developed to reduce or eliminate the risk.

The method selected will depend upon the situation and the risk. A trade-off analysis can be accomplished to determine the best method of handling a risk.

Monte Carlo is an analytical method that is meant to imitate real-life systems, which randomly generates values for uncertain variables over and over to simulate a model. This method can be used effectively for risk strategizing. There are also established questionnaires that can be used effectively for risk management and strategizing.

As discussed previously, this is an on-going process that should be accomplished throughout the Process Improvement effort as well as any effort undertaken by an organization.

Tools for Success: Techniques, Methods, Models, and Databases

There are a good many tools and databases that can be beneficial to any project; this is especially so with an accelerated Process Improvement effort. It's hard to make any progress if you don't have the right tools to get there. The key to selecting the right tool is to ensure that you are getting the "bang for the buck." This section will discuss a few of these useful tools.

Project Management Databases

A database is the optimal method for managing various aspects of a project. A simple spreadsheet can also be very effective but databases hence facilitate smooth management of key areas. There are several good commercial tools that are available but creation of a "homegrown" database will give the user exactly what they are looking for if the expertise and time is available. These tools have many advantages over a simple listing including:

- Ease of search
- Smooth management of elements
- Provides for an "authorized" record of project elements
- Change control
- Metrics collection with minimal effort
- Can be used for any needed documentation.

Some databases that can be very beneficial include:

- *Process Development Tracking Database*—can be convenient for tracking processes that are being developed for the Process Improvement effort.
- *Mini-Assessment Database*—can be useful for several purposes such as tracking mini-assessments, mini-assessment results, progress reports, baseline mini-assessment results.
- *Process Organization Database*—provides an effective, easy-to-use method of organizing processes.

- *Organizational Asset Database*—provides an effective method of organizing the numerous other organizational assets such as management reports, estimating data, historical data, approved tools, approved lifecycles, and any other information for project and organizational use.
- *Historical Database*—method of archiving project and organizational historical information.
- *Training/Staff Skills Database*—very useful tool for keeping track of the skills that the organizational staff possess and their training needs.
- *Task Management Database*—can be effectively used for managing tasks assigned as well as a method for keeping track of the status of each task.
- *Action Item Database*—very effective tool for managing issues, problems, complaints, etc., for a project or organizationally.
- *Risk Management Database*—provides an easy-to-use method of tracking, calculating, and managing risks for a project or organizationally.

Techniques, Methods, and Models

Stop Light Charts/Assessment Index

The baseline results from a mini-assessment can be effectively maintained through use of stop light charts that depict the status of each project and the organization for each Process Improvement requirement. Other types of tables can also be used effectively that indicate the status of each project and the organization. Instead of using red, yellow, and green indicators, percentages assigned also work well. These should be updated following each progress mini-assessment and can be used for regularly reporting to the Executive Steering Committee.

Mini-Assessments

These can be used very effectively for determining the status of the Process Improvement effort. Mini-assessments will be discussed in detail in later chapters.

Process Notebook/Implementation Matrix

These can be used for each project and organizationally to ensure that Process Improvement element requirements are being met. This allows a mapping of each process area to the organizational processes and procedures, thus ensuring that goals are met. This is a good tool to be used during a mini-assessment to identify strengths and weaknesses. There are off-the-shelf tools and databases that can be useful for maintaining the Process Notebook/Implementation Matrix for organizations that select the CMMI® or CMM® as their Process Improvement model. Wallcharts also work well especially if there is a "war" room available for the Process Group to work.

Brainstorming

This is usually a meeting where ideas are offered freely. A key is to avoid any criticism of ideas no matter how outrageous. Typically discussions are held until all ideas are on the table. They can be very useful in uncovering all possible ideas and approaches. These sessions are sometimes called Cerebral Popcorn.

Criteria Grid

This can be used effectively for many different purposes, such as peer reviews, decision making, idea rating, or anything that has criteria to be evaluated. Tables 8-1 through 8-3 illustrate some typical Criteria Grids.

FishBone

Also called a Cause and Effect Diagram or Ishikawa Diagram, this useful issue/ problem resolution tool was developed by Kaoru Ishikawa in Japan at the Kawasaki shipyards. It examines the potential or real causes that result in a single effect. Figure 8-4 illustrates a typical fishbone. The lines coming from the main horizontal line are the main causes and the lines coming from those are the subcauses. The causes are drawn according to their importance. This can help identify the root causes or areas where problems exist. It also compares the importance of relationships with various factors influencing issue or problem.

Table 8-1   Sample Criteria Grid 1

Weak	Satisfactory	Strong	Criteria	Reviewers Comments
			Assertion: clarity, importance	
			Evidence: relevance, strength, credibility	
			Organization: arrangement of ideas	
			Mechanics: spelling, grammar, punctuation	
			Overall effectiveness	

Table 8-2 Sample Criteria Grid 2

Criteria	Weak	Fair	Strong	Comments
Layout/Organization				
Table of contents/page numbers?				
Structure (organization by sections, subsections, appendices)?				
Figures and tables (clearly labeled and professional)?				
Clearly stated purpose and objective(s)?				
Accomplished its purpose?				
Good overall structure? Ideas ordered effectively?				
Transitions used?				
Introduction and conclusion focus clearly on the main point?				
Paragraphs right length?				
Development and Support				
Major ideas/topics well developed?				
Supporting material persuasive?				
Adequate references and resource materials?				
Unnecessary repetition avoided?				
Style				
Topic and level of formality?				
Sentences and words varied?				
Wordiness?				
Grammar and Mechanics				
Grammar?				
Spelling?				
Punctuation?				
Recommend three specific changes:				
1.				
2.				
3.				

Table 8-3 Sample Criteria Grid 3

Criteria	1	2	3	4	5	Rating
Implementation	Extremely difficult	Very difficult	Moderately difficult	Somewhat easy	Easy	
Timing	Long term	Lengthy	Moderate	Reasonably quick	Very quick	
Cost	None	Some	Moderate	Significant	Large	
ROI	Extensively below limit	Somewhat below limit	Meets limit	Somewhat above limit	Extensively above limit	
Understandability	Extensive training needed	A lot of training needed	Some training needed	Little training needed	No training needed	
Fits organizational strategy	No	Minimally	Moderately	Well	Very well	
Resource requirements	Extensive	Significant	Some	Little	None	
Compatibility	No	Significant changes needed	Moderate changes needed	Minor changes needed	Yes	
Fits organizational culture	No	Some	Moderately	Very	Yes	

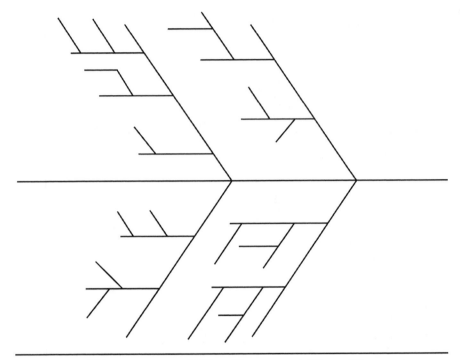

Figure 8-4   Fishbone, Cause and Effect Diagram, or Ishikawa Diagram

Force Field Analysis

A tool that analyzes opposing forces involved in change initiatives to facilitate decision making. Figure 8-5 illustrates this method. It is based on the premise that change is a result of a struggle between forces of resistance and driving forces.

forces impeding change → ← forces favoring change

This method helps to identify the best method to implement. The resisting forces are listed on one side and the driving forces are listed on the other. Either a score can be assigned to each or a decision can be made based on having the most or least forces. This method was developed by Kurt Lewin, who viewed organizations as systems where each situation is a balance of forces that act against change.

Nominal Group Process

A method for structuring groups to allow individual judgments to be pooled. These judgments are used when there is uncertainty or disagreement about the

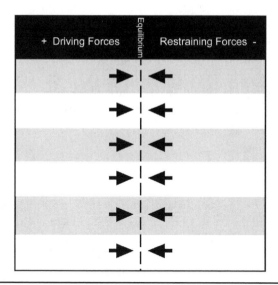

Figure 8-5   Force Field Analysis

nature of the problem and possible solutions. It helps in identification of problems, exploration of solutions, and establishment of priorities. It ensures a balanced participation of group participants. The process steps typically are:

1. Silent idea generation
2. Round-robin style sharing of ideas
3. Feedback to group from lead
4. Group discussions
5. Individual reassessment
6. Ideas are ranked by each participant
7. Number added and ideas prioritized from highest to lowest.

SWOT (Strengths/Weaknesses/Opportunities/Threats)

This focuses on the internal and external environments, examining strengths and weaknesses in the internal environment and opportunities and threats in the external environment. This tool is used in industry extensively to analyze their strategies but it can be used effectively for a Process Group with the external environment being the rest of the organization.

The rule of 7 Plus or Minus 2

This is based on the premise that individuals have limited processing capabilities and limited storing capacities. It says that individuals can store approximately seven pieces of information in their brain at any given time. It is the basis for "chunking," which is a method of grouping elements such as chunks of information on a page, number of items on a list, number of items on a web page menu, or number of controls. This theory was developed by George A. Miller, a Princeton University psychologist in 1956, based on research he conducted to test short-term/working memory. This is a great method to consider when developing processes, web pages, or plans.

Detailing the Master Schedule

In order to be an effective tool for managing a project, a schedule must be iterative or a "living" schedule. At this point, the WBS and Master Schedule that were previously developed should be detailed. Additionally, a critical path should be identified.

Each milestone and key event that was identified in the Launch step should be fully expanded to identify all tasks required to meet that milestone or event. Tasks are any distinct piece of work assigned to or expected of a person. Many times it is related to a deliverable or product but it may not be a physical entity, rather commitment to accomplish something tangible. As tasks are defined it helps to ask yourself "What will it take to call this milestone or event complete?" In other words, what accomplishments need to occur to complete that activity or what criteria are required to close that activity.

A critical path can be identified once the tasks have been defined. This path represents the sequence of activities which take the longest total time to ensure that the entire project finishes on time. Each task on the critical path becomes a critical task.

A delay on the critical path or a delay on even one of the critical tasks will cause a delay to the completion time for the project. A good rule-of-thumb is, if the schedule has more than 25% lag, it is a good signal of significant problems. There can be multiple critical paths or near critical paths that should be closely monitored. Risks should also be taken more seriously if they impact a critical path task.

As the schedule evolves, the critical path may change, so the managers need to be ever vigilant of a changing critical path to ensure that these tasks are put on a high priority for completion in order to make the schedule.

The critical path was developed by project managers in the 1950s and popularized in the late 1950s when it was adapted and improved upon by the US Navy for use on the Polaris missile project. John F. Kennedy, on May 27, 1961, said "I believe that this nation should commit itself to achieving a goal, before this decade is out, of landing a man on the moon..." Eight years after this famous speech, on July 20, 1969, the Apollo 11 landed two men on the moon. The careful planning accomplished by NASA revolved around a schedule which included a critical path. This careful production planning has been one of the key elements credited to the success of the project that led to the moon landing.

There are a good many off-the-shelf tools available for developing effective schedules, many of them creating a critical path. Once the schedule has been developed and a critical path identified, this becomes a key tool for management of the overall effort as well as management of individual task, event, milestones, deliverables, product development, and any other accomplishment required for the effort.

The schedule should always be maintained to include all current tasks, upcoming tasks, and potential tasks. Each current and upcoming task should be tracked to resolution to ensure appropriate resources are available to accomplish essential tasks as assigned. The master schedule should be developed and maintained by the Process Team to ensure soundness of the timelines. This will be a very important tool for success. It should be used daily by all Process Group members and Action Teams.

Measures for Success

Measures and metrics can be a key element to the success of any project, especially one that has multiple activities ongoing simultaneously like an accelerated Process Improvement effort. They provide insight into the stability of the effort providing early indications or real or potential impacts on resources, schedule, and budget. This early detection provides a window of opportunity for taking corrective action to eliminate or lessen the impact. Metrics are used to gauge the trends, successes, and areas of concern throughout the life of a project. By collecting and calculating metrics, a manager can resolve issues that may arise early to alleviate any impact on the project. By maintaining these metrics in a database trend analyses can be effectively generated.

Determining the right metrics to use can be difficult. You don't want to spend a great deal of time on useless metrics just for metrics collection sake. If they are going to give the management team the information they need to analyze the Process Improvement effort's progress and health, make sure it is useful and not misleading. Additionally, determining the right data to collect to generate the metric is just as important. Make sure the right metric is selected and the right data is collected before spending precious time with a metric.

The primary project entity that can be used as a measure of success is the schedule. Several effective metrics can be elicited from the schedule that is useful for measuring project status. A few key schedule-associated measures include:

- *Total slack or float*—the time available for an activity before there is an impact or a successor (following or later activity) activity is impacted. When there is a delay on an activity that goes over the total slack or float, the completion date on the project will be delayed as a result. This can change throughout the project and can be used a good monitor for the project.

- *Schedule Performance Index (SPI)*—this can be calculated to forecast the completion data at any given time on the project. This is an element of the Earned Value Method. It is where the Budgeted Cost of Work Performed (BCWP) is divided by the Budgeted Cost of Work Scheduled (BCWS).

$$BCWP/BCWS = SPI$$

- *Schedule Variance (SV)*—this measure indicates whether the effort is on, ahead, or behind schedule. When the project is behind schedule this can indicate that work-arounds need to be considered or a recovery schedule developed. This is an element of the Earned Value Method. It is where the Budgeted Cost of Work Performed (BCWP) is subtracted from the Budgeted Cost of Work Scheduled (BCWS). A SV percentage can be calculated by dividing the SV by the BCWS to indicate the percent ahead or behind schedule.

$$BCWP - BCWS = SV, \text{ where negative value means behind schedule}$$

If an earned value method is not being used, the schedule can still act as a good measure of the project's status if kept up-to-date. Many tools will mark the schedule's graphical portion as completed, which can be reviewed for a good view of the project's progress. Earned Value is a book in itself, so this book will not attempt to detail this useful project management metric, but will use some of the terms so the reader is familiar with some potential measures for a project.

Another tool typically used for measuring an effort is the budget with the same type of measures available when using the earned value method. A few key budget-associated measures include:

- *Cost Performance Index (CPI)*—this can be calculated to forecast the completion data at any given time on the project. This is an element of the Earned Value Method. It is where the Budgeted Cost of Work Performed (BCWP) is divided by the Actual Cost of Work Performed (ACWP).

$$BCWP/ACWP = CPI$$

- *Cost Variance (CV)*—this measure indicates whether the effort is on, over, or under budget. This is an element of the Earned Value Method. It is where the Budgeted Cost of Work Performed (BCWP) is subtracted from the Actual Cost of Work Performed (ACWP). A CV percentage can be calculated by dividing the CV by the BCWP to indicate the percent under or over budget.

$$BCWP/ACWP = CV, \text{ where negative value means over budget}$$

Some of the off-the-shelf tools combine the schedule and budget which can provide an effective method of managing these two important project management tools.

Several other measures can be used to determine a project progress successfully. A few successful ones include:

- *Actual versus planned metrics*—metrics that calculated the difference between the actual work (such as number processes, number of pilots, number of mini-assessments) over the planned work. This can be based on the number of elements actually developed over the number planned or size estimation. Remember that estimates are just that, estimates, and if too much time is spent analyzing, time can be wasted; in doing so don't spend a good deal of time on this unless highly warranted. Sometimes complexity is not taken into consideration.
- *Defect Rates*—defects discovered during peer reviews or during piloting (equivalent to software or systems testing). This metric can be misused too often but if used properly it can be beneficial. Always remember that finding defects is good so they don't cause problems later. There are many factors that should be taken into consideration when using defect rates.
- *Productivity rates*—measuring the time it takes to accomplish tasks, which is typically output divided by input. Input and output units can be in terms of dollars, time, actions, goals, and any element pertinent to the effort. This can be misleading however because complexity and other key elements are not considered so it should be used with care.

Metrics tolerances and thresholds should be established for all metrics. These are a range of upper and lower limits that indicate variation in performance. Figure 8-6 illustrates thresholds for identifying real or potential problems. Typically these should not be overly complicated or tight, except for high cost or high schedule time elements which should be tight to adequately monitor. When a threshold is exceeded, a simple action plan should be developed to determine the cause and evaluate alternatives for correction of any real or potential problems.

Selecting Projects for Process Improvement

Depending upon the size of an organization and the scope of the Process Improvement effort, an organization should select projects to be involved in the

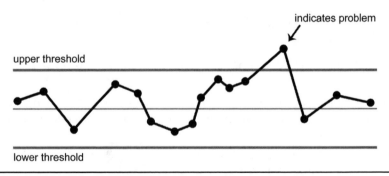

Figure 8-6   Thresholds for Metrics

Process Improvement effort. Some projects may not be in a position to be part of the Process Improvement effort. Not all projects in an organization need to be included for an organization to achieve a high level of maturity but, eventually, all projects, especially new ones, need to be part of the organizational process culture.

The following are a few elements to consider in selecting projects for involvement:

- *Schedule*—if a project is on a tight schedule the organization may want to consider waiting until there is adequate slack for that project to become involved in the Process Improvement effort.
- *Budget*—if part of the budget is being allocated from projects, an organization should consider what projects have sufficient budget to be involved in the Process Improvement effort.
- *Risk*—a project with a significant amount or some extremely high-risk areas; an organization may want to consider delaying involving until these risks are overcome.
- *Project phase*—projects that are at or near the end are not always good candidates for Process Improvement. These should be considered only if necessary.

Team Action Plan

During Planning, an overall Process Improvement Action Plan is developed as discussed, but a Process Action Team (PAT) Action Plan should be developed for each major activity for Action Teams. There should be a plan detailing the specific aspects for the activity. These must be accomplished at the start of the team so that everyone is on the same sheet of music and alleviate any misunderstandings and misconceptions. They should always be kept short and simple with just the right information needs to press forward. A typical Action Plan is in the toolkit. The Overall Action Plan should be used as a basis for these plans which should include the following information:

- *Problem Definition/Objectives/Purpose*—describe the activity that is being undertaken in a clear, concise paragraph or two so that the end results of the activity are understood.
- *Team Members*—each team member should be identified and their role on the activity effort is understood. Responsibilities could be added to this to ensure that each member's responsibilities are well-understood.
- *Piloting Strategy*—the strategy to be used to ensure that the activity meets the organizational needs should be defined.
- *Desired Results*—what the end result should be when the activity is completed.
- *Issues and Risks*—all issues and risks need to be defined including any constraints that impact the execution of the activity.
- *Timeline/Actions*—a simple timeline with the major actions required should be developed. This timeline should be added to the master schedule. In order to avoid redundancy, the actions could be defined in the master schedule and that portion included in the Team Action Plan.
- *Deliverables*—all resulting deliverables of the effort should be identified. This includes processes, procedures, policies, tools, templates, checklists, graphics, etc.

Organizational Kickoff Meetings

During the Planning step, additional Kickoff Meetings should be conducted to ensure that all organizational staff know and understand what is being accomplished and how it will impact them. Chapter 19 discussed some methods of "marketing" the Process Improvement effort that can be used as part of the presentations and throughout the effort.

The following two additional Kickoff Meetings should be conducted for the organization:

1. A special Kickoff Meeting should be accomplished for the mid-level management staff. This is where a mid-level management commitment is received, which is as important to the success of the effort as executive management. The mid-level management will ensure that things are done a certain way, such as using the processes developed by the process team. An affiliation with the mid-level managers who are typically the Project Managers and Key Leads can make the difference between success and failure. These individuals are typically the organization's social leaders who can set the direction for the rest of the organization. These individuals

will prove to be very important to the entire effort. Chapter 19 discusses building liaisons and this is the first step in starting that process.

2. A Kickoff Meeting for the entire organizational staff will provide the first opportunity to advertise the Process Improvement effort. Advertising the effort will be important to getting the entire organization on board with processes and the Process Improvement effort. Further advertising should be done throughout the process. Remember, the ultimate goal of Process Improvement is to change the way the organization accomplishes its work. If the staff doing the work are not on board and aware of the effort, the changes can not be accomplished. Chapter 19 discusses organizational change and some mechanisms to ease the process.

Establishing Regular Status Meetings and Reports

Communications and reporting activities convey information to various management levels on project status, potential/actual problem areas, and corrective action that is being or needs to be implemented. The Process Improvement Manager should be the focal point in all reporting activities. Several layers of reporting activities should take place starting at the staff level. Figure 8-7 illustrates typical reviewing and reporting levels and some responsibilities.

Process Group Team Meetings

If a team lead is assigned, they should get reports (verbal or written) from their team members and then report to the Process Group; typically, they are members of the Process Group. The Process Improvement Manager holds weekly or daily status meetings with the Process Group. During an accelerated Process Improvement effort daily meetings may be warranted during peak times. As with the Agile Programming Methodologies, eXtreme Programming calls these stand ups and Scrum call them scrums; these meetings can set the pace for the daily activities. Typically, management is not as involved with these meetings but they get a scrum report daily so that they know where the project is and can react as needed to any issues. This can work well for the APIM, with meeting onsite if co-located and on-line using web-conferencing if members are located at different locations. These meeting should be short (scrums are 15 minutes at the end of the day) and should focus on specific plans for the next day if held at the end of the day or on the day's work if held early. A quick scrum report to Action Team Leads and the Process Improvement Manager would also be beneficial. These meetings are beneficial for both the Action Teams as well as the Process Team, depending upon what actions are in progress at any given time.

Minutes should be taken and sent to each attendee to ensure that everyone is on the same sheet of music. In other words ensure that there are no

ACTION TEAM

▶ Report action status to Team Lead
▶ Attend Weekly or Daily status
  meeting
▶ Collect data for metrics

*Focus on
accomplishing
assigned actions.*

ACTION TEAM LEAD

▶ Report all team action status and
  issues to Process Group
▶ Attend Weekly or Daily Process
  Group meeting
▶ Collect/Calculate data for metrics

*Focus on managing team
actions and accomplishing
assigned actions.*

PROCESS GROUP MANAGER

▶ Plan and maintain plans
▶ Report all action status and issues
  to Executive Steering Committee
▶ Lead Weekly or Daily Process
  Group meeting
▶ Calculate and report metrics

*Focus on planning, tracking,
reporting, issue resolution, and
accomplishing assigned actions.*

PROCESS GROUP

▶ Report all action status and issues
  to Process Group Manager
▶ Attend Weekly or Daily Process
  Group meeting
▶ Collect/Calculate data
  for metrics

*Focus on planning,
tracking, and accomplishing
assigned actions.*

EXECUTIVE STEERING COMMITTEE

▶ Resolve issues
▶ Provide planning assist, as needed
▶ Track Progress based on reports and metrics
▶ Provide resources, as needed

*Focus on problem resolution,
tracking, and resources.*

Figure 8-7   Reviewing and Reporting

misunderstandings or misconceptions going into the effort. A sample agenda and minutes are located in the toolkit.

Executive Steering Committee

Inputs from the Process Team meetings and any unresolved issues should be used for reporting to the Executive Steering Committee. A formal review meeting should be held, at a minimum of monthly, to assess the progress of the effort and resolve any problems that have been unrecoverable at lower management levels.

On accelerated efforts, it might be beneficial to hold these reviews more often but always remember to eliminate as much of the red tape as possible. The Process Improvement Manager is responsible for reviews and reporting to the Executive Steering Committee.

The Executive Steering Committee is responsible for approving plans, reviewing results, monitoring the progress of the Process Group, obtaining the required resources to make the effort successful, and resolving issues that have been elevated to that level. In order to perform this role successfully, they need to have as much information as possible to make the right fact-based decisions. A presentation should be conducted regularly and on an event-driven basis to enable discussion of status, issues, and risks, to include technical and administrative matters. A presentation-style format should be used for all regularly scheduled meetings to ensure that nothing falls through the cracks and all significant issues are fully discussed. For event-driven meetings, the event that drove the meeting will also drive the format and agenda.

There are several areas that should be covered during the reporting process including:

- Status summaries
- Stop light charts
- Schedule (include discussion of critical path)
- Budget
- Risks and Risk Mitigation Plans
- Resources
- Metrics
- Issues, Concerns, Problems, Setbacks (Unresolvable—all issues should be resolved at the lowest possible level if possible)
- Accomplishments
- Recognitions of Individuals
- Action Items.

Minutes should be taken and sent to each attendee to ensure that everyone is on the same sheet of music. In other words, ensure that there are no misunderstandings or misconceptions going into the effort. A sample agenda and minutes are located in the toolkit.

Process Group Training

Training in general is a major key to success for any endeavor but, for the Process Group to accelerate a Process Improvement effort, detailed training is crucial. It must be accomplished as early in the process as possible so that you can get the Process Group off running to tackle the needed Process Improvement actions.

The Process Group training should include the following elements as a minimum:

- What is Process Improvement?
- What is Process Maturity?
- Process Improvement Methodology (Methodologies) Specific Detailed Training
- People Side of Process Maturity
- Implementing Process Improvement

  — Plan-Do-Study-Act (PDSA) Cycle
  — IDEAL^{SM} Model
  — Process Action Teams
  — Piloting

- Documenting Useable Processes
- Process Models
- Organizational Method Selected
- Process Development Cycle
- Enforcing Processes
- Roles and responsibilities of each team member
- Planning, tracking, and reporting needs from each team member
- Metrics for collection including what they will be used for.

During training it is important to keep open communications a constant. The training sessions should be open to questions, comments, suggestions, and even constructive criticism, in order to ensure that participants fully understand the material and agree upon the methods described for implementing Process Improvement. However, the trainer should be ever vigilant to balance this with ensuring participants get the training needed in the least amount of time possible without going into the weeds too far.

Trainers also need to sensitively handle any rabble-rousers, troublemakers, and hecklers since they can bring the whole group down. They, typically, are not going to be part of the Process Group but it needs to be dealt with promptly to avoid problems later.

Most of the Process Improvement models and methodologies discussed in previous chapters have excellent training programs available. It is wise to send at least one Process Group member, typically the manager, to that training so that they understand the intricacies that may not come about as part of other training efforts or by simply reading the materials provided. Once a Process Group member has attended formal training, they can effectively bring that training back to the organization in a train-the-trainer type of program.

Even if an organization has staff with some previous experience, it is very beneficial for the organization, especially in an accelerated effort, that they fully understand a model or methodology from the point of view of the developers.

In the end, it saves a good deal of time and money that could be wasted going down the wrong path.

Organizational Training

Process Improvement training is important for the organization. However, in-depth process model or Process Improvement implementation is not needed for all organizational staff. It, in fact, is counterproductive to train an entire organizational staff on Process Improvement or process models unless they are involved in the effort. What they need to know depends upon their position in the organization.

A Project Manager or Quality Assurance Manager would need to know more about Process Improvement and models than an engineer. In fact, many of these are in some way involved in the Process Improvement effort. They would require fairly detailed training. For each level of management, for example staff in lead positions, process training would be less in-depth. For the majority of organizational staff, a Process Improvement orientation would be the only process training needed. This orientation should include the basics of the selected process model and a general idea of how it is being implemented, but the key element should be to let them know how it will impact them and how they can help make it happen.

What is key for all organizational staff is the training accomplished to transfer knowledge on the developed processes. This will be the most important training for most of the organizational staff. Process Training is discussed in detail in a later chapter.

Summary

Planning has been proven as a major key to success. Take the time to ensure that the Process Improvement effort is properly planned but balance that with not going overboard. Planning is an iterative process, it doesn't start and stop with this step. This step provides the initial planning which should be built upon as the effort progresses and new insight is gained.

The important thing about this step is to set the stage for continued planning not to create a realm of shelfware. A balance needs to be found to ensure the project planning is adequate to kick the effort off to a good start and not so much that it takes away from getting started on the actions needed to make it happen.

Chapter Key Points

- Use a forward-looking planning philosophy to ensure enough flexibility to accommodate changing task priorities.
- Balance planning not too much but enough to get the effort off to a good start.
- An Overall Action Plan should be developed to identify how the effort will be conducted and manage activities.
- Communications planning helps manage information flow, define lines of communication, and ensure that all stakeholders are considered.
- Control of processes and other Process Improvement data items to ensure that things are not lost, overwritten, misidentified, unverified, or distributed improperly.
- A proactive approach should be used to handle issue/problem correction and prevention before they get out of hand.
- Peer reviews can be conducted with formal reviews or more information methods but they are important to ensure that processes developed meet the needs of the assigned actions.
- Determine the format of the processes and develop a template.
- Let Quality Assurance be the eyes and ears for the Process Group.
- Utilize a Risk Management process to identify and mitigate risks to avert events that have potential undesirable consequences.
- Use tool and techniques to get the most out of the Process Improvement effort.
- Using the initial master schedule, add details for each milestone and key event to identify all tasks required to meet that milestone or event.
- Use of measures and metrics provides early detection of issues and problems, thus providing a window of opportunity for taking corrective action to eliminate or lessen the impact. Identify thresholds.
- Select projects to be involved in the Process Improvement effort based on where they are in the development life cycle as well as other considerations.
- Develop Process Action Team (PAT) Action Plan for each major activity.
- Provide Kick-off meetings to facilitate buy-in from the entire organization.
- Plan for regular status meetings with Executive Management Committee.
- Schedule regular Process Team Meetings; the length and timing will vary on what actions are in progress.
- Training is an important consideration. Complete Process Improvement training for all members of the Process Group and varied training for the rest of the organizational staff.

Tips for Success

- Use a forward-looking planning philosophy.
- Planning is an iterative process.
- Keep the Action Plan short and simple.
- Know the who, what, when, where, and how to avoid misunderstandings and misconceptions.
- Use an Action Item Database to manage and track actions.
- Use peer reviews as another method of communication as well as defect resolution.
- Use a risk management database to manage and track Process Improvement risks.
- It's hard to make any progress if you don't have the right tools to get there.
- Use the critical path to ensure that the tasks on that path are monitored closely.
- Use metrics and measures smartly.
- Keep PAT Action Plans short and simple.
- Use various levels of training based on staff position.

Chapter 9

Maturity Phase: Step 1—Awareness

A mini-assessment will determine where an organization is and where it needs to go based on the selected Process Improvement model goals and requirements. The focus is on identifying the weak areas or gaps that need to be corrected or improved to meet the organization's Process Improvement goals. There are two levels of mini-assessments: initial mini-assessments and progress mini-assessments. These are sometimes called a gap analysis.

The initial mini-assessment is the first mini-assessment to be accomplished to identify weaknesses and gaps. It should be accomplished at the beginning of the Process Improvement effort for both selected projects and organizationally. For projects that are not selected as part of the accelerated Process Improvement, an initial mini-assessment should be conducted if or when they are brought into the effort. The initial mini-assessment will set the baseline for progress mini-assessments.

Depending upon the organization a self-assessment conducted by each project can be beneficial to kick off the Process Improvement effort. This can be accomplished either using questionnaires or by using a coach to help them get through the assessment process. Both methods will provide a place to start and a confidence building between the Process Group and the project staff. Again, minimal impact to the project should be the goal, so don't try to do it all in one mini-assessment or the project will be overwhelmed and in their view will take them away from their "real work". Develop a condensed version of the assessment needs and focus on some specific areas.

Progress mini-assessments should be accomplished for each iteration of the maturity phase as illustrated in the APIM diagram or on an event-driven basis. The initial mini-assessment baseline should be used as a yardstick and the areas that were identified as weak concentrated upon. Even though concentration is on the weak areas, the other areas should be assessed as well, much as you would when regression testing software to ensure there has been no impact to the areas since the previous mini-assessment.

Mini-Assessment Methodology

There are various mini-assessment methods that can be used. Figure 9-1 illustrates a mini-assessment method that was adapted from the SEI appraisal methodologies, the Standard CMMI® Appraisal Method for Process Improvement (SCAMPI^{SM}) [32] and the CMM®-Based Appraisal for Internal Process Improvement (CBA IPI®), [12] that has evolved over time based on lessons learned. The focus is upon finding weaknesses or gaps in relation to the selected Process Improvement model or methodology. In short, it consists of a records analysis as well as interviews with the process users. The length, size, and scope of the mini-assessment will

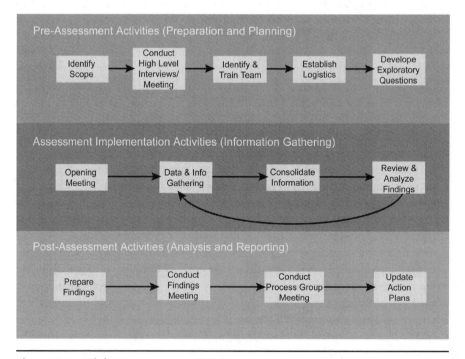

Figure 9-1 Mini-Assessment Process

be dependent upon the assessors' knowledge of the organization and/or project as well as the Process Improvement model. The mini-assessment process should minimize the involvement of organizational staff not on the process team, thus having minimal impact to daily operations.

Mini-Assessment Team Composition

The composition of the recommended Mini-Assessment team should include at least one experienced assessor as the lead and one assistant/coordinator to minimize the impact to the other organizational staff. If a project is being assessed, it is helpful to have the assistant/coordinator as a project team member. A mix of external and project-internal assessors has been proven to provide the most successful results by balancing the project knowledge with assessment/Process Improvement knowledge and experience. The assistant/coordinator should be responsible for assisting the experienced assessor in coordinating the activities of the Mini-Assessment. This includes locating and providing the agreed-upon documentation for review, assisting administering the questionnaires to selected staff if questionnaires are used, arranging for the staff interviews, arranging facilities, and helping schedule interviews.

Mini-Assessment Scope

The scope of the mini-assessment should be based upon the specific goals set by the organization. Depending upon the size of the Process Group and mini-assessment team, starting with a small number of the selected models goals is recommended. The exact scope should be determined early in the planning process since it will drive the rest of the planning.

Mini-Assessment Process

The Mini-Assessment Process consists of three major phases: Pre-Assessment, Mini-Assessment Implementation, and Post-Assessment. The Pre-Assessment is the planning and preparation, the Mini-Assessment implementation is the information gathering, and Post-Assessment is for the analysis and reporting.

Pre-Assessment Activities

As the names indicate, the Pre-assessment consists of the activities that need to occur prior to the conduct of the actual mini-assessment implementation for planning and preparation purposes. This is sometimes called Pre-Site Assessment when the assessment is conducted at a remote location from the Assessment Team. The specific steps included in this activity are discussed in Table 9-1.

Mini-Assessment Implementation Activities

The Mini-Assessment Implementation is the information-gathering phase of the mini-assessment. It is where the selected goals researched within the organization and on each of the projects selected as part of the Process Improvement effort. This activity should take place mostly at the organization and project location. During the consolidation task, some off-site work may be feasible, depending upon availability of appropriate resources and the need for coordination with organization or project staff. The specific steps included in this activity are discussed in Table 9-2.

Post-Assessment Activities

As the names indicate, the Post-Assessment consists of the activities that need to occur after the mini-assessment cycle. The activities are used following conduct of the actual mini-assessment for analysis and reporting purposes. The specific steps included in this activity are discussed in Table 9-3.

Mini-Assessment Tools

There are several proven tools and techniques to collect information for evaluating the current practices for organizations. Some of the tools that can be helpful during a mini-assessment are shown in Table 9-4.

There are a few tips that can help make a mini-assessment easier. Table 9-5 lists a few of these recommendations.

Strict confidentiality should be guaranteed throughout the entire mini-assessment thus preserving the integrity of the mini-assessment. The assessment team should ensure that all discussions held with participants, data that is reviewed, and the assessment outputs are subject to confidentiality. It's helpful when each participant, including assessors, coordinators, managers, interviewees, sign an agreement to that effect. It should be disclosed at the start of the mini-assessment as well as at the start of each interview session. It is important that everyone fully understands that anything they say will be held in the strictest of confidence and will not be disclosed outside of the interview session hence and that anything imparted is non-attributable. The assessors should ensure that any information that can identify the interviewee or their project is used for administrative purposes only, and held in strict confidence. Interviewees' answers should be used in summary statistical form but specific answers should never be identified by project, individual, or in any other manner. Confidentiality during any assessment effort

Table 9-1   Pre-Assessment

Pre-Assessment Activities

✓ Identify Scope—Define the scope of the mini-assessment including which projects will be involved and which goals will be evaluated.

✓ Conduct High-Level Interviews/Meetings—Conduct high-level interviews and/or meetings with senior management staff for the organization and projects to inform them of the goals and expectations for the mini-assessment and refine scope as needed based on discussions.

✓ Identify and Train Team—Identify the assessor, if not already accomplished, and assistant/coordinator. Train and/or mentor the assistant/coordinator in the conduct of the mini-assessment and potentially the Process Improvement model selected as it relates to the mini-assessment. Concentrate on identified goals.

✓ Establish Logistics—The assessor and assistant/coordinator establish the logistics for the mini-assessment including scheduling time, making staff arrangements for interviews and questionnaires, facilities including room, food and supplies as needed. A war room may need to be arranged for conduct and analysis purposes. The assistant/coordinator ensures that all arrangements for on-site visits have been made, that all documents to be reviewed are available, and that all pre-planned interviews have been scheduled and arranged. The appropriate Process Area Notebook needs to be either generated for an initial mini-assessment or made available for progress mini-assessments.

✓ Develop Exploratory Questions—Based on the scope of the mini-assessment and the goals established, develop the questions for the interviews to be conducted. The questions will be further refined as the mini-assessment commences. For the less formal interviews a set of kick-off questions should be developed and then let the discussion go from there, but a backup/ "hip pocket" set of questions should be available for situations where the informal conversation does not develop.

Inputs
- Mini-Assessment Process
- Lessons learned from previous efforts
- Mini-Assessment materials from previous efforts
- Process Notebook, if progress Mini-Assessment
- For Progress Mini-Assessment, baseline of initial or previous progress mini-assessment

Outputs
- Mini-Assessment Plan (not necessarily a documented plan)
- Logistics Preparation
- Interview Preparations
- Questionnaires, if used
- Process Notebook

Table 9-2   Assessment Implementation

Assessment Implementation Activities

✓ Opening Meeting—Conduct the opening meeting with management, as needed.

✓ Data and Information Gathering Loop—This loop is repeated until all data has been gathered to support the goals set for this mini-assessment. Two things to remember: (1) keep it short and simple, (2) minimal impact to organizational and project daily operations.

- Data and Information Gathering—This is one of the most critical but time-consuming steps in the mini-assessment process since it will directly impact the results. The Process Notebook should be used to specify adherence to selected goals. As data is found that substantiates a goal, notes should be put into the notebook including the who, what, when, where, and how. The data and information gathered includes:

  — Documents such as the organization's policies and procedures as well as project artifacts from the participating projects
  — Notes from the interviews of key staff members including project managers and groups of practitioners from the different functional specialties.

- Consolidate Information—The information gathered is consolidated. The consolidate information includes:

  — Combine data from various sources and summarize
  — Determine sufficiency for making judgment of maturity.

- Review and Analyze Findings—Review and analyze the consolidated data based upon the goals set for this mini-assessment. The review and analyze findings include:

  — Based on consolidated information, review and analyze the resulting consolidated data
  — Determine if enough information has been gathered to determine any weaknesses based on the goals identified for this mini-assessment
  — Determine if any other things were ferreted out that should be further investigated prior to closing the mini-assessment.

Inputs	*Outputs*
• Mini-Assessment Plan (not necessarily a documented plan)	• Weaknesses including any other useful information ferreted out as part of this mini-assessment
• Logistics Preparation	
• Interview Preparations	• Completed Process Notebook
• Questionnaires, if used	• Action Planning Data
• Process Notebook	

Table 9-3   Post Assessment

Post-Assessment Activities

✓ Prepare Findings—The final findings are prepared including recommendations for the Process Improvement effort and a rating based on goals.

✓ Conduct Findings Meeting—The final findings are briefed to senior organizational and project management. These may be briefed to the organization or communicated to them by other means such as a newsletter or other communications selected for organizational staff.

✓ Conduct Process Group Meeting—This session is conducted to discuss the next steps for the improvement program.

✓ Update Overall Action Plan—Based on the results, the Overall Action Plan needs to be updated to reflect the new information, with concentration on the short- and long-term goals as well as any new risks, issues, or constraints identified during the Mini-Assessment Implementation.

Inputs	*Outputs*
• Weaknesses including any other useful information ferreted out as part of this mini-assessment	• Weaknesses for tasking
	• Risks, issues, or constraints
	• Final Rating
• Completed Process Notebook	• Updated Action Plan
• Action Planning Data	• Lessons Learned

is essential to the success of the mini-assessment. It is key to the credibility and confidence in the findings.

Mini-Assessment Process Group Sessions

Another critical task of the mini-assessment is to conduct a work group session for the Process Group. This should be an approximately 2-hour brainstorming session focusing on the final report from the mini-assessment. The goal of this meeting is to discuss and determine what rating should be given for each area assessed, recommended high-level solution, and the next steps for the Process Improvement effort. The result should be assignment of actions to keep the ball moving to improve processes. The mini-assessment team should lead the session with attendees including the Process Group members, all of the assessment team members, and it can be beneficial to also include participating managers, and anyone deemed by management as needed to attend.

The goal of this meeting is not to solve the problems but to rate the areas and make recommendations. A Process Action Team will typically be assigned to solve the major issues which will be discussed later in the effort. Keep this meeting focused and don't go off on tangents that take away from the goal of the meeting to

Table 9-4   Mini-Assessment Tools

Tools	Brief Description
Questionnaires	A Questionnaire allows the team to focus the assessment and obtain personal information from staff members in textual form. A specific one can be developed and the SEI has a Maturity Questionnaire that can be used or tailored as needed if the CMM is the Process Improvement model selected.
Interviews	Interviews are conducted with various control groups so that different perceptions can provide insight to enable appropriate actions. Unlike the more formal CBA IPI and some levels of the SCAMPI appraisal, the interviews should be more informal and unstructured. It is recommended that some preliminary questions are asked but then allow the more informal random discussions. A side effect of a less focused interview session is that areas may be ferreted out that had not been considered as areas to tackle early. It also builds more buy-in from users since interviews become more conversational and staff feel less intimidated. Remember to keep these as short and concise as possible with the goal of minimal impact to daily operations. If the organizational style is more formal, a more structured interview session would be feasible.
Document Review	Various documents should be reviewed including the organization's policies and procedures and project artifacts (e.g. Software Development Plans, Quality Plans, and Configuration Management Plans, . . .) from the participating projects. The documents reviewed should include those that may be applicable to the selected areas of concentration.
Observation	General observation will provide the assessor with a sense of how business is accomplished on a day-by-day basis and institutionalization of process at the organization. Sometimes this can provide invaluable information to the assessor.

make plans for where to go from here. Look at the general meeting rules discussed in the previous chapter.

Mini-Assessment Results

The outputs for the mini-assessment are critical to kicking the Process Improvement effort off on the right path and for progress mini-assessments

Table 9-5   Tips for Successful Mini-Assessments

Make it fun
Bring food
Respect confidentiality
Be objective; there are alternatives
Avoid impact to daily operations
Keep it light but keep it focused
Don't point fingers
Find collaborating information for every item possible
Keep it Simple!

keeping it on the right path. The focus of the mini-assessment is on identification of weaknesses to enable the organization to make informed decisions. Some of the strengths of the organization may be included to form a complete picture based upon the organizational goals. Additionally, it can effectively ferret out issues, concerns, risks, and any constraints on progress that are invaluable.

The specific results should be as follows:

- Process Notebook
- Report/presentation identifying:

  — Organizational weaknesses
  — Potential high-level solutions to identified weaknesses
  — Other recommendations
  — Issues, concerns, risks, and constraints

- Updated Action Plan.

The baseline results should be constantly maintained to depict the status of each project and the organization. A great way of doing that is through the use of a Process Notebook. A Process Notebook, as described in Chapter 8, allows for mapping the model practices and/or goals to organizational and project processes and procedures. It also indicates where the information is located or maintained to support a practice or goal. This tool makes identifying weaknesses in the organization and on project much easier by organizing for ease of use.

The Process Notebook is very useful in the form of wallcharts if a big enough room is available for the Process Group. There are several good off-the-shelf tools available but creation of a "homegrown" database will give the user exactly what they are looking for if the expertise and time are available. These tools have many advantages over a hardcopy, or even wallcharts, including ease of search, smooth management of elements, provides an "authorized" record of project elements, change control, metrics collection with minimal effort, and can be used for any needed documentation.

An effective method is to have two levels in the Process Notebook. One level would be for the details and notes during the mini-assessment, with one for each participating project and one for the organization. The next level would provide a summary to easily reference when looking at the organization as a whole. Even though this is redundant when working from a hardcopy, or even wallcharts, the redundancy helps summarize the mountains of information being collected. The users of this tool need to ensure that it is consistently collated and maintained so that the correct information is available in both places. This is where a database would help alleviate that redundancy.

A presentation or simply a report should be generated for the management team of projects and organizationally. The Stop Light Charts or an Assessment Index should be used to report results. These further summarize the results and show where the project and organization falls based on the Process Improvement goals. At the end of each mini-assessment it is important to update these and keep them updated. This presentation or report should include a high-level solution for any identified weaknesses, other recommendations, and any issues, concerns, risks, and constraints identified during the mini-assessment.

The Action Plan should be revised to reflect updated short- and possibly long-term goals. During the mini-assessment some of the assumptions made early in the planning process will change, these need to be reflected in the plan. Remember, this is a living plan, not shelfware. Another key area to capture in the revised plan is any new or changed issues, concerns, risks, and constraints. There may be other areas impacted by a mini-assessment; the entire plan should be reviewed to ensure there are no other impacts based on the results.

Summary

One of the key success factors for Process Improvement is conduct of mini-assessments to determine where an organization is and where they need to go. The focus should be on identifying the weak areas, to generate actions to be accomplished by the Process Group to meet the organization's Process Improvement goals. Two levels of mini-assessments provide the optimal solution: initial mini-assessments and progress mini-assessments.

The initial mini-assessment should be accomplished at the beginning of the Process Improvement effort for both selected projects and organizationally to set the baseline for progress mini-assessments. For other projects, the initial mini-assessment needs to be accomplished as time permits to provide a baseline for further improvement.

Progress mini-assessments should be accomplished for each iteration or on an event-driven basis. The initial mini-assessment baseline should be used as a yardstick and the areas that were identified as weak concentrated upon.

Chapter Key Points

- Determine what method to use to conduct a mini-assessment including both an initial and progress mini-assessments.
- Composition of the Mini-Assessment team should include at least one experienced assessor to minimize the impact to the other organizational staff.
- Mini-assessment outputs are critical to kicking the Process Improvement effort off on the right path and for progress mini-assessments keeping it on the right path.
- Provide report of results to management using Stop Light Charts/Assessment Index.

Tips for Success

- Remember: minimal impact to the project.
- Use mix of external and project-internal assessors for mini-assessments.
- Sign confidentiality contract with interviewees. Adhere to it in order to maintain integrity with organizational staff.
- Use Process Notebooks with Stop Light Charts/Assessment Index to record and track Process Improvement.

Chapter 10

Maturity Phase: Step 2—Triage

As with most projects, the Process Improvement will be accomplished with the least amount of staff as possible. In order to be successful, the limited resources must be efficiently utilized with the goal to tackle the most important work as realistically as possible. For an accelerated Process Improvement effort, besides limited resources there is limited time. The key is to get the effort complete in short, succinct accelerated phases or cycles with time being measured in "internet-time," which is typically three to six months. The goal is to maximize the amount of work accomplished in the least amount of time. That's where triage plays an important role.

Triage for Prioritization

Triage is from an old French word, *trier,* which means "to sort". It has been used in the treatment of patients, especially battle and disaster victims, according to a system of priorities designed to maximize the number of survivors. Baron Dominique Jean Larrey, a famous French surgeon in Napoleon's army, is credited with the practice. He devised a method of quickly evaluating and categorizing soldiers that were wounded in battle. Baron Larrey would evacuate wounded soldiers that required the most urgent medical attention during actual battle with no regard for their rank.

In triage, patients are divided into three to five categories. Depending upon the method used the categories vary. Based on a typical three-category method the following categories may be used:

1. Those who will not survive even with treatment.
2. Those who will survive without treatment.
3. Those whose survival depends on treatment.

There is a more advanced version of triage that uses five categories, as follows:

- *Black/Expectant*—so severely injured that they will die of their injuries, possibly in hours or days, or in such life-threatening medical crisis that they are unlikely to survive given the care available; they should be taken to a holding area and given painkillers to ease their passing.
- *Red/Immediate*—require immediate surgery or other life-saving intervention, first priority for surgical teams or transport to advanced facilities, "cannot wait" but are likely to survive with immediate treatment.
- *Yellow/Observation*—condition is stable for the moment but requires watching by trained persons and frequent re-triage, will need hospital care and would receive immediate priority care under "normal" circumstances.
- *Green/Wait*—require a doctor's care in several hours or days but not immediately, may wait for a number of hours or be told to go home and come back the next day.
- *White/Dismiss*—They have minor injuries; first aid and home care are sufficient, a doctor's care is not required.

There are conditions where a reverse triage is warranted and the less wounded are treated prior to the severely wounded. In war, there are times when soldiers need to be quickly returned to the field and reverse triage is used to facilitate their return. This practice is common in the Russian military. Additionally, it is useful in war situations where the medical staff are among the wounded or need assistance from patients. For Process Improvement there may be times that reverse triage could work to the advantage rather than disadvantage.

By using triage, the treatment of patients requiring help is not delayed by useless or unnecessary treatment of those in the other groups. Triage originated in military medicine, when limited resources faced many wounded soldiers and time was critical. Hence, triage decisions are made after relatively quick examination; patients in lower-priority groups are reexamined periodically. Triage approaches have been used successfully in several business-related areas, such as:

- Financial planners to manage requests and electronic mail
- Toyota to speed up and manage car repairs
- For software development for areas such as prioritizing bug fixes and requirements
- For Y2K efforts to determine what needs to be fixed and in what order.

This same triage or sorting method can be used to accelerate Process Improvement efforts.

Once the Process Team has completed the mini-assessment, the resulting actions need to be established and prioritized. Much like the doctors on the battlefield, prioritization can be very effective and efficient by using triage. The prioritization categories would be a bit different with consideration for the potential impact and justified need, as well as the level of weakness and the effort required to strengthen it. This could be further substantiated by the needed actions of most value to the project or the organization as a secondary key consideration.

The key selection criteria should be based on three goals:

- Business goals
- Project goals
- Process goals.

The business goals are the goals that would impact the organization as a whole, such as budget, especially overhead budget, image, or overall resources. The project goals would include things that impact the project budget or schedule, project resources, or their ability to accomplish the technical tasks they are contractually obligated to accomplish. The process goals are the goals that have been set for the Process Improvement effort. Table 10-1 lists a typical triage prioritization index for Process Improvement.

Reverse triage may be warranted in some cases. The processes requiring very little to get them in place may be selected especially early in the Process Improvement effort. Some early, fairly painless Process Improvement successes would go a long way in gaining buy-in.

Whatever prioritization criteria are used, this should be done swiftly in order to get the organization where it needs to go as quickly as possible. Remember to practice tough love. Christopher P. Higgins, Bank of America National Manager Currency Services, based on his Army experience, said, "Make a decision! Make a decision! People are dying all around you!" Sometimes we tend to discuss things for so long, by the time a decision is made it's too late really to make a difference. Make a decision; if you make a mistake, correct it but make a decision and do something, don't just talk about it forever.

Learning from Mistakes

During the course of the Process Improvement effort the likelihood of mistakes being made is high, especially when you are accelerating the effort. The key is to get something done and not just sit around talking about it while the situation gets worse. Be prepared for mistakes and use them to help improve, they are not typically fatal and, in fact, most of the time are fairly minor. If you are afraid

Table 10-1 Process Improvement Triage Index

Process Improvement Triage Order	Medical Triage Order	Determining Factors
1. Processes getting immediate attention	Immediate/serious injuries	• Meet process improvement goals?
2. Processes that will be addressed in the short term (this APIM iteration)	Observation/stable but frequent re-triage	• Meet project needs? • Meet organizational needs?
3. Processes that will be addressed in the long term (probably next APIM iteration)	Wait/walking Wounded	• How much effort needed? • How much cost needed? • How much time needed?
4. Processes that will not be addressed until much later in effort	Expectant/dying	• Impact to projects? • Impact to organization?

of making small mistakes then things are never accomplished or they take much more time to accomplish.

Spencer Johnson summed this up well in his book, *The Present*. He created three visions to help people be more successful: being (present), learning (past), and creating (future). These same visions can be used during any effort but are especially appropriate for a process improvement effort. The first one he discusses is being, which he states:

"Be In The Present
When You Want To Be Happier And More Successful
Focus On What Is Right Now.
Respond To What Is Important Now."[20]

He emphasized that by living in the present and simply being, people are better able to focus on what is important. However, the past is important so that people can learn from mistakes and problems encountered along the way. He explains:

"Learn From The Past
When You Want To Make The Present Better Than The Past
Look At What Happened In The Past.
Learn Something Valuable For It.
Do Things Differently In The Present." [20]

According to Johnson, besides examining the past and living in the present, people also must look at the future and create it. By creating the future, people are able to visualize the future and realize it. He states:

"Plan For The Future
When You Want To Make The Future Better Than The Present
See What A Wonderful Future Would Look Like.
Make Plans To Help It Happen.
Put Your Plan Into Action In The Present." [20]

Whether it is a Process Improvement effort or any other effort at work or home, these sayings are great inspiration to live by. Try to use these ideas during the Process Improvement effort to help make it more successful.

Keeping it Agile

One of the key Agile Programming methods is the planning accomplished to meet the project requirements. Figure 10-1 shows a typical flow of requirements to development teams. A Release Planning Meeting, also called Stand-Ups,

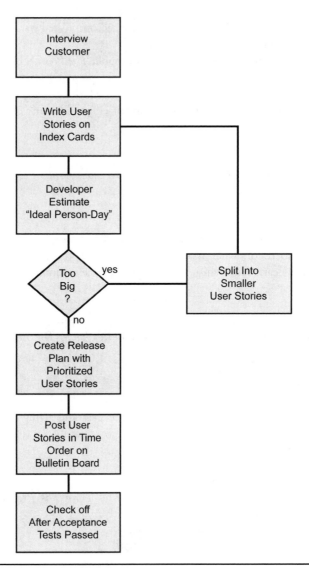

Figure 10-1   Typical Agile Release Planning Process

is typically conducted daily which keeps it flexible. Flexibility is just as important for action planning.

Triage planning could take some pages out of this key agile process. Accomplishing prioritization with the use of index cards on a wall, whiteboard or wallcharts, can be a good prop for allowing the Process Group to visualize the actions. This prop helps in generating logical, flexible plans. Remember to include the actions not accomplished from the previous mini-assessment and reevaluate the prioritization assigned.

Another element that works well for triage is splitting actions into smaller chunks when they go over a certain time. For accelerated Process Improvement, a good rule of thumb is actions that would take longer than two to three weeks. Chunking down is a term used for decomposing a problem into smaller chunks that are easier to solve. This technique of decomposing problems can be used effectively in decomposing actions into workable chunks. Figure 10-2 illustrates an effective approach to accomplishing triage in an agile manner.

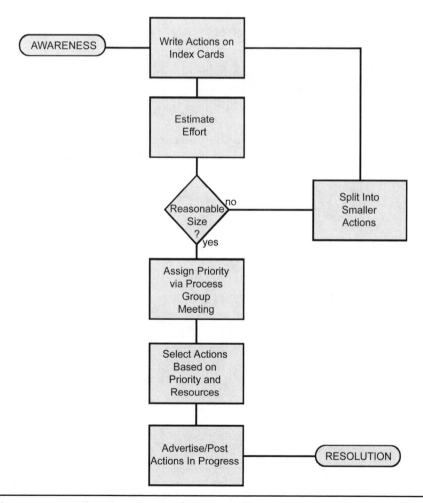

Figure 10-2   Agile Triage Approach

Triage Process Group Meeting

Most of the time the lead for a Process Action Team (PAT) will be part of the process group; if they are not, potential leads should be invited to the Triage Meeting to assist in prioritization. This Triage Meeting should be longer than just 15 minutes like the Agile Stand-Ups but they still should be kept as short and concise as possible.

Determining how long it will take to complete a Process Improvement action is a bit more difficult than for a software component. Most Process Team members will not have the experience to determine how long each action may take and, as a rule, most of us tend to underestimate. The most effective method to determine timing is a Delphi-like method, combined with Nominal Group Process-like discussions about each action. The recommended steps, illustrated in Figure 10-3, for this method are as follows:

1. Discussion of Prioritization Index to ensure full understanding of each triage order category and the determining factors (this should be done at each meeting, not just the first one, since it is the key to making good prioritization decisions)
2. Round-robin style sharing of ideas concerning the actions (can do this one action at a time or groupings of actions but remember to include the actions from previous APIM iterations that were not accomplished)
3. Group discussions
4. Individual reassessment and round-robin sharing of revised ideas
5. Process Group participants provide three estimates (optimistic (E1), pessimistic (E2), and probable (E3)) for each action (should be independent and anonymous)

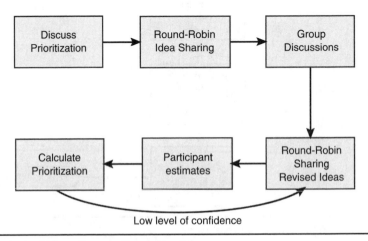

Low level of confidence

Figure 10-3   Triage Process Team Meeting

6. Determine prioritization for each action by:

$$E = ((E1 + E2 + (4E3))/6)/\#\text{participants}$$

7. Repeat steps 4 and 6 until an appropriate level of confidence is met.

Round-robin is a method of handling group discussions so that each person gets a chance to contribute equally. Typically, the discussion starts with one person and goes around the room until everyone gets a chance to share without interruption. A time limit can be set so that it does not go too long.

Managing Actions

The necessary actions determined during the mini-assessment need to be managed along with their prioritization. There are several good methods of accomplishing this, especially a database that is set up that can correlate various elements. These tools have been discussed in previous chapters. Whatever tool is selected, it needs to maintain the list of actions and the prioritization of each one. This prioritization may change following the next progress mini-assessment.

The ones selected for this APIM iteration should be managed on a daily basis to ensure that they are being accomplished in an agile manner as planned.

Summary

In order to be successful with limited resources and time for Process Improvement, triage helps prioritize actions. The key is to get the effort complete in short, succinct accelerated phases or cycles with time being measured in "internet-time," which is typically three to six months.

The business goals, project goals, and process goals should be the primary drivers for prioritization. Reverse triage may be warranted to get processes requiring very little to get them in place to gain buy-in. Whatever prioritization criteria are used, this should be done swiftly in order to get the organization where it needs to go as quickly as possible.

In short, triage provides a method of quickly prioritizing the Process Improvement effort into succinct stages or cycles. It can make a huge difference in the success of an accelerated effort and can be beneficial during any Process Improvement effort as method of prioritization.

Chapter Key Points

- Triage is a good method to use for prioritizing actions needed for Process Improvement based on the mini-assessment results.

- The key selection criteria should be based on three goals: business goals, project goals, and process goals that would impact the organization as a whole, such as budget, especially overhead budget, image, or overall resources.
- Conduct Process Group Meeting to prioritize actions using agile techniques.
- Manage the actions with prioritization for completion during this cycle or another one.

Tips for Success

- Make key selection criteria simple.
- Use of index cards on a wall, whiteboard or wallcharts to visualize the actions.
- Use chunking down for decomposing a problem into smaller chunks that are easier to solve.
- Use a database to manage actions.

Chapter 11

Maturity Phase: Step 3—Resolution

Once prioritization has been established, the selected actions need to be resolved. Typically, a Process Action Team (PAT) is assigned by the Process Group to accomplish the resolution for each task based on priority. The number of actions that are tackled at one time will be dependent upon the resources available to the Process Group. For some of the smaller actions that don't require a large amount of effort, the Process Group may simply resolve these or assign a Process Group member to resolve them as needed. For the larger efforts, the PAT will be assigned and an Action Plan developed for accomplishment. It is important that the PATs be monitored to ensure that actions are being accomplished in a timely manner, especially for an accelerated effort. As with the whole Process Improvement effort, flexibility is key, changing priorities will be a constant and must be managed.

Process Action Teams (PAT)

A PAT is established to tackle the actions for the Process Improvement effort. They are typically selected based on their knowledge and experience with a specific area as well as their availability.

The general responsibilities of this team include:

- Resolve process action or issue as assigned
- Develop action plan

- Report status and any issues
- Propose a solution to the problem
- Train staff involved in pilot
- Pilot test the solution mentoring staff throughout
- Assist in rollout of solution to the rest of the organization.

These important teams can be formed by members of the process group or other organizational staff. The members that form this team will be dependent upon the skills needed to resolve the process action as well as resource availability. If the process or action being tackled is a management issue, managers, especially middle managers, should be selected to resolve the action or issue. A good mix of skills for any action or issue will provide some objectivity so a good cross-functional team is the ideal. It is important to find PAT members that are enthusiastic about the Process Improvement effort to properly resolve the action or issue. The PATs will be discussed in detail in Chapter 18.

PAT Mentors/Coaches

PAT Mentors or Coaches when staff selected are not from the Process Group can be very beneficial in assisting PATs in resolving assigned actions or issues. They can help the PAT overcome any problems encountered and set them on the right path quickly. When problems are encountered during the process, they can help them avoid any damaging results from problems that can slow the action resolution progress. In short, a coach can help cut through the clutter, accept the problems, focus on them, and resolve them in a timely manner.

Mentoring has been used throughout history in many ways but, typically, it is considered a planned pairing of a more skilled or experienced person with a lesser-skilled or -experienced person to accomplish an agreed-upon goal and develop specific abilities in the lesser-skilled or -experienced person. Originally, the word mentor came from Homer's Odyssey. Telemachus was the son of Odysseus, king of Ithaca, [Ulysses] and Penelope. Mentor was Odysseus' wise and trusted counselor as well as tutor to Telemachus. When Odysseus left for the Trojan War he asked Mentor to look after, educate and train his son to fulfill his birthright. Telemachus grew up listening to stories about his famous and heroic father. When Telemachus came of age, he set out on his own odyssey to find his father. With a ship and a crew of 20, Telemachus traveled to Sparta and Pylos, searching for news of his father. Based on this story, mentor has come to mean teacher, counselor, advisor, or guide.

For Process Improvement, a mentor/coach can work in many different ways with the PAT. They can work as a member of the PAT Team and form a partnership to work side-by-side with the PAT in resolving the action or problem. They can, also, be available on the sidelines as needed by the PAT to help resolve problems. Any one or a combination of these works well with teams that don't have the knowledge or skill established yet to quickly work through their assigned actions or problems. The method used will be dependent upon a team's needs and the availability of the appropriate mentor/coach. It can be either a temporary or permanent situation throughout the action resolution process, depending on needs and availability. If the availability is not there it would still be beneficial if a coach is available at the start to kick the team off in the right direction.

A mentor/coach should be selected based on their skills and knowledge. This may be skills and knowledge of the Process Improvement effort, the process model, the organization, a specific project, or a specific skill needed to resolve the action or problem. Careful selection of this person should be undertaken since the wrong person can actually cause more problems than help.

Selecting a good team leader for each PAT is important to ensure that the tasks required are accomplished in a timely manner with the least amount of impact to the organization or projects involved. They must be effective leaders to lead an effective team in their day-to-day action/problem resolution. A key is the ability to promote communications and cohesiveness for the team and with the Process Group.

Building High-Performing PATs

We have already discussed the forming, storming, norming, and performing in a previous chapter but another term being used extensively for building teams is high-performance teams. This term becomes important for the PATs since they will be working very closely with each other on a daily basis and trying to accomplish things quickly.

It is easy for a team to get out of sorts. When there are a lot of decisions that need to be made and problems to be resolved quickly, it can cause teams to disengage just as quickly and become an impediment rather than an asset. Be ready to make changes as needed.

In order to counter some of the inherent problems and focus on the tasks at hand, it is important for PATs to learn how to work as a team. This doesn't mean long drawn-out training courses in team building. It means providing a short, concise awareness session for new teams. These sessions can be beneficial in making them aware of what it takes to become an effective team and to understand that it is normal for conflicts to erupt. They need to know how to resolve these eruptions quickly before they become an impediment to getting the needed tasks accomplished.

Some of the things that help are making teams aware that each of them brings their own personality, style, background, and issues. The sooner that is accepted about team members the sooner they can start becoming a team. There are many good proven techniques for accomplishing effective team-building. Some of the techniques that can be acquired to help build effective teams include:

- Understanding of group dynamics
- Leading in a team environment
- Identifying problem-solving approaches used by teams
- Developing a team-based decision-making process.

There are a good many books available on these and other team-building issues. This book will not attempt to go into these topics but recommends further research be accomplished to build effective teams that are able to accomplish assigned tasks quickly.

Pair Programming for PATs

In eXtreme programming and other agile methodologies, the code is developed by two people who work together at one computer. It is recommended that they slide the keyboard and mouse back and forth, allowing each one the opportunity to contribute either physically or tactically. The one not at the keyboard thinks through the problem to solve it while the other one accomplishes the physical inputs of information. They take turns doing and thinking. It is important that both members are able to see the monitor most of the time or it isn't true pairs programming.

This has been proven as a very successful method of developing code, since they tend to provide positive peer pressure to each other in order to get the best code possible and they are not as likely to deviate from requirements and standards as an individual. The University of Utah has studied this technique and determined that pair programming does produce code in less time with a higher quality. A side effect is that the people involved enjoyed the work more and felt more self-confident, hence making them more productive.

Depending upon the size and scope of the problem or action, as well as the available resources, a pair programming-like process development could be beneficial for the Process Improvement effort. This is especially true for an accelerated effort.

PAT Action Plan

The PAT Action Team is a separate document from the Overall Process Action Plan. One is required for every assigned action or issue. Its purpose is to outline the plan of action for that specific task. This is an extremely important plan and should not be overlooked but at the same time too much time spent can delay action being taken to correct. Keep it short and concise but put in information needed to ensure that the team has a direction and a plan of action prior to undertaking the effort. The size and scope of this plan will be dependent upon the size and scope of the assigned task but keep it as simple as possible.

- Problem Definition/Objectives/Purpose
- Team Members
- Piloting Strategy
- Desired Results
- Issues and Risks
- Timeline/Actions
- Deliverables.

The WBS should be used to define overall tasks for the timeline. Once the schedule is approved, it should be merged into the overall Process Improvement schedule so that it can be tracked to conclusion. The schedule or timeline is a "living" tool for tracking a task's progress.

This plan should be accomplished by the PAT Team Lead and submitted to the Process Group for approval. Approval can be accomplished either at meetings or online via email, a portal, or other means of communications selected for the team. Just like the Overall Process Improvement Action Plan, this should be a "living" plan and not shelfware. Change it as new information is learned and use it as a tool to accomplish the tasks needed for resolving the assigned action.

Resolution How-To's

Actions assigned to the PAT can be either an issue to resolve or a process action. Each of these has different steps to be accomplished. Whatever the problem, the PAT needs to "roll up their sleeves" and figure out the problem. The worst thing that can happen is that they simply throw things over the fence and ask project staff or organizational staff to develop a process. The PAT has the responsibility to develop the process with inputs from the staff, so get in there and get your hands dirty. Remember, the key is to minimize impact to staff as much as possible.

If the assignment is an issue as opposed to a process action, it is important to determine the cause and the nature of the issue prior to trying to resolve it. This will vary based upon the problems but some of the tools discussed in the previous chapters, such as interviews with staff involved, brainstorming sessions, Criteria Grid, FishBone/Cause and Effect Diagram, or Force Field Analysis.

For process actions, the following steps, illustrated in Figure 11-1, are recommended.

1. Start where you are; determine what is currently accomplished in relation to the assigned process. Leverage what is already in place; start with what you find to develop the process. This can be accomplished using the tools discussed in previous chapters such as interviews with staff involved,

brainstorming sessions. If there are existing processes, use a Refactoring method to improve them as described later in this chapter.

2. Determine where this process meets the process model selected.

3. Fill any gaps in the process by determining what the methods are that will work best for the project or organization to meet the model goals. This can be accomplished using the tools discussed in previous chapters such as interviews with staff involved, brainstorming sessions, Criteria Grid, FishBone/Cause and Effect Diagram, or Force Field Analysis.

4. Document process including: process flows, policies, procedures, forms, and templates. Reference previous chapters for developing processes.

5. Coordinate with appropriate managers and leads as needed. The idea is to build buy-in when processes are developed and the best way to do that is to coordinate with the staff that actually have to do the work when the PAT is disbanded. Most of the PAT members will walk away to another assignment but the staff that the process is developed for will have to live with the results, so make sure it works for them and be willing to compromise as long as the process model goals are met.

6. Obtain approval from the Process Group.

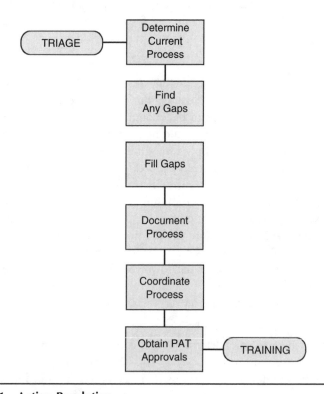

Figure 11-1   Action Resolution

Developing Processes

During resolution the process should be developed that may include process flows, policies, procedures, forms, and templates. Previous chapters have discussed various methods for developing processes effectively but this chapter will cover a few other issues concerning the actual process development. The key again is simplicity, KISS. As in agile programming: "Do the simplest thing that will work." This is done by Refactoring existing code and is a method that is essential for accelerated Process Improvement.

Refactoring

If previously developed complex processes are used, you should use a technique called Refactoring. In agile programming, as well as other programming methodologies, Refactoring means "making the code clearer, cleaner, simpler, and elegant." This does not mean changing the functionality or rewriting processes but simplifying them for easier use. It is often used in writing as well as code development. The idea of Refactoring in writing means improving the readability or structure with the explicit purpose of keeping the same meaning intact. It is often called "cleaning it up" or changing the internal consistency and clarity. This same practice is key when using existing processes. Prior to changing the process, Refactor it so that it is easier to understand and use. According to some agile programming methodologies, Refactoring should be "merciless" since it keeps the design simple and avoids "clutter and complexity." This makes the code easier to understand, modify, and extend. The same is true for processes. Refactor mercilessly!

Testing/Prototyping Processes

Just as with code development, it is important to ensure that the process developed works as written. Set up a simulation of the process prior to sending it to the Process Group for approval. This will ensure that all the steps in the process, procedures, and templates are feasible and all steps make sense. This is an inexpensive, easy method that can save a good deal of time and effort later in the effort.

Peer Reviews

A quick peer review method should be used to finalize processes for approval. Chapter 8 discussed this key process. It will ensure that the process is ready for piloting. It can be accomplished using a formal method or an informal method but it should be accomplished before it is coordinated with managers and leads. Again keep these as simple and short as possible. Don't go overboard and introduce a lot of bureaucracy otherwise you will move away from accelerating the Process Improvement effort. Some paperwork or other means of documenting the effort should be archived to track this important process and ensure it is accomplished.

This is another place where communications can expose problems and issues not considered previously. This will be dependent upon how the peer review is conducted. It must be done in a non-adversarial way so that there are no hard feelings. People become emotionally tied to the work they have accomplished and it is easy to hurt feelings if not careful, especially in a formal peer-review environment. Many times the developer, whether it's code, a document, or a process, feels ganged up on. Even small suggestions can feel personal, which can have a very negative impact on their morale, hence the work suffers. It is important to use care with peer reviews and in this situation a less formal peer review may work to the advantage.

Monitoring PATs

During this iteration of the APIM, it is important that the PATs are monitored and their progress tracked to ensure that the work is being accomplished in a timely manner and to resolve problems early. It is especially important to discuss risks at each meeting to ensure that they do not negatively impact progress. If you wait, it may be too late to change.

Regular status meetings should be in place to monitor PATs. These can be incorporated into the Process Group meetings or be a separate meeting. Each PAT should be given an opportunity to status the Process Group in much the same manner as described for the Process Group to brief the Executive Steering Committee. The toolkit includes a sample agenda and minutes for this meeting, which can be tailored for the PAT status briefing to the PAT.

The schedule is the key tool in tracking action progress. As discussed earlier, this is a "living" tool that can make the difference between success and failure. If things change, change the schedule. There are a couple of methods used for revising schedules when problems are encountered. They are called fast tracking and crashing a schedule.

Fast tracking is a method of compressing the schedule by doing some or all of certain activities in parallel that would normally be done in sequence. This method is only effective when the resources are available to accomplish the fast tracking. Crashing means to decrease the duration of a critical activity by means of increasing resources or some other means of reducing the duration. Both of these methods require extra resources so neither may be feasible if the budget is not available to handle them.

Summary

Resolution is typically accomplished by assignment of a PAT but can be accomplished by an individual, depending upon the size and scope of the action or issue. Smaller actions may be accomplished as a group depending upon the action or issue at hand. The number of actions that are tackled at one time will be dependent upon the resources available to the Process Group. Most of the actions should have an associated Action Plan to identify the key planning elements such as piloting, timelines, and risks or constraints. PATs' progress must be monitored to ensure they are being accomplished in a timely manner with the quality needed to make the solution successful. Flexibility again will play a role so the Process Group must be prepared to change course as needed to get the most out of the effort.

As with the rest of this methodology, the key is agility and keeping it simple. Avoid bureaucracy unless highly warranted, it is time consuming.

Chapter Key Points

- A Process Action Team (PAT) is established to tackle the actions for the Process Improvement effort based on their knowledge and experience.
- PAT Mentors or Coaches, when staff selected are not from the Process Group, can be very beneficial in assisting PATs in resolving assigned actions or issues.
- It is easy for a team to get out of sorts; monitor PATs closely for any problems.
- Outline the plan of action for that specific task in a PAT Action Plan.
- Develop processes and pilot the processes to ensure they are effective.
- Regular statusing should be accomplished for all PATs.

Tips for Success

- Use pair programming-like solution for PATs as feasible.
- Use short, concise team awareness sessions to build effective teams.
- Key is keeping it simple.
- Remember agility; always be ready to change course as needed.
- Avoid bureaucracy unless highly warranted, it is time consuming.
- Use refactoring in developing processes to keep them simple and clean so they are easy to use.

Chapter 12

Maturity Phase: Step 4—Training

Training can play a pivotal role in the acceptance or rejection of a developed process. Special care should be taken with training in order to get buy-in from the process users. This period of time should be used to tailor the process to meet any specific user needs as well as train the user on the process. Proper training will make the difference between whether the process is used or shelved. If it is understood and easy to use, it will be used.

Training Methods

There are some great techniques and methods that can be used to accomplish training. The proper tool will be dependent upon the trainer, the organization, the staff, and the available tools for accomplishing the training. Some helpful methods are discussed below.

Classroom versus Workshops versus Online Training

Video conferencing, CD-ROM, and the Internet are throwing open the doors of access to training. Classroom training is typically more of a lecture type of training, whereas workshops bring some level of hands-on experience to the participants and online training is accomplished using a computer. Any of these methods are effective but each one has advantages and disadvantages.

Instruction-led training such as classroom or workshop training does not ensure that the same training is given every time, whereas online training ensures that training is consistent. Online training has been gaining in popularity mostly due to:

- Ease of use
- Consistency
- Content integrity
- Scalability.

If the resources are available, this type of training can be effectively used for process training. Not only would it be available for current project and organizational staff but also for newcomers.

Classrooms and workshops have an advantage in the interaction between the trainer and participants. For processes, this is important during this stage since it also should be used to gain buy-in to the developed processes. This is where elements of the processes may change as a result of new information that comes about during a training session. Workshops can also be effective in promoting teamwork.

At this point in the Process Improvement effort, workshop training is optimal to allow participants to use some elements of the processes in a classroom setting with a key side effect of ensuring that they execute as developed. Later in the effort an online training curriculum would be optimal. For remote participants video conferences work well, if available. There are many services on the internet that provide video-conferencing for reasonable costs.

In-House Versus Off-Site

The next consideration is to where to conduct the training—in-house, where the staff conduct their day-to-day jobs, or off-site. There are advantages and disadvantages to both methods.

When training is being conducted in-house, it allows staff more convenience and time, plus it is familiar territory for them. However, the chances are that they can be pulled away from the training much easier than if it were off-site. When training is conducted off-site, it allows staff to concentrate on the training that is being conducted much better with less potential interruption. However, it can be inconvenient and take more time.

These advantages and disadvantages need to be balanced. There will be other considerations as well, such as available facilities and training resources. The key is to get the most out of the training provided, whichever method is selected. If you make coming to the training a worthwhile event participants will be excited to come to the training and look forward to it, but if it is perceived as a nuisance any inconvenience will be too great.

Training Conduct

Conducting training can be difficult. The objective is to ensure that all participants leave with the knowledge and understanding of the topics presented. There are methods that help achieve this goal. Many studies have shown that adults learn significantly better when they are actively involved. Training strategies have been developed to facilitate this principle. A balance of lectures and exercises can make a huge difference in understanding as well as making the learning fun. As Confucius said in 500 BC, "What I hear I forget, what I see I remember, but what I do I understand."

SAVI

Many training organizations are using an accelerated learning technique called SAVI which applies basic brain principles to learning. These brain principles are:

- Somatic (S)
- Auditory (A)
- Visual (V)
- Intellectual (I).

These principles are related to learning in order to provide the optimal learning experience. Many training organizations are calling their courses "SAVI-compliant training."

The various brain principles can be applied to development of training sessions for process improvement to ensure that the participants walk away with the knowledge they need to understand and accept the developed processes. SAVI is related to learning as follows.

- *Somatic—Learn by Doing.* Some have related this to physical activity and even the use of the body in some way to enhance learning. This is also called kinesthetic learning.
- *Auditory—Learn by Hearing/Talking.* This has been related to social interaction as well as simply hearing.
- *Visual—Learn by Seeing.* This can be watching or listening.
- *Intellectual—Learn by Thinking.* Some have related this to reflection and analysis of materials.

Lecture versus Exercises

Studies have shown that students learn better when they are actively involved. There has been a good deal of research into the theory of learning that has been published in several good training books. Some of these theories have become well-known and proved successful in the classroom. Table 12-1 discusses a few of the more successful theories.

Another key consideration is breaks. There are several theories concerning breaks but the best rules of thumb are ten minute breaks every hour or 15 minute breaks every one and a half hours. These must be carefully controlled since they tend to be abused extensively. This is especially so when training is being conducted on-site.

Table 12-1 Learning Techniques

Theory	Brief Description
90-20-8 Rule	People can listen for 90 minutes with understanding. People can listen for 20 minutes with retention. Bob Pike, Creative Training Techniques, theorizes that trainers need to involve people every 8 minutes to reinforce the learning. Pike promotes the use of "window panes" to anchor learning points. He suggests that simply by asking direct questions of participants or engaging participants in discussion can enhance the learning experience, especially targeting those that aren't as actively involved.
20-40 Rule	Based on the same research, this theory of learning recommends talk for 20 minutes out of every hour and use the rest of the time for reinforcement, skills practice or discussion.
15/85 Rule	Devote 15% of your time to lecture or presentation, 85% of the time should be devoted to small-group activities and large-group sharing and exploration.
Pictures	Our minds visualize/think in pictures.
400–600 words per minute	Adults can generally think at a rate of 400–600 words per minute.
120–140 words per minute	Adults generally speak at a rate of 120–140 words per minute.
Working memory	Primacy is our ability to remember the beginning of a list, sequence or presentation and Recency is our ability to remember the end.
Review six times	Maximize retention by reviewing key elements at least six times.
Anxiety vs Retention	Retention of material is directly proportional to the level of anxiety. If anxiety in learning is high, retention is low.

Typically, the process training should be kept fairly short so that it does not impact the daily operations of the organization or a project. It may be best to break the training up into smaller less time-consuming pieces. The issue is making sure all participants attend the training.

Making it Fun

For any type of training, the more fun it is the more participants tend to learn and retain. A balance between just having fun and learning needs to be controlled. There are several ways to make it fun. Group activities where participants are broken into working groups can be an effective method of getting participants involved. Games can help not only the learning process but also can act as a test of sorts. Another thing that keeps it fun is bring food, this seems to be the cure-all for all meetings and training sessions. Table 12-2 discusses some of the more popular methods of keeping training fun and interesting which in turn promotes understanding and retention.

Standard Contents for Training Sessions

When developing the contents for a training session there are a good many things to keep in mind. A key aspect is to remember that the best design for any training program is one in which participants spend the most time doing the thing they are supposed to be learning.

Preparing For Training

Training preparation can be daunting. There are several elements that most successful training sessions incorporate. Remember, don't go overboard, keep it simple; this is an accelerated effort and many times too much time spent on preparing training can be counterproductive, but at the same time balance that with ensuring the participants' understand and retain the most information possible to do their job. Table 12-3 describes some of the key elements required for effective training sessions. Use organizational training standards if they are available.

Organizing Ideas

Organization of the ideas and information for training can be a key to its success or failure. Disorganized training sessions can be a detriment rather than a benefit. There are a good many methods and strategies for organizing the data that need to be imparted to a group of people.

Table 12-2 Games for Learning

Keeping it Fun Techniques	*Brief Description*
Jokes and stories	Breaking the information up and including jokes and stories can enhance listening and help keep participants from getting bored.
Role-playing	Role-playing can be accomplished in a number of ways but can be very useful to demonstrate how a process or method is accomplished and some of the roadblocks that can occur.
Popular TV game shows	Some very popular games are ones that are recognizable, such as tailoring Jeopardy or Who Wants to Be a Millionaire using a database tool such as MSAccess or a presentation tool like MSPowerpoint.
Participation poker	Playing cards are handed out to participants. Cards can be earned for several reasons, such as: ✓ ask a question or offer a comment that contributes to the session ✓ volunteer to assist training session ✓ somehow behave in a positive way ✓ timely returns from breaks ✓ participating as the group spokesperson during exercises The object at the end of the day (or a specified segment) is to have the best five-card poker hand. The participant holding the winning hand gets a prize.
The memory game	The memory game is useful when there is a list of things you want participants to remember. It uses a ball or another object that is passed or tossed and the receiver must name an item on the list then pass the object to another person.
Gallery walk	Post charts you've used during the class and have participants do a "gallery walk" from chart to chart in groups of three as they discuss what meaning the charts hold for them, and how that impacts their daily work.
Crossword puzzles and find-a-word	When a number of terms are involved in the learning process, crosswords can be a good method for testing understanding and fun for participants.

(continued)

Table 12-2   Continued

Keeping it Fun Techniques	*Brief Description*
Top ten lessons-learned	Top ten lessons-learned Lists can be a fun way of summarizing sessions and enhancing retention of information.
Feedback wallcharts/ parking lot	At the beginning of a session, ask participants what knowledge they expect to come out of the session. Use this at the end or at various intervals during the session to ensure that participants' expectations are being met or explain why this is an unrealistic expectation.
Parking lot	If questions are asked during a training session that will be covered later the parking lot acts as a method of ensuring these questions are answered. Go back to the parking lot at various intervals to ensure that all participant concerns are met.

Some methods used to organize ideas either for a presentation or for supporting data such as a workbook include:

- *Chronological*—sequential order according to when a step occurs
- *Topical*—organized by sub-topics that are of equal importance. Remember the recency, primacy, and middle topic discussed previously
- *Spatial*—arranged according to location and direction
- *Cause and effect*—identifying a situation and discussing the resulting effects (cause/effect) or presenting a situation and exploring the causes (effect/cause)
- *Problem and solution*—exploring how a problem is solved.

There are some techniques that can help organize a presentation to make it easier to understand by participants. Some of these include:

- *Signposts*—a list detailing what is to come and providing direction through the presentation
- *Previews*—statement of what is to come
- *Transitions*—these can be either verbal or non-verbal
- *Summaries*—these can be accomplished at various intervals throughout the training session or at the end of the training session.

Table 12-3   Elements of a Training Session

Element	Brief Description
Lesson plan	Describes the topics that will be discussed during the training session. These can be phrases or two or three words and backed up with a more detailed statement or statements of more specific contents.
Session objectives	Objectives help the participant understand where the training is heading so that they understand when the target is reached. If testing is involved, they can act as a guideline for testing. They should state something about what should be understood at the end of the training session.
Presentation slides	Presentation slides should be kept fairly small depending upon the size of the course. They should be used to guide the trainer through the training session but not act as a tool to read to the participants. If a workbook is used they should correlate with the information provided in the workbook.
Workbook	A workbook provides a method of transferring more detailed information in written format. This can enhance the training experience and be used after training for reference. This can be a key element of process development to help the understandability of processes.
Exercises	Exercises provide that key ingredient of training, the somatic or kinesthetic learning. Examples of effective exercises can be gleaned from the elements in Table 1 and 2.
Terms, acronyms, and definitions	By providing these separately, it enables students to easily find and understand the Terms, Acronyms, and Definitions that are key to the training session.
Supplementary resources	When a training session is over, many times participants find topics that are of interest to them and want to find more detailed information concerning the topic(s). This provides them a place to start.
Cover sheet	This is a simple addition to a training session that gives it a more professional look and feel. This perception can make the training session seem more important to the participants.

(continued)

Table 12-3   Continued

Element	Brief Description
Table of contents	This provides the participants an easy method of finding information in a training package.
Evaluation form	Getting feedback concerning the training session will help improve later training sessions and may indicate the need for some follow-up training.

Training Survey/Evaluation

A post assessment of a training session helps the overall effectiveness of training in general. It provides a method of ensuring that the participants have the information needed to go out and accomplish their job based on the processes developed. It may indicate a need for some follow-up training sessions(s) to reinforce the information.

The evaluation should cover evaluation of the materials, instructors, facilities, and overall effectiveness of the training. They should provide a method of statements of what they liked best and what they disliked the most. Recommendations should be encourage to make the sessions better and more useable in the future.

Use Training To Gain Buy-In

Several methods can be used to gain buy-in from participants. A simple brainstorming session during training allows participants to provide some ideas for improving what has been developed for their job. This encourages a feeling of ownership which can be important to ensuring use of the processes developed. A good method is to use a whiteboard or wallchart to "tick off" what the brainstorming session comes up with and then add your own to the list and discuss these aspects of the process. Another successful method is to ask participants to describe various situations that are related to the topic or process and discuss how it was resolved and how this new or revised process might make it better. Finally, role-playing offers a good somatic exercise to show how a situation might work and how it might work better.

Buy-in will make the difference between using a process and shelving a process. The training session offers a great forum for enhancing that buy-in.

During the training session, take the ideas generated from the group to help improve the process that was developed. Remember that the whole objective of process improvement is to improve processes; they are not written in stone and should be changed as needed to make them work for the process users. This, of course, must be balanced with the elements of the selected process models.

Summary

Training can be one of the best tools a Process Group can use to obtain buy-in for development processes. It is critical that staff that will be using a developed process fully understand the process and associated artifacts such as templates, guidelines, tools, etc. If conducted properly training can also be used to tweak the processes as needed to meet the needs of the organization as well as a particular project.

Proper training will make the difference between whether the process is used or shelved. If it is understood and easy to use, it will be used.

Chapter Key Points

- There are some great techniques and methods that can be used to accomplish training.
- Video conferencing, CD-ROM, and the Internet are making training more accessible and less expensive. These can be in the form of classroom-style training or workshop training sessions.
- Training should be a balance of lectures and exercises to be most effective.
- Use the many training techniques and methods developed which help people learn easier and retain the information they learn.
- Balance providing enough training with going overboard. This is an accelerated effort and many times too much time spent on preparing training can be counterproductive.
- A post-assessment of a training session helps the overall effectiveness of training in general.

Tips for Success

- Carefully weigh the advantages and disadvantages of in-house versus off-site training.
- Remember to apply SAVI (somatic (S), auditory (A), visual (V), intellectual (I)) which are the brain principles to learning.
- Make training fun.
- Don't go overboard, keep it simple.

Chapter 13

Chapter 13

Maturity Phase: Step 5—Deployment

Piloting processes is much like testing software. You wouldn't put software into an operational environment without ensuring that it functions properly first. Processes should be piloted on a project, or somehow within the organization, prior to being added to the organization's process repository. It is important to ensure that the process will work in a real situation instead of just in theory. There will be situations where a pilot is not called for based upon the size, scope, or type of action or issue being resolved. This is a judgment that should be made during the Action Planning and approved by the Process Group.

Process Piloting

A project or individual in an organization should be selected as the target pilot. This process should be accomplished during the Action Planning step.

The piloting plan can change as a result of events that impact a project or individual in a way that cannot support the pilot any longer, so a PAT needs to be prepared to select another project or individual if feasible. An alternative is to simulate the process execution; this will especially apply when a process or part of a process is not used extensively or very much of the time.

If not feasible, the Process Group can make the decision to implement the process or not for the rest of the organization depending upon what the impact will be to the organization. All issues, risks, and concerns should be weighed to make that decision.

Several things should be considered in selecting a project or individual for the piloting step including:

- For a project, the selection will depend upon where they are in the project life cycle compared to the process to be piloted.
- Selection of either a project or individual(s) will depend upon their enthusiasm. If staff are not enthusiastic about the Process Improvement effort or that particular process, they will not make a good pilot subject.
- Impact to schedule, resources or budget. Project and individuals must have the time to accomplish the steps required and make appropriate measures and judgments to be effective.

The amount of time to allot for a pilot will depend upon the phase in which the process is implemented and where in the phasing a project or individual currently is operating. It will also depend upon the time available from the project or individual. This needs to be determined early and monitored to ensure that it does not take so long that it is counterproductive.

Once a project or individual is selected the piloting begins. This should include, as illustrated in Figure 13-1, the following steps:

1. Determine criteria to evaluate success or failure.
2. Set or reset set schedule. This should be documented in the action plan and changed as needed to always reflect the current schedule.
3. Mentor staff who will be accomplishing pilot.
4. Staff should implement processes as required.
5. Make changes or tweak processes as needed based on pilot results.
6. Document results based on criteria.
7. Repilot as needed until it functions satisfactorily for PAT.
8. Submit to Process Group for final assessment and repiloting as needed.

Evaluating the Process Effectiveness

Criteria should be selected to prove the effectiveness of a process. A great method for accomplishing the evaluation is through use of the criteria grid discussed in Chapter 8. Selecting the appropriate criteria is key to determining success or failure. The following are some things to consider for effective effectiveness criteria:

- What are you trying to accomplish with the process?
- Exit and entry criteria for process.
- Inputs and outputs of process.

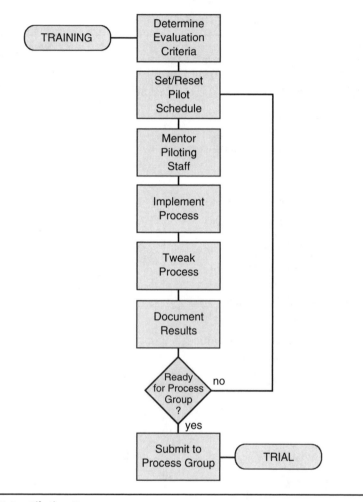

Figure 13-1 Piloting Processes

- Are there any associated or indirect criteria that should be evaluated?
- Clarity and strength.

Table 1 illustrates a sample criteria grid for piloting a process. If more than one staff member is involved in the piloting, each one should submit a Piloting Success Criteria Grid to the PAT with their comments and evaluation of the process.

Besides observation to determine if criteria are satisfied, the PAT may opt to use questionnaires, interviews, or brainstorming sessions to get users' opinions. These tend to bring out things that may not get revealed through observation. A combination of these tools is optimal.

Table 13-1   Piloting Success Criteria

Criteria	Weak	Fair	Strong	Comments
Layout Organization				
Structure (organization into sections, subsections)?				
Figures and tables (clearly labeled and professional)?				
Clearly stated purpose and objective(s)?				
Process steps orderly?				
Accomplished its purpose?				
Good overall structure?				
Paragraphs right length?				
Process Intent				
Major ideas/topics of process well understood?				
Supporting material appropriate?				
General process description?				
Graphical depiction clear and correct?				
Unnecessary repetition avoided?				
Entry Criteria				
Exit Criteria				
Inputs				
Outputs				
Associated or Indirect Criteria				
Clarity and Strength				
Was the overall process easy to use?				

(continued)

Table 13-1 Continued

Criteria	Weak	Fair	Strong	Comments
Was the overall process adequate to accomplish the tasks?				
Recommend any changes:				

Process Group Mentoring Piloted Processes

The Process Group, in particular the PAT or a member of the PAT, should act as a mentor/coach for the project when piloting processes. Frequent check-ups should be accomplished to ensure that it is being used as developed and to ensure a complete understanding of each step, template, deliverable, process, procedure, tool, etc.

Summary

Processes should be piloted on a project, or somehow within the organization to ensure that the process will function properly in an operational environment. Once the piloting has been accomplished and the results approved, the processes can be added to the organizations' process repository.

Chapter Key Points

- A project or individual in an organization should be selected as the target pilot. This process should be accomplished during the Action Planning step.
- Make changes or tweak processes as needed based on pilot results.
- Repilot as needed until it functions satisfactorily for PAT.
- Criteria should be selected to prove the effectiveness of a process. A great method for accomplishing the evaluation is through use of the criteria grid.

Tips for Success

- Select projects for pilots carefully.
- Mentor staff accomplishing piloting.
- Use criteria grids for pilot success criteria.

Chapter 14

Maturity Phase: Step 6—Trial

Once the process has been piloted, the Process Group should assess the effectiveness of the processes developed for the selected actions. At this point they can either approve or reject them. Depending upon the severity of the findings, they may be immediately improved and approved or improved and repiloted during the next iteration. As always, collect lessons learned for making later iterations easier, better, and even more agile.

Putting Processes on Trial

The steps for putting a process on trial, illustrated in Figure 14-1, are as follows:

1. Evaluate the processes submitted by the PATs using the criteria they have selected.
2. Approve or disapprove the process as submitted for deployment to the organization.
3. If approved, deploy selected process(es) to the organization.
4. If disapproved, send the process back to the PAT to accomplish the resolution and repiloting as needed again.
5. Evaluate organization's readiness for a formal appraisal by conducting a progress mini-assessment. If the Process Improvement goals are not met, go into the Triage step. If goals are met, determine if a formal

appraisal is needed. If goal is not a formal appraisal, evaluate readiness for continued Process Improvement through other methods rather than the APIM.

6. If not ready for formal appraisal or continued Process Improvement, evaluate whether there are more actions to be implemented in this iteration of the APIM Maturity Cycle.

7. If there are more actions in the queue for evaluation, assign PAT and go to resolution.

8. If there are no actions designated for this iteration of the APIM Maturity Cycle, accomplish a progress mini-assessment and start a new cycle.

9. Prepare for appraisal.

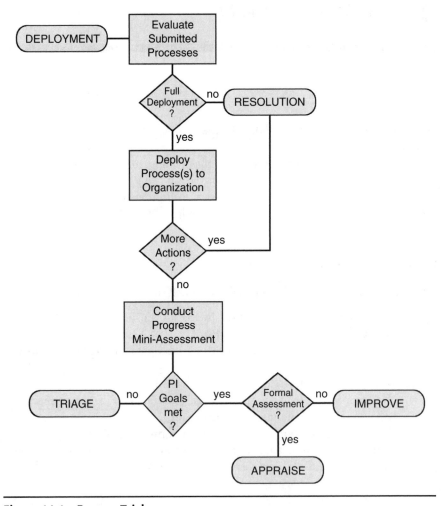

Figure 14-1   Process Trials

Evaluating Effectiveness

The process and all process artifacts, along with the completed Piloting Success Criteria Grid(s), should be submitted to the Process Group by the PAT. This should be accomplished using the communication mechanism that has been set up for the approval process. The Piloting Success Criteria Grid(s) should be used by the Process Group to evaluate the processes developed for each action submitted for final approval. This can be accomplished by a group meeting or other means of communications as established. The group should weigh the factors that have been selected by the PAT in combination with the comments submitted by the piloting staff. If further information is needed, the staff involved in the piloting should be contacted for further comment. A brainstorming session would be a good tool to discuss any issues or comments. Risks should be revisited to ensure that no new risks have been introduced and evaluate the priority of the existing risks. Due to the new or revised process, some risks may become null and void at this point.

Final Approvals

The Process Group should be the final approval for all piloted processes or processes that do not require piloting prior to deployment to the rest of the organization. The Process Group may choose to deploy the process to the organization or to send it back to the PAT for further work.

If a process has some risks, the Process Group may choose to accept the risk(s) and rework the process at a future time. If the risks are not major, this is recommended. The primary goal is not to develop perfect processes but to develop processes and improve them over time. Get something on the table to start with and then go back to make it better. Too many times we spend so much time trying to make it perfect that it is extremely counterproductive. The key here is to keep the long-term action list up-to-date so that nothing falls through the cracks later. Even if something does fall through the cracks eventually the staff using the process will make sure that any problem they encounter gets attention. This may fall out during an audit by the Quality Assurance staff.

A Process Group may decide that the success criteria do not support the deployment of the process. At that point, they would ask the PAT to reevaluate the criteria and resubmit the package again.

Ideally, the Process Group will approve the process and deploy it to the organization. At this point the PAT may be disbanded or they may be asked to tackle another action on the prioritized list. This will depend upon the synergy of the PAT and their ability to meet the assigned goals set for the assigned actions. If new skills are needed, take care in the individual selected and ensure that the PAT still work well together. Monitoring the team for a period of time might be feasible until there is confidence in their ability to complete the assigned task.

Deploy Processes

Once a process has been approved by the Process Group it is ready to be deployed to the rest of the organization. The process artifacts need to be put into the Process Library and archived. If the action replaces an existing process these artifacts must be archived for historical purposes using the Configuration Management process discussed previously for version control.

This is where the liaisons established with Project Managers, as discussed previously, become very important. Each project needs to be evaluated to determine if the process should be deployed to that project at this time, at a later time, or at any time. This will be dependent upon many project variables including:

- Phase of the life cycle
- Schedule flexibility
- State of the budget
- Available resources
- Impact the process would have on the project (positive or negative).

Any new projects will tailor the process as needed based on the tailoring guidelines.

Once a decision is made to roll the solution out to the rest of the organization, training should be conducted to those that will be using the process or have a stake in the process such as a key interface. Everyone should be aware of all the processes but not everyone needs to know the gory details about all processes. The training should already be accomplished as described prior to the piloting step and would be tested out and revised as needed during piloting.

Because the process is now in the Process Library does not mean it is written in stone; continued Process Improvement means constantly adjusting elements as needed to make them perform better for the staff that need to use them. Don't be afraid to change them even at this point; depending upon the change, the process may or may not need to go through this entire process for every change. Sometimes changes can be put on the long-term actions list for completion later as time permits.

Formal Appraisal or Not

At this point, the Process Group needs to determine where they go from here. If all of the actions for this iteration of the APIM Maturity cycle are not completed, actions should be assigned to a PAT based on the assigned priority. The PAT would start evaluating the action at the resolution step and continue to this point until all actions designated for this iteration have been worked.

If all of the actions designated for this iteration of the APIM Maturity cycle have been accomplished, a Progress Mini-Assessment should be started.

If the Progress Mini-Assessment indicates that the Process Improvement goals have been met and all actions have been completed, the Post Maturity phase begins.

If the Process Improvement goals have not been met, the Triage step should begin.

Prior to starting the Process Improvement effort, the decision would be made if the goal is to achieve a formal maturity level or simply improve the way the organization does business. Both of these are good reasons to accomplish a Process Improvement effort. This is a decision that the Executive Management staff would make with advice from the Process Group.

If a formal appraisal is selected, the preparations for this need to be accomplished at this point. Chapter 15 will discuss these preparations in detail.

If a formal appraisal is not the goal, the method to be used for continued Process Improvement needs to be instigated. Chapter 16 will discuss this in detail.

Lessons Learned

It is important to always collect lessons learned so that the same mistakes aren't continuously made. This is a good point to discuss lessons learned with the Process Group and have the PAT and staff that were involved in piloting submit lessons learned. These should be archived in the Process Library. However, they should not be shelved, they should be revisited and correlated as time permits to maintain a concise list of lessons for each new team and even for older teams to remind them of what does and does not work. The lessons may be lessons that are unique to an organization or project but they may also be lessons that are typical of Process Improvement or a particular process.

Summary

Prior to deploying processes to the rest of the organization they should go through an approval process. The approval process should evaluate the effectiveness of the processes developed and piloted by PATs. The findings should be used to determine if the process should be immediately improved and approved or improved and repiloted during the next iteration. Lessons learned during the Maturity cycle can make later iterations easier, better, and even more agile.

Chapter Key Points

- All process artifacts, along with the completed Piloting Success Criteria Grid(s), should be submitted to the Process Group for approvals.
- Evaluate effectiveness by weighing the factors selected by the PAT in combination with the comments submitted by the piloting staff.
- Risks should be revisited to ensure that no new risks have been introduced and evaluate the priority of the existing risks.
- Once approved deploy processes to the rest of the organization. Place process artifacts in the Process Library.
- Collect lessons learned so that the same mistakes aren't continuously made.

Tips for Success

- Use brainstorming sessions to discuss any issues or comments during evaluations.
- Use Configuration Management processes to control processes and process artifacts.
- Don't just shelve lessons learned, use them to make things better and even more agile.

Chapter 15

Post Maturity Phase: Step 1—Assess

The final phase is the Post Maturity Phase, which starts with the formal assessment if the organization has decided to conduct one. This decision should have been made before or at the beginning of the Process Improvement effort. The ultimate goal of Process Improvement should be to achieve process maturity that works for that unique organization with the formal level achieved secondary. If a formal assessment is the goal, it should be accomplished when the progress mini-assessment indicates readiness. Even if the goal is a formal assessment, an organization may or may not be ready for it at this point.

The ultimate goal may be a formal assessment but, as the Process Improvement effort progressed, some long-term actions were identified that make it unfeasible to undergo a formal assessment at this point. The organization may want to go into continued improvement while the long-term actions are being achieved, but some of the methods used for accelerating the effort may still work well for continued improvement. This will depend upon the revised goals of the organization.

The method of assessment will be dependent upon the Process Improvement model or methodology selected but it will be key to identifying strengths and weaknesses from an outside source. Some formal assessments use organizational staff and some use staff from outside the organization or company. These are decisions that need to be made prior to preparation for the formal assessment.

Some Formal Assessment Methods

The formal assessment method will be dependent upon the model selected for Process Improvement. This chapter will briefly discuss some of the formal assessment methods based on the models discussed in this book. Each one has an associated publication that discusses the assessment methodology as required.

Software Engineering Institute's (SEI) Capability Maturity Models Integration (CMMI®)

The CMMI® uses a series of assessments called Standard CMMI® Assessment Method for Process Improvement (SCAMPI[SM])[32], with the purpose to provide "benchmark quality ratings." Appraisal Requirements for CMMI® (ARC) provide the requirements for CMMI® appraisal methods. It "consists of a set of high-level design criteria for developing, defining, and using appraisal methods based on CMMI® models." It was influenced by the various models and methodologies that make up the CMMI®. SCAMPI[SM] is ARC compliant.

SCAMPI[SM] comes in three different versions, each developed for various purposes. The three versions are:

- SCAMPI[SM] Class C → approach

  — Quick check of organization based on Process Improvement goals, similar to an initial mini-assessment described in this book
  — Focus on getting initial reading for Process Improvement
  — Results in initial process maturity, not a level but a general idea of where they need to go from there.

- SCAMPI[SM] Class B → deployment

  — Less comprehensive, similar to a progress mini-assessment described in this book
  — Focus on specific area
  — Results in status of Process Improvement progress.

- SCAMPI[SM] Class A → implementation

  — Fully comprehensive
  — Thorough model coverage
  — Results in maturity level.

Details of this assessment method can be found in the Standard CMMI® Appraisal Method for Process Improvement (SCAMPI[SM]), Version 1.1: Method Implementation Guidance for Government Source Selection and Contract Process Monitoring Handbook CMU/SEI-2002-HB-002.[32] This document is combined to meet the needs of source selection and contract monitoring by the Government.

Software Engineering Institute's (SEI) Capability Maturity Models for Software (SW-CMM®)

The SW-CMM® SEI-authorized assessment method is the CMM®-Based Appraisal for Internal Process Improvement (CBA IPI).[12] This model is no longer supported by the SEI and has been replaced by the CMMI® but many organizations continue to use this successful model and the assessment method associated with it. However, the CMMI® has incorporated many of the lessons learned from the SW-CMM® so that it reflects more up-to-date best practices for organizations.

Software Engineering Institute's (SEI) Personal Software Process (PSP^SM) and Software Engineering Institute's (SEI) Team Software Process (TSP®)

There is not a specific assessment method associated with these models but they are typically measured by the higher performance ranges of:

- Post-release defects/KLOC
- System test duration
- Defects/KLOC in acceptance test
- Schedule deviation
- Effort deviation.

Due to being based upon the CMM® and use of best practices for system development, organizational staff members and teams trained in use of these two models would facilitate an organization's maturity growth based on the CMMI® model.

Software Engineering Institute's (SEI) People Capability Maturity Model (P-CMM®)

The People Capability Maturity Model^SM (CMM®)-Based Assessment Method is the method used to determine the level of people management according to the P-CMM® practices. It is an on-site assessment accomplished with a P-CMM®-Based Assessment Method. It examines the key process areas and achievement of them. It is intended as a precursor to organizational improvement activities. As discussed previously, the people involved in the Process Improvement effort can make the difference between success and failure of the effort.

International Organization for Standardization (ISO) 9001

ISO 9001 requires a registration audit for which an organization becomes ISO-registered. The audit teams are authorized professionals that audit an organization looking for any nonconformances based upon the 20 elements identified by the ISO Standard. This is achieved through interviews, "desk checking," reviews of evidence, and following trails as they arise. The key here is that this is an audit not an assessment, you either do it or you don't.

Software Process Improvement and Capability dEtermination (SPICE)

SPICE Assessments assess conformance with the requirements of ISO/IEC 15504—Software Process Assessment. It is conducted by an assessment team with the goal of providing a maturity level much like the CMMI® but with more of a software focus.

Project Management Institute's (PMI) Project Management Body of Knowledge (PMBOK®)

The PMI provides a Project Management Professionals (PMP®) Certification Program for Project Managers. A Project Manager receives PMP® credentials when they satisfy education and experience requirements as well as demonstrate an understanding of the PMBOK®-defined project management processes. The understanding is based on successful completion of a certification examination by the PMI.

The examination is based upon the PMBOK®-defined processes:

1. Initiating Processes
2. Planning Processes
3. Controlling Processes
4. Executing Processes
5. Closing Processes.

Once the PMP® credentials are achieved, the Project Managers must show "ongoing professional commitment to the field of project management." This is accomplished by adherence to the PMI's Continuing Certification Requirements (CCR) Program.

Microsoft® Operations Framework (MOF)

Microsoft® provides a free online tool for organizations with a Microsoft operational environment to perform a self-assessment. It consists of a series of questions that evaluates recommendations. It is separated into the model's four basic operational functions:

1. Changing
2. Operating
3. Supporting
4. Optimizing.

Control Objectives for Information and related Technology (COBIT)

COBIT provides Audit Guidelines to evaluate the achievement of desired goals and objectives. COBIT consists of 34 high-level IT control objectives grouped into four domains: planning and organization, acquisition and implementation, delivery and support, and monitoring. Organizations may select some or all of these objectives for the audit depending upon their goals.

Assessment Preparations

The preparations for an assessment will vary depending upon which models and methodologies are selected. The optimal combination of models and methodologies is CMMI®, ISO 9001, and PMP® Certified Project Managers. This chapter will concentrate on the CMMI® preparation and touch on ISO 9001 preparations since that is the recommended process model as discussed previously. PMP® certification is an individual goal, as opposed to an organizational goal, so that will not be included as part of this section.

CMMI® Appraisal Preparation

CMMI® Appraisal preparation can be very challenging but a good, organized appraisal can save time and money for the organization. Several areas need to be considered in preparation: resources, logistics, and data availability.

Resources for CMMI® Appraisal

The first thing that needs to be decided is how the assessment team should be composed. First, an SEI-authorized Lead Appraiser needs to be selected. The SEI provides a list of authorized lead appraisers on their website. Even though they are listed as an SEI-authorized appraiser, an organization should make sure that particular appraiser is a good match for their organization and meets their needs. They should make sure that the appraiser has some experience in similar types of organizations and experience with the model type selected: staged or continuous.

Finding out some specifics about how they conduct an appraisal can also be very helpful in selecting the right SEI-authorized Lead Appraiser. A Lead Appraiser has many tailoring options and an organization needs to ensure that these meet their needs and match their organizational business goals.

An organization has the tailoring option of using any mix of internal and external staff needed for the assessment. The selected Lead Appraiser can help make the right decision for each organization and suggest some additional external appraisers as needed. There are advantages and disadvantages to both methods as listed in Table 15-1. Each organization must decide which option works best based upon their organizational goals.

If a mix of some internal and external team members is selected, the SEI can also be helpful in providing additional appraisers for an appraisal. One option is lead appraisers that are in SEI lead appraiser training. Lead appraisers in training at the SEI are required to have a significant amount of experience and expertise

Table 15-1   Internal versus External Appraisal Teams

Advantages of Internal Team	Advantages of External Team
Lessons learned from the experience are invaluable in maintaining and continuing Process Improvement.	No preconceived notions concerning the organization and, normally, few or no preconceived notions concerning implementation of the model.
Able to fully understand what needs to be accomplished to correct problems encountered after the appraisal.	Complete independence from organization—no vested interest or threat of negative consequences based on results of appraisal.
Less costly than bringing in external team.	Ability to better prepare the organization for outside appraisal by the customer, if applicable.
Less coordination required to bring team together.	For a service organization, provides more credibility to findings in many customers' view, if that is a consideration for the organization.
Decreased preparation time for appraisal since members familiar with the organization and processes.	Can provide the organization with other best practice perspectives based on various areas of expertise.
More trained staff members in assessing the organization later.	Many times internal members are too close to the problems to see them, whereas an external team would be much more likely to readily spot a problem.

in the process model so they would be a good addition to any team. Many larger organizations may have trained or experienced process staff at other locations not involved in the organization's Process Improvement effort. These staff members are also good candidates for supplementing a team with external appraisers.

An appraisal team should consist of between four and nine members. The qualifications of these members are listed in Table 15-2.

Personnel needed to participate in activities or perform tasks in a SCAMPI[SM] appraisal include the sponsor, the SEI-authorized Lead Appraiser, the Organizational Unit Coordinator (OUC), the appraisal team members, and selected participants. There are several roles defined by the SEI that are typical on an Appraisal Team. Table 15-3 discusses these roles that are typically assigned by the Lead Appraiser and their associated responsibilities.

Table 15-2   Appraisal Team Member Qualifications

Key Area	Qualifications
Required	
Training	SEI-authorized CMMI training
Engineering experience	Average of six years in the various disciplines covered in the appraisal with the total team having 25 years' experience
Management experience	As a group team must have at least 10 years of experience, with one team member having at least six years' management experience
Life-cycle experience	At least two members should be practitioners that have used the organization's life-cycles.
Direct supervision	Cannot be the manager of a project selected for appraisal or have direct supervision of any potential interviewees.
Optional	
Communications	Good written and oral communications skills.
Previous appraisal experience	Half the team members should have previous appraisal experience.
Credibility	Sponsor should perceive team members as credible.
Personal characteristics	Dynamics of the overall team need to be considered based on personalities and character types.
Lead appraisers	More than one lead appraiser can be used as needed.

Table 15-3 Appraisal Team Roles and Responsibilities

Team Role	Brief Description
Team lead	Responsible for planning, training team members, monitoring, reporting, and overall conduct of the appraisal.
Organizational Unit Coordinator (OUC)	Responsible for the technical, logistics, and administrative aspects of the appraisal team. The Team Lead will assign most of the duties to the OUC. This person may or may not be part of the appraisal team.
Librarian	Responsible for management of the data associated with the appraisal. This person may or may not be part of the appraisal team.
Process Area Mini-Teams	The Team Leads assigned Process Areas to a subset (usually two or three people) of the Appraisal Team called Process Area Mini-Teams. They are responsible for all data needs and information for verification of the assigned Processes Areas.
Facilitator	Responsible for conducting interviews of selected interviewees.
Timekeeper	Responsible for keeping time during interviews and other key time-constrained activities.

Collecting Objective Evidence

Organizations must provide evidence that the selected Process Areas goals have been met for the organization and processes selected for appraisal. The Objective Evidence is defined as "qualitative or quantitative information, records, or statements of fact pertaining to the characteristics of an item or service or to the existence and implementation of a process element. It is based on observation, measurement, or test, and can be verified." [32] The objective evidence is evaluated as part of the appraisal in order to determine the organization's strengths and weaknesses. A rating will be provided based upon the evidence and interviews conducted during the appraisal.

Logistics Considerations

There are several areas that are key to a successful appraisal. Typically, the Lead Appraiser will coordinate these with the OUC assigned. Some logistical areas to consider include:

- *Working Space*—a comfortable room needs to be scheduled for the appraisal team to accomplish their work. It should be private to ensure confidentiality of interviews and other activities. It should be able to be secured to provide privacy of all team notes and other appraisal and personal items. Finally, it should be large enough to accommodate all the data collected and the interviewees if a separate area is not designated for interviews. If a separate area is for interviews, it must be private. Remember that the room should be as comfortable as possible since this team tends to spend long days and sometimes nights working.
- *Food and Beverages*—Meals, snacks and beverages need to be provided for all team members so that they can continue working as needed.
- *Supplies*—Office supplies for all team members such as pens, pencils, paper, stickys, wallcharts, etc.
- *Equipment*—Computer equipment will depend upon the needs of the appraisal team which could also rely upon the method in which the processes are organized.

Preparing Interviewees

Potential interviewees should be provided with some training or awareness sessions prior to the appraisal team arriving so that they know what to expect. This does not mean that they should be told what to say, the processes should speak for themselves. What they need to understand is what is expected of them in general. A mock interview session can help make them less apprehensive about the effort. They also should understand that anything they say will not be attributable and there will be no adverse results from their comments in interviews. At this point the organization should be using the processes that were developed and that will come across in the interviews. If it doesn't, the organization still has some work to do so that they meet the Process Improvement goals.

SCAMPI^{SM} Appraisal Conduct

A SCAMPI^{SM} Appraisal consists of three phases. The phases, as illustrated in Figure 15-1, include:

- *Planning and Preparation*—This is a critical phase of the appraisal since it will set the stage for the rest of the appraisal execution. Since the organization puts a good deal of budget into this activity, it is important that the time is taken to ensure that everything is prepared for the Appraisal team on day one and the preparations facilitate an easy appraisal.

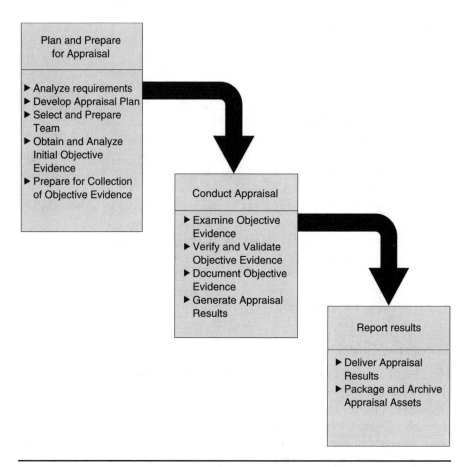

Figure 15-1   Appraisal Phases

- *Conducting Appraisal*—The length and effectiveness of this will depend upon the organization's preparations and readiness for the appraisal. It is important that everyone involved be available to accomplish their responsibilities as defined and possibly redefined.
- *Reporting Results*—the ultimate rating and identification of strengths and weaknesses will be reported to management. They will be responsible for passing this information to the organization as they see fit.

ISO Audit Preparations

In summary, a Gap Analysis should be accomplished prior to an ISO auditor visit, with the goal of process examination to ensure they meet the 20 ISO elements as needed for the organization, interviews of staff, and records review to ensure that records are being maintained properly. A checklist based on the applicable ISO elements should be used to ensure that the organization is prepared for an ISO Audit.

There are two key activities that will be critical to ensuring that an organization is prepared for a ISO audit:

1. *Organizational Audits*—continuous organization audits will ensure that processes are used and that records are maintained. This is also a good tool for CMMI® to ensure that processes are being used and records maintained. The toolkit has a sample Audit Plan, Audit Checklist, Audit Report, Audit Schedule, and a Gap Analysis Checklist. These items should be kept online using a database or portal, if that technology is available, but the toolkit will indicate the information needed.

2. *Corrective and Preventive Action System*—this will ensure that any action needed for correction during an audit problems are tracked to correction, the root cause of problems are analyzed, and an implementation plan generated to proactively correct and prevent future problems.

Summary

This activity in the final phase, the Post Maturity Phase, will be dependent upon decisions made early in the planning phases of the Process Improvement effort. The key to any Process Improvement effort is maturity of the organizational processes and an appraisal will help the organization understand where they are based on these goals. Combined with other process models and methodologies, they will allow the organization to know where they need to go to continue maturing the organization, based on identified weaknesses and strengths. A progress mini-assessment prior to going into this phase should result in readiness. The optimal combination of models and methodologies is CMMI®, ISO 9001, and PMP® Certified Project Managers.

Chapter Key Points

- The optimal combination of models and methodologies is CMMI®, ISO 9001, and PMP® Certified Project Managers.
- A decision to conduct a formal appraisal should be made early in the Process Improvement effort.
- SCAMPI^{SM} is the Appraisal method used for CMMI®.
- A successful progress mini-assessment should precede a SCAMPI^{SM}.

Tips for Success

- Take preparations for a CMMI® Appraisal seriously.
- Don't over-prepare interviewees.
- Ensure all participants on the Appraisal Team fully understand their obligations to the organization and the appraisal team.
- Don't skimp on the logistics planning and preparations for an appraisal.
- Combine the skills of a certified PMP® Project Manager with those of the Process Improvement staff.
- Use audits effectively for both ISO and CMMI®.

Chapter 16

Post Maturity Phase: Step 2—Improve

Now you're CMMI® Level 2 or CMMI® Level 3 or ISO certified, or maybe not, whatever the case may be depending upon the organizational Process Improvement goals. So, where do you go from here? If you met your goals, how do you keep it that way? If you did not make your goals, how to do you get there from here?

Not meeting your goals is not a bad thing. Even when the ultimate goals aren't realized, the road to get there, more than likely, made some significant positive changes for the organization. The key now is to keep the momentum going and not get caught in the what-ifs and why-nots. A decision needs to be made as to what new road to take. The APIM works well for continued Process Improvement but may need some tailoring or the organization may choose a more traditional method of Process Improvement.

So what if you made your goals? It is important to provide continuous improvement to an organization. Don't let the momentum of the success get lost in the clouds. Use the momentum to keep things on target with the organization's ultimate Process Improvement goals. These goals should, at a minimum, be to continue improving. The accelerated Process Improvement effort puts the initial processes needed in place as a foundation for further improvement. In order to continue being agile and keep costs at a minimum, the accelerated Process Improvement method can continue to be used. Since needed processes will already be in place, it may need to be tailored for meeting future process needs as opposed to initial process needs or a more traditional Process Improvement method can be used to effectively build on the momentum of success.

Keeping the Momentum Going

At this point, an organization does not want to lose the wave of change that has been initiated by the Process Improvement effort. First and foremost, don't disband the Process Group, even if resources are such that the team needs to be minimized; don't disband the team, it is critical to continued improvement that the team remain in place even if at a smaller scale. There are some tactics that can be used to maintain the momentum:

- Make the changes visible to all staff including both management and practitioners, even the small ones. This can be accomplished using some of the tools that were put in place for the Process Improvement effort or other means. Some suggestions:

  — Process-oriented newsletter
  — Any other organizational newsletter
  — Posters
  — All-hands presentations
  — Status meetings
  — Advertisements on the portal, if used.

- Celebrate even the baby steps toward complete process maturity

  — Bagels or donuts in the morning
  — Small parties or luncheons
  — Special events such as a Chili Cook-off, Italian Day, Potlucks, etc.

- Compare today's process-centric environment to yesterday's chaotic way of life

  — Show all organizational staff what progress has been achieved
  — Include management and practitioners.

- Reward those involved regardless of results; let the organization see the importance of the effort

  — Process Improvement Manager
  — Process Group
  — Appraisal participants
  — PATs
  — Executive Steering Committee
  — Project Managers involved
  — Practitioners involved.

Whatever you do, don't stop improving processes; chances are the working environment has improved and it will show. Regardless of the situation, if things go backward it will cause more pain later to correct.

Changing Over Time

Organizations change, staff change, business goals change; many changes take place in organizations, sometimes very quickly and processes must continuously keep up with these changes.

A Continuing Process Improvement Plan should be developed to incrementally continue improving the organization. The APIM works well for continuing improvement and many of the same critical areas need to be continued. Continuing the momentum of communications that are critical to Process Improvement should be leveraged. Some of the things that should be considered for the improvement effort include:

- Periodic Progress Assessments
- Updated Risks
- Updated Budget
- Updated Action Plan
- Task completion criteria
- Improvement measures
- Audit Plans
- Audit Reports.

Progress mini-assessments will play a key role in the continuing Process Improvement, these should be planned incrementally for the organization. They will identify any weaknesses and ensure that areas previously worked are still in place.

Any weaknesses identified during a formal appraisal and long-term goals identified by the Process Group should be actively monitored and accomplished as needed. Even if the goal is not to achieve a rating but to achieve process maturity for process maturity sake, it is important to follow through with the process goals both long term and short term. Depending upon resources available these may be on-going for some time.

The critical aspect of the APIM of project mentoring should continue. Again, this may be minimized from the previous situation but this critical program should be continued, especially for new projects and projects in crisis.

Auditing for Process Adherence

Sometimes, even with the best of intentions, organizations slip back into old habits. Audits reinforce the shift to process use and ensure processes continue to be used by organizational staff. Besides being a requirement of most good Process Improvement models, audits are a good way for management to ensure that the business is progressing as they envisioned. Additionally, they can help identify issues, problems, and risks prior to their occurrence.

Training Assessment

An assessment of training needs would be a good idea at this point to determine what additional training is needed. This should be accomplished incrementally to ensure that staff are always ready to tackle the organization's needs using current technology and methods. A Training Assessment Survey to identify areas of training can have a positive impact on an organization. The information collected can uncover hidden needs of the staff, as well as help organizations conquer the challenges that many times arise from growth and changes. An effective assessment should offer a detailed analysis to determine the strengths, weaknesses, and opportunities in the organization. The outputs help pinpoint specific training gaps.

Summary

Whether the goals set for this Process Improvement effort have been realized or not, it is important to keep the ball rolling. Chances are, regardless of the outcome, there have been significant changes made to the organization. The APIM can be used effectively to continue Process Improvements with or without some tailoring or a more traditional method may be selected.

The key is to continue down the road to further and continuing Process Improvement. Even with a more traditional Process Improvement method several aspects of the APIM should be retained, such as the keep it short and simple, especially in the case of processes. As time goes on and more improvements are added to the existing processes they tend to get more complicated as you go on, remember refactoring!

It is important to provide continuous improvement to an organization. Don't let the momentum of the success get lost in the clouds. Use the momentum to keep things on target with the organization's ultimate Process Improvement goals. These goals should, at a minimum, be to continue improving.

Chapter Key Points

- Don't let the momentum of the success get lost in the clouds, continue providing Process Improvement.

- Processes tend to get more complicated over time, use the KISS principle to keep them easy to use.
- Not meeting your ultimate Process Improvement goals is not a bad thing, some significant positive changes have occurred for the organization.
- Don't disband the Process Group, minimize it if needed but don't disband the team, it is critical to continued improvement.
- Regardless of the situation, if things go backward it will cause more pain later to correct.
- Organizations change over time, sometimes very quickly; it is important to keep an eye on processes to ensure they keep up with the organization.
- Any weaknesses identified during a formal appraisal and long-term goals identified by the Process Group should be actively monitored and accomplished as needed.
- Continue process mentoring program.
- Progress mini-assessments will play a key role in the continuing Process Improvement.
- Audits reinforce the shift to process use and ensure processes continue to be used by organizational staff.
- Incremental assessment of training needs helps ensure staff are continuously ready for all organizational needs.

Tips for Success

- Keep the momentum going.
- Don't get caught in the what-ifs and why-nots.
- Don't disband the process group.
- Make the changes visible to all staff.
- Celebrate even the baby steps.
- Compare today's process-centric environment to yesterday's chaotic way of life.
- Remember refactoring.
- Reward those involved regardless of results.

Chapter 17

APIM Checklist

The APIM provides a method of accelerating Process Improvement using some of the very popular Agile Programming techniques to accomplish many of the needed activities. It is a great method to use to kick the Process Improvement effort off to a good start or to continue improving the processes. It all depends upon the organization's ultimate goals.

Table 17-1 provides a quick overview for each step in the APIM. A checklist is provided in the toolkit.

Table 17-1 Accelerating Process Improvement Steps Overview

Phase	Step	Objectives
Pre maturity	Launch	• Executive approvals • Set process improvement goals • Task authorization • Executive steering committee • Initial resources/appointments • Budget • Kickoff meeting(s)
Pre maturity	Planning	• Develop brief action plan • Communications planning • Data management planning • Issue resolution planning • Process peer review planning • Process format planning • Quality assurance liaison planning • Risk management planning • Tool planning: databases, techniques, methods, and models • Detail master schedule • Develop metrics and measures • Select projects • PAT action planning • Establish regular status meetings and reports • Process group meeting planning • Executive steering committee • Plan and conduct training: organizational and process group
Maturity	Awareness	• Conduct mini-assessment to identify strengths and weaknesses—initial and progress • Select mini-assessment methodology • Compose mini-assessment team • Conduct pre mini-assessment activities • Conduct mini-assessment activities • Conduct post mini-assessment activities • Baseline mini-assessment results
Maturity	Triage	• Prioritize actions using triage approach • Develop key selection criteria • Conduct process group meeting to prioritize • Manage actions

(continued)

Table 17-1   Continued

Phase	Step	Objectives
Maturity	Resolution	• Establish process action teams • Develop action plan • Resolve process action or issue as assigned — Develop processes (remember KISS) ✓ Process flows ✓ Policies ✓ Procedures ✓ Forms ✓ Templates • Conduct peer reviews • Report status and any issues • Propose a solution to the problem • Train staff involved in pilot • Pilot test the solution mentoring staff throughout • Manage actions
Maturity	Training	• Determine methods to be used for training • Prepare training materials • Conduct training • Accomplish post training assessment
Maturity	Deployment	• Pilot processes to selected project • Tweak processes, as needed • Mentor pilot project(s)
Maturity	Trial	• Assess effectiveness of processes • Determine outcome • Deploy processes • Collect and analyze lessons learned
Post maturity	Appraise	• Determine maturity level • Identify strengths and weakness for future improvement
Post maturity	Improve	• Keep the momentum going • Develop continuing process improvement plan ✓ Improvement measures ✓ Audit plans ✓ Audit reports ✓ Periodic progress assessments ✓ Updated risks ✓ Updated budget ✓ Updated action plan ✓ Task completion criteria • Audit processes • Training assessment

IMPLEMENTING APIM

Joe sat at the table waiting for the waitress to bring his Coke while he shot the breeze with some coworkers, more relaxed than he had been in months. Uncle Tony's Pizzeria seemed like a great retreat from his cramped office.

As the waitress finished taking their order and was walking back to the kitchen, Joe saw the bright red door open and recognized his buddy Mark.

About that same time, Mark spots Joe as he is scoping out the tables for a place for he and his friends to sit. "Hey Mark," Joe says, greeting his friend and coworker.

"They let you out of that padded cell for lunch, huh?" Mark laughed, walking over to where Joe was sitting.

"Yeah, you too!," Joe says, getting up to shake Mark's hand.

"Yes, it's actually getting to be a pretty nice habit now," Mark answers, noticing his friend waiting. He introduces her to Joe as a newbie and asks her to find them a table for six since they have more folks from the office joining them, before saying to Joe, "Can you believe, I was able to schedule a vacation next month? Sunny beaches here I come! The wife says she'll believe it when she sees it, we have not been able to have a vacation in years."

"Wow, that is cool, we're definitely seeing some changes around there lately," Joe exclaims, "I kind of like what I'm seeing."

"Me too," Mark replies, "what do you think is going on?"

"It's that process improvement we've been hearing so much about the last few years. I heard they were trying a new method to make things happen faster," Joe says excitedly.

"Yes, I've been seeing some very nice changes, I can find things that help me get my job done faster and better," Mark replies.

"Really, that is just what we've been wanting for years, huh?" Joe remarks, "What do you hear from other folks around the office?,"

"It's all good," Mark answers, "Mary told me the other day that she loves the new portal that was put up recently. She said she knows what's going on and feels like people are working better together these days."

"That's what I'm hearing, things are getting documented and I can find much of the information I need now," Joe agrees, "Of all people I heard Steve say that the processes the process group is putting in place helped his project out when they were short staffed."

"This could really turn out to be a great company after a while," Mark says, "So, a few months ago you told me you were putting in your application, you just couldn't take it anymore, you're still here."

"Yeah, I actually did put my resumé out to several places and got some really great bites. I even got a few bona fide offers, pretty good ones really, but then I started seeing some things changing around here. I liked what I was seeing and hearing from other folks. I decided to stick around and see how it pans out. You know what they say about leaping? Out of the pan into the fire," Joe explains, "I actually got home at a decent hour the other day and the wife thought someone was breaking into the house, don't want to mess up a good thing now."

"I agree," Mark laughs, spotting his lunch buddies coming in the door, "Hey Joe, good to see you again, let's do lunch sometime soon," Mark says as he leaves to join in a much-deserved lunch away from the office.

"Sounds good to me, give me a call", Joe answers, sitting back down to enjoy his lunch.

Remind you of a project you've been on?

Chapter 18

The People Side of Process Improvement

The people aspects of Process Improvement can be more challenging than the Process Improvement aspects. They are key to success and failure but finding the right people for the various roles can be difficult. Unfortunately, some organizations put people on the process team because they don't have another area for them at the moment instead of based on their skills. That is a mistake. The Process Staff should be the best of the best in order to smooth the progress of the changes needed for an entire organization.

Process Improvement Effort Staffing

Figure 18-1 illustrates the key Process Improvement staff. Everyone in the organization is responsible for the Process Improvement effort but these folks are the ones that take the actions to make it happen. In an IT organization, most of the staff will have significant technical skills but a different set of skills is required for accomplishing Process Improvement. Make sure that the staff selected to realize the Process Improvement goals are armed with the appropriate skills and expertise to make the difference that executive management envisions. Figure 18-2 illustrates which team is the focus during each step of the APIM Maturity cycle.

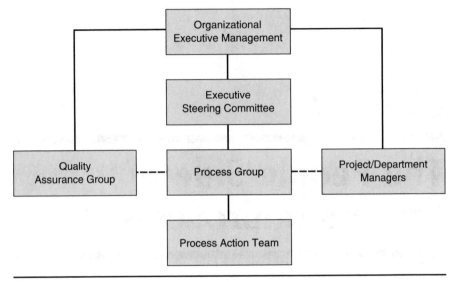

Figure 18-1   Process Improvement Hierarchy

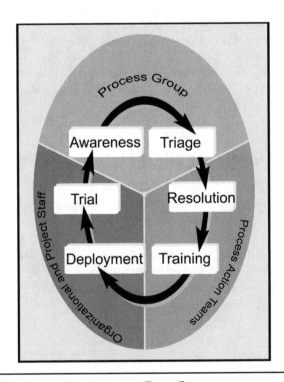

Figure 18-2   Key Process Improvement Team Focus

Process Improvement Manager

This is the most significant role for the Process Improvement effort. In short, they spearhead the effort. Just as any Project Manager, perhaps more so, they must employ a forward-looking philosophy to ensure that the process group is prepared for each task, while ensuring enough flexibility to accommodate changing task priorities.

Some confuse facilitation with management. A decision must be made as to whether this is the role of a facilitator or a manager. The difference according to Merriam-Webster:

- Facilitator → to make easier help bring about
- Manager → a person who directs a team.

The role of a manager is not to make recommendations but to set the direction and direct the team to make a difference. This must be a full-time management position with all the privileges and responsibilities that holds. There must be a level playing field in order for the Process Group to make a difference. As discussed previously, the Process Team, in particular the Process Improvement Manager, should be armed with the authority to make decisions and changes needed to meet the Process Improvement goals. If they are seen as equal to other Project Managers this goes a long way to easing change.

The responsibilities of the Process Improvement Manager are diverse and ever-evolving. Some of the key responsibilities of the Process Improvement Manager include:

- Ensuring appropriate resources are made available to accomplish essential Process Improvement tasks
- Plan and lead the Process Improvement effort
- Conduct presentations to senior management and all organizational staff concerning Process Improvement
- Report progress to Executive Steering Committee
- Elevate issues and problems if irresolvable to Executive Steering Committee
- Make team assignments for Process Improvement tasks
- Coordinate and conduct process group team meetings
- Track and mange action items to closure
- Replace process group and PAT team members for performance or attitude problems; it only takes one "bad apple" to ruin the whole batch
- Act as a focal point to provide key communications to all organizational staff
- Conduct, track, and ensure process training for all organizational staff
- Accomplish Process Improvement tasks as needed
- Share expertise, act as mentor and coach for rest of organization
- Manage and conduct mini-assessments and track results
- Manage actions needed as a result of mini-assessments

- Ensure that all Process Improvement staff adhere to the keep it short and simple (KISS) principles
- Arrange for and manage the formal appraisal
- Oversee development and maintenance of all process libraries and tools
- Approve all Action Plans.

This is the focal point for the Process Improvement effort. The skills and personal traits required to accomplish the activities needed to realize the Process Improvement goals are challenging. Some of the key elements that enhance chances of success include:

- Hands-on technical experience in system development and project management
- Proactive and willing to take reasonable chances when necessary
- Organized/Ability to organize without over-organizing (avoid bureaucracy)
- Visible, respected member of the organization
- Willing to bend when necessary and knowing when it's necessary
- Easy-going but not too easy-going that things don't get done
- Ability to communicate at all levels from managers to practitioners
- Good listener, open to others' opinions
- Confident without huge ego
- Non-argumentative
- Detail oriented
- Totally committed to Process Improvement itself and the organization
- Immense drive/motivation and ability to drive others
- Ability to work in stressful situations
- Able to withstand criticism from all levels
- Ability to keep a proper perspective (don't get angry)
- Focused
- Adaptable—Be able to roll with the punches
- Never lose sight of goals
- Credibility with senior management and even more importantly practitioners
- Ability to maintain confidentiality
- Ability to lead as well as follow depending on circumstances (must recognize when each is appropriate)
- Quick learner/ability to become an "expert" in many different areas that are not their normal field of expertise—ability to be self-taught

Process Group

All Process Improvement revolves around this group. They are just as key to the success as the Process Improvement Manager. They must be composed of a group of organizational staff with diverse skills spanning all areas associated with the Process Improvement goals. They should also include members from as many projects in the organization as possible. They should possess many of the same skills and personal traits as described above for the Process Improvement Manager. A majority should come from the middle managers in the organization. If nothing else, the staff selected for this team should be innovators, or at least early adopters, and enjoy trying new ways, things, technologies, and tools.

One key is that this is usually a part-time position for all members except the Process Improvement Manager, so they must be committed and make every effort possible to attend meetings and participate in the Process Improvement activities. One of the major issues with Process Groups is this dueling role they have on their projects and the Process Group.

Some of the responsibilities of the important group are:

- Accomplish Process Improvement tasks and issues as assigned, either as part of a PAT or independently
- Provide Process Improvement training in general and for all processes
- Keep open communications at all levels of the organization
- Promote the Process Improvement effort throughout the organization
- Elevate issues and problems if irresolvable to Process Improvement Manager
- Share expertise, act as mentor and coach for rest of organization
- Conduct mini-assessments
- Assist in formal appraisal as needed
- Assist projects in tailoring organizational processes
- Form liaisons with Project Managers to ease change.

Process Action Teams (PAT)

The PATs can be made up of members of the Process Group or they may come from other parts of the organization. It depends upon the skills and knowledge required to resolve the assigned action or issue. There may be skills needed from a subject area expert that a process team member does not possess, or the process group resources may be stretched thin and others are available to assist. A good rule of thumb is to use mostly middle managers for these groups.

A PAT size will depend upon the action or issue assigned. It can consist of two to four staff members with a mix of full- and part-time members. A PAT Lead should be appointed to manage and direct the team as well as report progress to the Process Group. Even when a PAT team member is not part of the Process Group, they should attend Process Group meetings during execution of their assigned actions. If there are potential PAT team members designated prior to the Triage step, they should participate in that procedure.

The skills required for this position ideally would be similar to that described above for the Process Improvement Manager, but care should be taken to ensure that the staff assigned are of the process-oriented frame of mind as well as adhering to the keep it simple principle.

The responsibilities of the PAT are diverse since they may be assigned varying actions and issues. Some of the typical responsibilities include:

- Develop an Action Plan for the assigned action depending on size and scope of the assigned action or issue
- Determine cause of assigned problem or issue, as needed
- Analyze the nature of the problem, as needed
- Leverage of work previously accomplished and method currently used, as applicable, before creating new methods
- Propose a solution to the problem
- Develop processes, policies, procedures, guidelines, templates, tools, and anything else required for the development of a process to meet the assigned needs
- Pilot processes as planned
- Report progress to the Process Group
- Elevate issues and problems if irresolvable to Process Group
- Share expertise, act as mentor and coach as directed by the Process Group.

Quality Assurance

Quality Assurance should definitely have at least one representative as part of the Process Group, but besides that role, as described above, they also play another critical role for the Process Improvement effort. Just as they act as the eyes and ears of Project Managers and executive management on a project, they play the same role and more for the management of Process Improvement efforts. It is critical that the Process Group forms an important liaison with the Quality Assurance Group. They should work hand-in-hand to develop processes and ensure usage of them. The Quality Assurance Group should also remain independent and neutral so they can evaluate the effort and progress of effort just as on any other project. Remember, these are the folks known as the protectors of the organization.

Some of the key responsibilities of the Quality Assurance staff as it's related to the Process Improvement effort include:

- Conduct of audit to ensure usage
- Track issues to resolution
- Publish audit results
- Participation in process reviews to ensure process standards are followed
- Track issues to resolution

- Publish review results
- Elevate issues to Executive Management, as needed
- Develop Quality Assurance processes and ensure that all organizational staff are aware of their role in the organization.

Many times the Quality Assurance Group will take responsibility for the Organizational Corrective Action System to ensure all organizational corrective and preventive actions are corrected, based on a root cause analysis, and analyze any trends. This coordination with the Process Group will be key to improving processes throughout the organization.

Project Manager

It is important to build alliances with Project Managers. They will be the ones that ultimately ensure that their staff follow the processes developed by the process group. They should have good representation in the Process Group. Even though these are usually very busy folks, they need to take the time to be part of this group. Sometimes this may take a little encouragement by executive management. It will depend upon how the process team is perceived by the organization.

The Process Group should form a liaison with all of the Project Managers to ease the deployment of processes to their projects and facilitate the training of project staff. The logical liaisons are the folks assigned as project process mentors. The roles should go hand-in-hand. Chapter 19 discusses liaisons in more detail.

Executive Steer Committee

This important committee will set the direction and goals for the Process Improvement effort. They will ensure that the appropriate resources are available for the process group which is key to success; without the proper resources nothing can be accomplished even with the best of intentions. This committee is typically formed prior to the Process Improvement effort to accomplish the early planning efforts and kick the project off. Once the Process Improvement effort has started they will act as the in-between for the Process Group and Executive Management.

One thing to look out for with an Executive Steering Committee is ensuring that the process group doesn't get the Process Group bogged down in a cumbersome approval process; in other words avoid bureaucracy, unless highly warranted. It can slow the effort down immensely. It is important to keep this group's interest in the Process Improvement effort since they can facilitate or impede a Process Group as they see fit. The Process Improvement Manager will be the interface with this group so it is incumbent upon that individual to maintain this key relationship.

This group is typically composed of higher-level managers. Some of the their responsibilities include:

- Provide leadership and encouragement to the Process Group as well as other organizational staff in relation to the Process Improvement effort
- Establishing the Process Group and making initial assignments
- Monitoring progress of the Process Group through regular status meetings with the Process Improvement Manager
- Providing staffing resources for the Process Group and PATs
- Providing funding and other needed Process Group resources
- Resolving issues that have been elevated by the Process Improvement Manager
- Keeping senior management informed of the progress of the Process Improvement effort
- Ensure the strategic goals of the Process Improvement effort are being met
- Approve the Overall Process Action Plan
- Collaborate with Process Group to resolve any process issues related to organizational executive management.

Executive Management

Executive Management has been quoted as the primary key to success of any Process Improvement effort. This is because they provide the needed resources and funds required to accomplish the process goals. They also typically set the goals. It is important to maintain good credibility with these folks. The Process Improvement Manager will provide this important role.

The critical thing with Executive Management is to ensure their interest is maintained on the effort. By using the APIM, the results of Process Improvement can be seen quicker and, therefore, a lot of time doesn't pass before they begin to see even small improvements. That, in itself, will keep their interest.

All Organization Stakeholder

Every single person that works for an organization will in some way be impacted by the actions of the Process Group. The marketing techniques in Chapter 19 will help ensure that they come on board and stay there. These are the people that will ultimately be using the processes developed so it is important that they be kept "in the loop."

One of the keys to making any changes is forming habits. Habits have been formed prior to the Process Improvement effort that should be leveraged in order to improve. The rule of thumb in changing habits is that it takes 21 days to develop a habit. Usually, changing a habit takes a combination of knowledge, skills, and desire. Considering what it takes to change a habit may help in determining a piloting and mentoring strategy.

Summary

Considering the people side of Process Improvement is just as important as the actual implementing of the effort. The right people assigned can make the difference between success and failure. Select the right people to do the job because they are the best of the best and not because they don't have another job right now. Make assignment to this important team a career booster as opposed to a career buster. It's all in the perception of the job and that is set by management. Reward the individuals through recognition at key organization events to let the rest of the staff realize that this is a key appointment and not just a weigh station, as it is treated sometimes in organizations.

Chapter Key Points

- The Process Group Manager is the focal point of the Process Improvement effort. Selection of this individual should not be taken lightly. There are many soft skills that should be considered.
- Select the right people for the process group with varying skills and knowledge.
- Quality Assurance plays a key role in ensuring that processes are being used.
- Strategic liaisons should be formed with Project Managers to ensure processes will be taken seriously on projects.
- You can't do it without executive management, keep them happy.

Tips for Success

- Assign the best of the best to the Process Group.
- Level the playing field for the Process Group.
- Replace process group members when needed; it only takes one "bad apple" to ruin the whole batch.
- Appoint Process Group members who are committed.
- Form liaisons with Quality Assurance and Project Managers.
- Avoid time-consuming approval processes that slow things down.

Chapter 19

Organizational Change

As discussed previously, Peter F. Drucker stated "It is not true, as a good many industrial psychologists assert, that human nature resists change. On the contrary, no being in heaven or earth is greedier for new things. But there are conditions for man's readiness for change. The change must appear rational to him...".[15] The key here is that any change must appear rational, especially when trying to effect an entire organization by making it more effective with documented and used processes. At the onset, the process engineers must realize that there will be resistance to change but, if it is promoted properly, the resistance can be minimized and controlled.

Process Improvement is Like Cat Herding

Many have heard the old saying that "managing programmers is much like cat herding." Process Improvement is even more like cat herding; it's not easy but it's ultimately very satisfying. There are many challenges connected with transitioning any new ideas and changes to an organization. By studying marketing trends and methods, we can use some of the more effective methods for marketing Process Improvement and the resulting processes. Table 19-1 lists some marketing methods and their effectiveness according to the Forrester Research.

In addition to the more traditional organizational change methods, some of the science theories are also being used successfully in discussions of organizational change. Some of the more effective methods discussed below include Everett Roger's Adoption Curve for dissemination of ideas as well as the detractors of this

Table 19-1   Popular Marketing Methods Rankings

Rank	Technique	Popularity	Effectiveness
1	Affiliate programs	17%	4.3
2	Email to customers	77%	4.3
3	Public relations	45%	4.1
4	Television	30%	4.0
5	Outdoor	17%	3.7
6	Email (opt-in lists)	23%	3.5
7	Magazines	34%	3.4
8	Radio	32%	3.4
9	Direct mail	30%	3.4
10	Sponsorships	34%	3.3
11	Buttons	55%	3.2
12	Banners	89%	2.8
13	Newspapers	32%	2.6

theory, Roger Chiocchi's Inductive marketing theory, the Perspective Factor to ensure that each stakeholder's perspective is considered, some of the varied sociotechnical theories, and the Science of Organizational Change.

The Science of Organizational Change

Experts have been relating organizational change to other arenas. This research helps us further understand methods for becoming successful organizations that are flexible enough to make effective changes. Some of the new ideas for managing organizational change are coming from some seemingly unlikely arenas such as the Chaos Theory, Relativity, Quantum Physics, Mathematic, Chemistry, Biology, and Open Systems.

One of the most relevant ideas is the Chaos Theory. The Chaos Theory is about finding the underlying order in apparently random data. It comes from the fact that the systems that the theory describes are apparently disordered but having an underlying order.

In Ancient Greece thousands of years ago the cause and effect rules were introduced as a philosophical belief. Sometime around the 1500s this concept was accepted as a scientific theory. Issac Newton's laws implied that everything that would occur would be based entirely on what happened right before. Henry Adams is credited with first describing chaos as, "Chaos often breeds life, when order breeds habit."

In 1846 the planet Neptune was discovered, which had been predicted from the observation of deviations in Uranus' orbit. Oscar II, King of Sweden and Norway, initiated a mathematical competition in 1887 to celebrate his 60th birthday in 1889. He challenged anyone to prove or disprove that the solar system was stable. Henri Poincaré, sometimes called the "Father of Chaos", was awarded the prize for his three-body problem in celestial mechanics where he provided the first mathematical description of chaotic motion. However, when a colleague found an error in his theory, the prize was taken away until he could find a new solution. After much consultation with colleagues he found that there was no solution including use of Newton's Laws. Poincaré had been trying to find order in a system where there was no order, hence this error is now regarded as marking the birth of Chaos Theory.

Edward Lorenz, a meteorologist at MIT, has been called the first true experimenter in chaos in the 1960s while he was working on a weather prediction problem. Lorenz set up a computer with 12 equations to simulate the weather. This program theoretically predicted the weather but, when in 1961 he wanted to see the sequence again but wanted to save time, he started in the middle of the sequence and let it run. This sequence diverged from the original pattern. What he found was that the number had been stored with six decimal places in the original sequence and when he reran the program he rounded the six decimals to only three decimal places to save paper. Where he should have gotten a sequence very close to the original, it had a huge effect on the resulting pattern. This is known as sensitive dependence on the initial conditions, which he found changes the long-term behavior of a system. He found that small changes on things lead to changes on a large scale. It was the classic example of chaos.

This theory of chaos is directly related to managing organizational change. You can't always predict what a system will do next but you can put things in motion in smaller ways to perpetuate changes on a large scale. How a pattern eventually looks is very dependent upon the initial conditions that are set up.

In his book *Chaos—Making a New Science*, James Gleick related chaos to the motion of a water wheel and found that "water drips steadily into containers hanging on the wheel's rim. Each container drips steadily from a small hole. If the stream of water is slow, the top containers never fill fast enough to overcome friction, but if the stream is faster the weight starts to turn the wheel."[17] This holds true with accelerated Process Improvement as well. You must get things moving fast enough and keep the momentum going in order to make the organizational changes needed. Gleick points out that "The rotation might become continuous. Or, if the stream is so fast that the heavy containers swing all the way around the bottom and up the other side, the wheel might then slow, stop, and reverse its rotation, turning first one way and then the other."[17] The key is to keep the momentum going fast enough to effect change. Never let things settle down enough to stop the momentum, since sometimes it's even harder to get the momentum going again and it can reverse the progress already made.

Dr. Helene Uhlfelder holds that organizations are much like the human body and our planet. Many are starting to look at organizations as open systems to help define their structure. The use of the term open systems for defining organizations comes from the comparison to the human body or our biological cells, as well as our solar system, in that they are all engaged in active transactions with their environment. Dr. Uhlfelder states that "An open system has certain characteristics that need to be understood if one is going to work in and change it."[36] Some of the characteristics that she defines include:

1. Open systems are porous and have permeable boundaries.
2. Open systems are interdependent with surrounding systems and are composed of interdependent parts.
3. Open systems need to be dynamic and fluid to survive.
4. Open systems are interactive with their environment and must be adaptable.
5. In an open system, the whole is greater than the parts.

A key to organizational change in Dr. Uhlfelder's theory holds that closed systems can result in entropy. "Entropy is an inverse measure of a system's capacity for change and means the system will eventually die from a lack of energy. Because open systems can import energy and can be dynamic and fluid, open systems can grow and change."[17]

Dr. Uhlfelder contends that systems should never strive for equilibrium and should always maintain a certain amount of disequilibrium as a necessity to foster change. She states that "Organizations that are designed for high control, stability, and constant equilibrium are destined to die or become non-competitive. Being an open system and taking advantage of open system characteristics can be a positive thing for organizations."[17] As with ecology she finds that departmental interdependency is a key to success; in other words "what happens in one department affects what happens in another department."[17] The key is for an organization to become an open system that is adaptive to allow "input and output with the environment, political and social institutions, and world events."[17] Dr. Uhlfelder's Open System Organizations is illustrated in Figure 19-1.

Margaret Wheatley in *Leadership and The New Science* uses quantum physics to apply to leadership. The new science of quantum physics describes a universe "where order and change, autonomy and control were not great opposites that we had thought them to be. It was a world where change and constant creation signaled new ways of maintaining order and structure."[37]

Wheatley relates the field theory to organizations which asserts that "fields are unseen structures, occupying space and becoming known to us through their effects."[37] She holds that "All employees, in any part of the company, who bumped against the field, would be influenced by it. . . . their energy would link with the field's form to create behavior congruent with the organization's goals."[37] She believes that if we "think of ideas as fields" it will permeate the entire

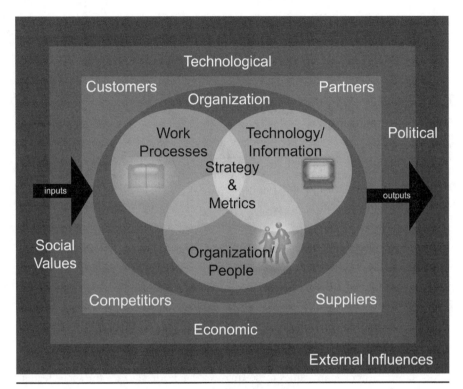

Figure 19-1   Open Systems

organization. She states that "We need all of us out there, stating, clarifying, discussing, modeling, filling all of the space with the messages we care about. If we do that, fields develop—and with them the wondrous capacity to bring energy into form."[37] This is especially appropriate for Process Improvement, where participation of the process users is a critical key to success of the process and the Process Improvement effort as a whole. Wheatley says that an organization's vision is actually a culmination of all the people that make up the organization as opposed to handed down from management. The concept of ownership is a key where she discusses that "the best way to build ownership is to give over the creation process to those who will be charged with its implementation."[37] She holds that "It doesn't work to just ask people to sign on when they haven't been involved in the design process, when they haven't experienced the plan as a living, breathing thing."[37] Participation in creating processes is a must for Process Improvement; it is a must in understanding and accepting a process. This can be accomplished in many ways as described in the Process Improvement implementation section.

Everett Roger's Adoption Curve

Everett Rogers, the author of *The Diffusion of Innovation*[31], which is currently in its third edition, is a professor of communications at the University of New Mexico. The theory that he discussed in this book concerned how new ideas are disseminated and accepted by groups of people. Even though many have shown that there are some issues with the Roger's Adoption Curve, it is still a good rule of thumb for adoption of new technologies and ideas. His theory holds that, given a normal population distribution, people accept new ideas and innovation at a different rate. Rogers defines an innovation as "an idea, practice, or object that is perceived as new by an individual or other unit of adoption."[31] He defined various adopters as follows:

- 2.5 percent → innovators
- 13.5 percent → early adopters
- 34 percent → early majority (early mainstream)
- 34 percent → late majority (late mainstream)
- 16 percent → laggards.

This distribution of adopters results in a bell curve as shown in Figure 19-2.

The innovators are the few who first take up a new practice or listen to a new idea. The early adopters come along next and are great for communicating the effort to others since many times these are the social leaders. Once the social leaders take up a new idea, the early majority takes up the idea fairly quickly followed by the late majority. Finally, the laggards are typically the last to consider a new idea; they tend to adopt innovation very slowly and late. You must always account for a few laggards to bring up the rear.

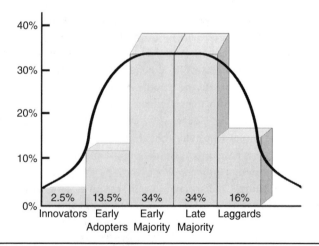

Figure 19-2   Adopters

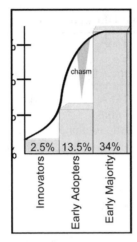

Figure 19-3 Adopters Chasm

A "chasm" has been defined between the early adopters and the early majority. Figure 19-3 illustrates the "chasm." This "chasm" implies that the transfer of information flows from innovators to early adopters easily, but that it is difficult to translate that into action and acceptance by the early majority, which is sometimes called the early mainstream. This is where the marketing of the effort and the resulting processes becomes most important; you have to get the word out to get results.

Universities use this to define the effort required for each category to recruit and retain adopters of new information and provide the appropriate training. Table 19-2 summarizes some of the data collected and used by universities.

This theory is not too much different than the characters in *Who Moved My Cheese?* [21] Scurry would be the innovator, Sniff would be the early adopter, Haw the early to late majority, and Hem the laggard. The key to using this theory is to know where to focus your resources. It also tells you who may be interested in helping advertise your effort; word of mouth is a key way of getting others on board.

Even though different people accept innovation at different rates, and you tend to want to focus on the early adopters and early majority, don't lose sight of the late adopters, and possibly the laggards, since they could end up being your greatest allies. Sometimes it takes one thing to pull a late adopter or laggard on board and they may end up being the key to success. Perhaps they need the "seeing is believing" before coming on board, but once they do they are all there and bring other late adopters and potential laggards along. As the effort progresses people may move from one adopter's level to another based upon the current tasks being accomplished and the successes. This may be due to false expectations or maybe the reality sets in. Sustained involvement in the effort may be more prevalent in the later adopters than the early adopters. The early adopters may move on to other things once the honeymoon period has passed and the newness has worn off.

Table 19-2   Adoption Curve Effort and Learning

Adoption Curve Category	Learning Curve	Effort Required for Adoption	Continued Support of Effort	Retention of Adopter
Innovator	Rapid learners	No recruiting effort	May be low	Steadfast: long term
Early adopters	Rapid learning	Minor effort	Moderate and in spurts	Dependable: will probably stick with it throughout
Early majority	Reasonable learning curve	Substantial effort	Higher and continuous	Fickle: may drop out if early expectations not met
Late majority	Trainable but slow	Major effort	Highest level of continuous support needed	Brittle: may drop out after minor failure or problems encountered
Laggards	Typically uninterested	Typically uninterested	Not feasible	

Rogers defined five key factors that can determine the rate of adoption of innovations. Table 19-3 defines the key factors.

The "Convergence Model," Roger's latest model, is also worth exploring. It "emphasizes the need for a continual process of interpretation and response, leading to an increased degree of mutual understanding between sender and receiver."[31]

Table 19-3   Roger's Key Adoption Factors

	Key Adoption Factor	The Degree to Which:
1	Relative advantage	the innovation is perceived to be better than the idea it supersedes
2	Compatibility	an innovation is perceived as consistent with the existing values, past experiences, and needs of potential adopters
3	Complexity	an innovation is perceived as relatively difficult to understand and use
4	Trialability	an innovation may be experimented with on a limited basis
5	Observability	the results of an innovation are visible to others

Chiocchi's Inductive Marketing

Roger Chiocchi[11] is executive vice president of The Lord Group and has been responsible for several very successful marketing efforts, including "The Softer Side of Sears," Advil, and Bell Atlantic. He has developed a marketing theory he calls Inductive Marketing.

Chiocchi contends that previously marketing was accomplished using a deductive method but inroads have been made by using a more inductive type of marketing strategy. With deductive marketing, the marketer presumes what the customer wants based on their needs, whereas inductive marketing in essence tells the customer what they want or induces products onto the market. Both the inductive and deductive method can work well for Process Improvement. The internet has been partly responsible for this shift toward inductive marketing which is a great tool to use for Process Improvement.

Top–down and bottom–up are two of the approaches described by Chiocchi. He defines the top–down approach as using "mega-dollars creating an avalanche of push-pull power"[11] by forcing products through advertising, public relations, and trade events. Conversely, the bottom–up approach is when a product finds its market through use of web sites and chat rooms or other special market niches. The bottom–up approach typically takes longer to see results but both are "hit-or-miss," with the results usually either enormous or completely off the mark with the customer as the determining force.

The inductive method works well for Process Improvement when you are trying to accelerate the effort, since you don't always have time to find out what's needed through the more laborious deductive method. Chiocchi states that it is "folly to ask consumers to be visionaries"[11] which stands true for Process Improvement. One key concept to accelerating Process Improvement is keeping the team small, since many times too many opinions can slow progress sometimes to a screeching halt. As I discussed previously, mistakes will be made and some products or processes will miss their mark but those mistakes can be corrected easily with close communications with the process users. Chiocchi points out that it took radio 38 years, TV 13 years, cable TV 10 years, and the internet only 5 years to reach 50 million users. The previously gradual process of getting products to market has been accelerated which has a positive impact. He states that "Today, products induced upon the marketplace have a better opportunity to find their market"[11] more quickly. While it is still the survival of the fittest, the gestation period has been shortened. This is true for the Process Improvement, get the products out and let the users try them and then evaluate the results. Of course, you must have the right people on the Process Improvement team who can determine the right processes to put out, which was discussed in a previous chapter. Chiocchi also discussed a new term he calls innopreneurs to describe the people who embrace this approach to marketing.

Finally, Chiocchi points out that "a fear of social incompatibility fuels product growth as certain segments of consumers fear missing out on the latest trend. This fear of incompatibility serves to further accelerate the consumer adoption process and, consequently, the inductive marketing tidal wave."[11] This is another important consideration for Process Improvement; fear of incompatibility can play a key role in marketing processes.

The Perspective Factor

MC Escher is famous for his Optical Illusion Art from the 1940s to the 1970s. He was well known for his impossible structures. A favorite is called Relativity that basically tells us that what you see is relative to where you're standing. When dealing with others' realities, we have to see things from their perspective and make it relative to them.

Each stakeholder is going to see something different, it is important to discuss a process based on their perspective. It all depends upon each of our perspectives. How you see a thing depends on what vantage point you're coming from. We all look at things differently based on our background, education, experience, and simply from where we are standing at the moment. It is key to Process Improvement that process development staff and users work as a team to develop effective processes in order to develop effective products. If we look at things from each other's vantage point, the chance of success grows by leaps and bounds. Open communications and respect for each other's position is crucial for success.

As a process engineer developing processes for a project or organization, the key is to let the user know that when you're done you can simply walk away, but they need to be able to use the developed processes to accomplish their job. The process engineer must work with users to make the processes work for them, keeping in mind their perspective, at the same time working with them to meet the selected model or methodologies requirements.

Sociotechnical Theories

Sociotechnical theories vary widely, but many of the concepts, methods, and theories can be applied to Process Improvement to effect organizational change. Organizations may use more than one sociotechnical method within the same organization, some emphasizing more of a technical focus and others emphasizing more of a social focus. The term sociotechnical combines social and technical aspects, in that social is concerning groups of people and technical is based on physical sciences and their application, combining to mean technical works involving significant social participation, interests, and concerns as illustrated in Figure 19-4.

The origin of sociotechnical theories goes back to the 1940s in London through work at the Tavistock Institute of Human Relations. The Tavistock Group was

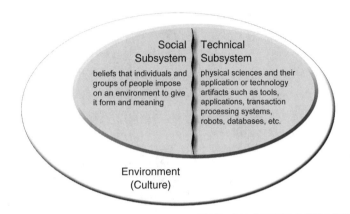

Figure 19-4   STS Overall

examining the effect of mechanized, mass-production systems on workers in the coal mining industry. The work resulted in consideration of users, work quality, and skill development.

A core component of sociotechnical theories is the active participation of all stakeholders. Most of them combine the softer issues of people participation to the harder issues of the more technical aspects. In considering organizational change, both the soft and hard issues must be addressed. The sociotechnical theory that we are going to discuss consists of five components: People, Tasks, Technology, Structure, and Environment (culture). Figure 19-5 illustrates this theory.

Some of the principles of sociotechnical theories are summarized below:

- There is no optimum organization.
- Upper management should set goals, supply resources and manage the culture.
- Organizational design must fit goals.
- Employees must be actively involved in designing structure of organization.
- Design the Socio and Technical systems simultaneously and jointly.
- Subsystems must be designed around relatively self-contained and recognizable units of work.
- Support systems must fit in with design of organization.
- Design should allow for high quality of working life.
- As the environment, culture, people and technology change, so should the organization.
- When selecting people for a workgroup, strive for homogeneity in their backgrounds and work attitudes.
- Reduce wide variations in knowledge levels and variety through cross training.

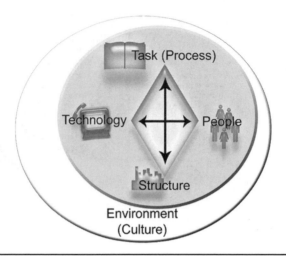

Figure 19-5   Sociotechnical Theory

- Achieve high performance through commitment rather than minimal compliance. Use more carrot than stick.
- Allow teams to manage the daily work.
- Build commitment by involving people in the shaping of their future.
- Begin and end a work group's technical boundary at a discontinuity.
- Coach and facilitate rather than supervise. Coaches should manage the team boundaries.
- Provide opportunities to satisfy unfulfilled higher-order needs. Use the intrinsic motivators.
- Learning occurs primarily through experience.
- Integrate learning on the job through advisors, facilitators, and guided application.
- Control variances at their source. Control of variances in production or service must be undertaken as close to their source as possible.
- Ensure that the detection of a variance and the source of that variance occur in the same work group.
- Maintain quality by detecting variances in the process rather than in the final product.
- Monitor inputs as carefully as outputs.
- Match technological flexibility with the product mix.
- Match technology scale with production volume of the work groups.
- Give workers larger and more varied tasks and increase cycle time.
- Integrate support functions within work groups to the largest possible extent.
- Optimize the system rather than the system's components.
- Changes should continue to be made as necessary to meet the changing environmental pressures.

All of these principles can be used effectively in building the organizational environment for Process Improvement as well as for managing the Process Improvement team. One of the key resources in Process Improvement is the staff driving and involved in the improvement.

Frederick Herzberg states "The quickest way to get an employee to do something is to ask, but if the person declines, the next solution is to give them a kick in the a– (KITA). . . . The employee . . . does move . . . but KITA does not lead to motivation, it only leads to movement."[41] He does not believe that money and benefits motivate employees but that continuous job enrichment is what ultimately motivates them. Herzberg identified Motivation Factors significant to staff motivation and performance:

- *Responsibility*—staff must accept responsibility for work accomplished. For Process Improvement, this can be characterized by responsible autonomy. The Process Improvement staff must take responsibility for the tasks at hand to achieve Process Improvement success.
- *Achievement*—opportunities for achievements and the actual achievement of a goal is one of the most important motivators. When small successes are achieved during a Process Improvement effort it sets the stage for further successes and motivates the organizational staff to meet the Process Improvement goals. The momentum is like a train on a downhill track, picking up speed with every success.
- *Recognition*—this is an area that many organizations fail to accomplish but people doing a task want and even need recognition even if it is in a small way.
- *Growth/advancement*—staff growth and advancement is the goal of most staff members. This is especially true for the movers and shakers within an organization. If this is withheld they will find this growth and advancement elsewhere.
- *Interest in job*—tasks should have sufficient challenges to fully utilize staff's abilities.

Of all the sociotechnical concepts these last four factors are the most important to remember. A strong, empowered team can make the difference between success and failure.

Tools and Strategies to Effecting Organizational Change

There have been numerous tools and strategies defined for effecting organizational change. The advanced computing technology we see today and the tools for dissemination of information opens the door to some very useful tools for Process Improvement. Some of the more popular are discussed in this section.

Information Portals

Webster's Dictionary defines a portal as a "doorway, gate, or entrance." In the information forum, an enterprise (intranet) portal solution provides an open environment for managing and delivering knowledge, applications, and services. It provides a single integration point in order to provide a multitude of varied information to diverse users. There are many types of portals defined but the portal discussed here refers to the enterprise or intranet portal for organizations to manage applications and information, or also called business to employees (B2E) portals, which can provide access to other portals such as Business portals, personal portals and public portals. As a tool for Process Improvement, a portal can prove to be one of the most important tools for many uses.

Portals are described as the "kitchen-sink application for the enterprise" by Michael Desmond, *Portals Magazine*.[14] Simply put, they provide a framework for pulling together information, applications, and services in a web-based environment. Portals have been defined as a "shining oasis of growth" in today's depressed technology market. The Giga Information Group predicts "portals will become the dominant means by which all users access corporate business content, processes, and services in 2005."[14]

A portal can be tailored for each user depending upon their specific needs. There are a good number of tools available for developing portals and many organizations may already have the capability to affect a portal. A trade study should be accomplished to determine the appropriate tool for each organization's computing environment. One thing that should be considered is avoiding duplication of applications or applications that already exist in a similar form and provide the same or like services. As the list of vendors grows, the likelihood of duplicate applications increases. Figure 19-6 illustrates a typical BI solution. Some of the Basic Portal Features are shown in Table 19-4.

Business Intelligence

Business Intelligence (BI) software can virtually provide users with information on demand. This technology is gaining steady popularity in providing timely access to relevant data from a variety of data sources. BI software can be especially effective when integrated with other tools such as portals, content managers, etc. As BI tools continue to gain popularity, it opens the market up to even more innovation in this arena. Predictions for the future of BI are encouraging as business intelligence transforms and grows.

There are various schools of thought on exactly what BI is and is not. The concept has become confused over time. BI software is sometimes defined as a combination of the following tools/technologies:

1. End User Query and Reporting tools—ad hoc data access and report building

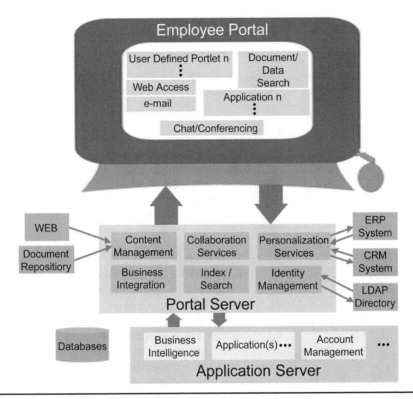

Figure 19-6   Portals

2. OLAP tools—multidimensional data management environment used for modeling business problems and analyzing business data
3. Data Mining Software—used to discover relationships in data and make predictions that are hidden, not apparent, or too complex to be extracted using statistical techniques
4. Packaged Data Mart/Warehouse Products—combine data transformation, management and access in a single package, usually with business models included
5. Executive Information Systems (EIS).

For the purposes of this book, BI is defined as a method of providing ready access to data that is stored in a variety of formats such as databases, regardless of the database tool used. In essence, BI provides a means of obtaining data from various sources and collating it into meaningful reports for users. Most organizations have numerous data sources in a multitude of databases and other data storage and retrieval tools. For Process Improvement, it is key to have the ability to pull all this diverse data together. Figure 19-7 illustrates a typical BI solution.

Table 19-4 Portal Basic Services

Service	Description
Content management	As repositories of unstructured text grow, simple search engines fail to meet all the information retrieval needs of users. Content Management gives large numbers of users access to large amounts of information. Content Management provides templates for capturing and publishing information in an organized way across the entire organization, with workflow and version-control, and a central repository for managing information. Information extraction is an area to keep an eye on since it is beginning to emerge as part of Content Management tools.
Business process automation/business integration	A business integration engine acts as a foundation for the entire portal, routing transactions across many systems, as opposed to creating processes for every application in every business unit.
Identity management	Virtually every Web application authenticates users and develops its own identity profile of their roles and privileges. Deploying an identity management system as a foundation service for all the applications developed within the portal allows users to navigate between applications and information without repeatedly logging in, and creates a common identity profile of user roles and privileges on which all the applications can draw. With an identity management system, security can be more consistently and easily enforced across the portal, which is a key consideration for all organizations today.
Index/search	The ability to search both structured and unstructured repositories is another key consideration for portals along with automated indexing of content and data. Search is deployed with almost every portal. Deploying search ensures that the content created by every application, the documents submitted to every collaborative project, the information routed through every process, can be easily found. Search can also index all the information stored in traditional systems in a knowledge management application, such as the document directory, with a set of categories that users can browse.

(continued)

Table 19-4   Continued

Service	Description
Collaboration	The majority of applications are collaborative, with facilities for tracking projects, sharing documents, assigning tasks, exchanging ideas or sending messages. By offering collaboration as a foundation service, the Portal can recognize dependencies between projects, and combine tasks and documents from different projects for each user, allowing users to work together across traditional organizational and network boundaries.
Personalization	Personalization provides finely tuned, customized digital dashboards that integrate critical parts of applications and services. It allows users to select specific information, regardless of source, that exactly meets their personal requirements. Users provide criteria such as key words that can be used in continual searches. This service is normally provided as part of a portal package but is a key service for the users so should be considered carefully.
Development environment	The development environment will be key to being able to stand an effective portal up for any organization in a timely manner. The primary element of the development environment is the tool to develop the portlets. Portlets are a component of the portal and, essentially, are custom-written APIs (Application Program Interface).The information displayed by portlets includes applications (i.e., specific links to enterprise applications) and collaboration tools (i.e., mail and chat) to content (i.e., data feeds) and whatever data particular employees need to do their jobs. Portlet development kits allow users and developers to create, edit, and deploy portlets. The advantage of portlets: you can integrate internal data sources as needed. Unfortunately, even though they're traditionally written in Java, Javascript, ActiveX, or XML, you can't take a portlet created with one application and move it to a different one. You're locked into that vendor's proprietary technology to access the data. Several vendors are actively working on the issue of standardizing and making portal solutions interoperable. This will be another area to keep a close eye on. If an organization were to become dissatisfied with the performance, reliability, or cost of their vendor choice, the elimination of proprietary portal APIs would take a significant amount of pain out of switching to a different portal solution.

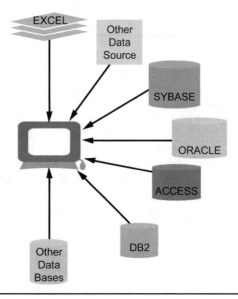

Figure 19-7 Business Intelligence

Process Improvement Focused Newsletters

A newsletter focused on processes and the Process Improvement effort is a great way to disperse information and spread the word. It can also be used as a training and knowledge dissemination tool. An effective newsletter should be published at the very least quarterly but a monthly newsletter is the optimal solution as time and resources permit. A bulletin can be used in between to make important announcements to keep the momentum going in the organization and keep the focus on the Process Improvement effort.

A newsletter is an effective tool to help facilitate the exchange of information if the door is open to authors outside of the Process Improvement group. There are many ways to use a newsletter such as:

- How-to description for processes, techniques, or methods
- Informational to describe a methodology, Process Improvement in general, or specific practices or processes
- Status dissemination to inform the organization of progress made on the Process Improvement effort
- Advertisement for new processes, tools, or other resources key to the Process Improvement effort
- Method for proving a feedback mechanism for organizational staff
- Method for collecting recommendations, suggestions, and comments from organizational staff

- Advertisement of successes; this is a great way to build and maintain momentum for accomplishing the Process Improvement effort; always advertise even the smallest successes
- A reminder of where various tools, resources, processes, etc., can be located for the organization
- Key lessons learned to help others in the organization from making the same mistakes
- Advertise upcoming events.

Whatever the focus of the newsletter the key to making it successful is to make it fun. Make articles interesting so that they will be read. Include a section for jokes, or funny stories, true or made up. One of the more interesting sections can be one where games are played such as puzzles, true or false, word games, etc.

Getting the newsletter read is important to its effectiveness. Dissemination can be accomplished either on-line or in hardcopy form. A combination of both is recommended for maximum benefit of the information provided. The key is to get it out and get it read by the largest percentage of people; if it's interesting most of them will read it.

Bulletins

Bulletins are effective methods of getting information out in a smaller way than the newsletter. They can be used in between the newsletters to encourage participation, announce events, advertise successes, or disseminate new or significantly updated processes or tools, or simply the location of such processes or tools.

Posters

A poster can be used to advertise the effort as well as other aspects of the program. They should be displayed in areas where they will get the most exposure and be the most effective within the organization. Don't leave any areas out of the process. You never know where a great resource may develop. Everyone likes to be kept informed.

Emails

Emails are another great tool for disseminating information. Care must be taken in using this important tool so that your good intentions are not seen as intrusions like SPAM. Don't overwhelm staff with too many emails. Use the tool sparingly for it to be most effective. When overused, staff members will just erase your messages without even reading them. Keep the messages sent short and to the point. A little humor here doesn't hurt either to maintain interest.

Using Staff Meetings Effectively

Presentations and announcements during staff meetings, such as all hands meetings for the entire organization, or smaller meetings, such as staff meetings, can be used to advertise status as well as successes. It's a great way to get the word out. Word of mouth is very effective in obtaining support and institutionalizing the processes. Again, make these presentations fun so that people listen. Play games; some effective games to be used during presentations or during training sessions have been included in the Toolkit.

Short training sessions at the end of a staff meeting for training or a questions-and-answers session can provide a means of disseminating a good deal of information to organizations. These should be kept fairly small and short to get the maximum benefit out of the sessions without inundating staff with too much information.

Polls

Take polls to determine if processes are being used as well as being accepted. These polls can take many forms. They can be on-line or paper-generated. They can cover a multitude of areas from the Process Improvement effort as a whole to specific processes or tools. It is a great way to determine where you really are in the Process Improvement effort.

Form Affiliates

Just like in marketing products or services, Process Improvement can benefit from the formation of affiliations. These affiliations can be most effective with projects and especially with the project managers and leads. Typically, these are the social leaders who control the direction for the rest of the group. As previously discussed, these are the folks that determine if, when, and how a process will actually be used. Process Improvement staff members can make effective liaisons to the projects. A little hand-holding in their territory can build valuable one-on-one relationships that will prove a major benefit to the entire effort. These liaisons are valuable in explaining some of the intricacies of processes and tools, acting as a mentor or sponsor for the project, determining their unique project needs, support the project as needed, return valuable information concerning use of processes and tools for planning the next actions needed to be most effective, and prepare them for any upcoming appraisals and mini-assessments.

Keeping an Eye on the Future

If you don't keep a close eye on the flurry of activity in the technology market, you will get left behind as technology progresses. Organizations must always keep an eye on technology changes to be ready to apply it to various areas, but for our purposes here, to Process Improvement. Every day exciting new inroads are made in providing better and faster communications as well as information storage and access. These are critical aspects for accelerating a Process Improvement effort.

The key is to determine what to tackle and when to tackle it to provide the most reliable, flexible systems possible for storing and dissemination of the multitude of information related to Process Improvement. The goal should be a move toward interactive, network-centric, web-based applications and capabilities, in order to provide the Process Improvement team the appropriate tools for developing processes and tools as well as storing them for easy use by organizational staff. There are a few areas showing great promise to keep an eye on that could have far-reaching impacts to a Process Improvement effort. These are discussed briefly in Table 19-5.

Planning and Managing Change

Planning and managing change as a part of the Process Improvement effort will be important to make the changes last and institutionalize them. Action planning and maintenance of the Action Plan as discussed in previous sections is key to that success. During any Process Improvement effort, numerous changes are being made in an organization, many times simultaneously. Monitoring those changes to ensure that the organization is not being inundated with too many changes to effect lasting change will be important. A risk management strategy will help to mitigate these or point the Process Improvement team in another direction. It will provide some key digressions to monitor. These have been discussed in the planning section.

Summary

Organizational change is very difficult. It is a matter of finding the right methods to use to make staff realize that the changes are rational and work in their favor. To paraphrase Drucker, human nature does not resist change if it seems rational. We are, in fact, by nature ready to try new things. For Process Improvement, the key is make the organizational staff understand what's in it for them.

Chapter Key Points

- Process Improvement is even more like cat herding; it's not easy but it's ultimately very satisfying.
- Some of the science theories are being used successfully in discussions of organizational change.

Table 19-5 Keeping an Eye on Future Technology

Methodologies/Technologies	*Brief Description/Potential for Future*
Portal technology/ enterprise information portals	The promised benefits of EIPs are the same as those of the Internet; in general a simple Web interface that helps users rapidly sift through information managed by a large distributed computer network. Portals offer significant potential to organizations to leverage information for their business benefit.
Artificial intelligence/ data mining	Data Mining, sometimes referred to as "machine learning," is based on automated methods for pattern discovery and general learning from data. This emerging technology can play an important role in removing some of the human intervention in systems.
Data warehousing	Data Warehousing can be very useful in the right environment but careful evaluation must be conducted. Data Warehousing is a viable solution when ad hoc queries and reporting tools are being run against a variety of data sources. Data Warehouses are the foundation of applications that make sense of large amounts of data.
Business intelligence	Business Intelligence tools are key to opening up data, collating it into meaningful reports and making it visible to decision makers.
Knowledge bases	Knowledge Bases and Knowledge Management are areas to watch in the future. A lot of headway is being made in this area. Where Artificial Intelligence has not shown enormous success, other ways of achieving the same results are being investigated and this concept is showing promise. Raw data in the form of numbers, characters, strings and so on, is not information until placed into meaningful context using semantics or relationships.
Clustering	Also known as "unsupervised learning," clustering is used to find groups in data. This method can be used for image compression and to increase the speed of data access.
Databases	Databases feed Web-based dynamic content and facilitate page updates; they reuse data across multiple applications and reduce redundancy; they also store in data warehouses information that's culled, mined and aggregated by business applications and knowledge-discovery tools. The potential for the new databases and database technologies is open.

- Some of the new ideas for managing organizational change are coming from some seemingly unlikely arenas such as the Chaos Theory, Relativity, Quantum Physics, Mathematic, Chemistry, Biology, and Open Systems.
- You can't always predict what a system will do next but you can put things in motion in smaller ways to perpetuate changes on a large scale.
- Roger's Adoption Curve holds that, given a normal population distribution, people accept new ideas and innovation at a different rate.
- The internet has been partly responsible for this shift toward inductive marketing which is a great tool to use for Process Improvement.
- Each stakeholder is going to see something different, it is important to discuss a process based on their perspective.
- The sociotechnical theory that we are going to discuss consists of five components: People, Tasks, Technology, Structure, and Environment (culture).
- The advanced computing technology we see today and the tools for dissemination of information opens the door to some very useful tools for Process Improvement. Examples include portals, business intelligence, process-focused newsletters, bulletins, posters, email, etc.
- Presentations and announcements during staff meetings, such as all hands meetings for the entire organization, or smaller meetings such as staff meetings, can be used to advertise status as well as successes.
- Just like in marketing products or services, Process Improvement can benefit from the formation of affiliations.

Tips for Success

- Participation in creating processes is a must for Process Improvement.
- Use both inductive and deductive marketing techniques.
- When dealing with others' realities, we have to see things from their perspective and make it relative to them.
- A strong, empowered team can make the difference between success and failure.
- Keep a close eye on the flurry of activity in the technology market, you will get left behind as technology progresses.

Chapter 20

Bottom Line

Mark and Joe are fictional characters in this book but scenarios much like those described are happening at organizations across the country. Process Improvement can make a huge difference in people's day-to-day life. Many times we spend more time at work than anywhere else so it is important that that be a positive experience. The method of achieving Process Improvement will be the first key decision that needs to be made to kick the Process Improvement effort off.

Slow and Easy versus Accelerated Process Improvement

The SEI has long recommended allotting 18–24 months per CMM® level. It found that the average is two years to get to SW-CMM® Level 2. Watts Humphrey recommends one to three years per level.[19] Each organization must weigh the importance of the advantages and disadvantages, based on their unique environment, to determine whether to take it slow and easy or accelerate Process Improvement. Table 20-1 compares some typical advantages and disadvantages of accelerating processes to taking it slow and easy.

Lessons Learned

There are many lessons learned from both successful and unsuccessful Process Improvement efforts. The Internet is full of hard-learned lessons and provides

Table 20-1 Accelerating Process Improvement Advantages and Disadvantages

Accelerating	Slow and Easy
Quicker return on investment	Institutionalization more likely
Success early fuels improvements later and keeps the ball rolling for more successes	More time for improvement successes but people may tire of the effort early and Process Improvement never reaches completion
Failures early jeopardize later efforts	Easier recovery from failures
Tendency to keep things simpler	Tendency to create bureaucracy
Less time	More time
Processes in place quicker	Processes more staggered
Requires research to levy lessons learned from other organizations	More time to learn from lessons and collect historical data
Process Improvement staff need to be both process savvy and have an agile temperament	Time to learn Process Improvement how-tos

a great tool for levying others' lessons learned. There are also many lessons learned from successful accelerated Process Improvement efforts. Use the tools and techniques developed and shared by others to help make your Process Improvement effort successful, as well as the hard lessons learned to help avoid making the same mistakes.

Keys to Remember

Keeping costs reasonable and time optimal is the key advantage of APIM. This method has proven to keep Process Improvement costs lower and time minimal. However, it is key to remember a few key tips:

- "Create the future" by planning but keep the plan flexible in order to "roll with the punches"
- Keep teams small; small, agile process teams are able to get more done, quicker
- There should be very little project impact due to the Process Improvement effort
- Keep organizational staff informed and involved
- Keep it Simple, use KISS to your advantage
- Listen to the water cooler talk to know the key staff care-abouts
- Let go of the past and learn from it to build a better future.

The only impact to projects should be in improving the way the projects operate. Otherwise, the cost savings will be minimal if seen at all. The bottom line is: Do not sacrifice productivity to meet Process Improvement goals. This will counteract any of the advantages achieved by using the APIM.

Bottom Line

Finally, always consider, "What is the bang for the buck?" If the return from each step, form, or plan, is not worth the time it takes to do it, then it should probably not be accomplished.

Do not let bureaucracy stop achievement of the ultimate Process Improvement goal: Mature processes for a smoother, more effective working environment!

Try it for a while and see if it works for the organization. Chances are most organizations will be surprised by the results. Once implemented, it's an easy step to the more traditional methods of Process Improvement and can set the organization on the right road to successful Process Improvement. Also, once an organization has gone through a few maturity cycles to set the foundation, they can always move to the more traditional methods with a few good successes under the belt.

Whatever you do, Always Remain Agile!

ACCELERATING PROCESS IMPROVEMENT METHODOLOGY TOOLKIT

This toolkit contains items to assist in the accelerated process improvement effort. The following lists the tools and guidelines included:

A. Work Breakdown Structure.
B. Wideband Delphi Estimating Method.
C. Schedule Checklist.
D. Budget Checklist.
E. Initial Executive Management Kickoff Meeting Agenda.
F. Initial Executive Management Kickoff Meeting Minutes.
G. The Goose Story.
H. Overall Process Improvement Action Plan.
I. Major Activity Action Plan.
J. Process Template.
K. CMMI® Process Stop Light Charts.
L. Process Group Meeting Agenda.
M. Process Group Meeting Minutes.
N. Executive Steering Committee Review Meeting Agenda.
O. Executive Steering Committee Review Meeting Minutes.
P. Process Notebook Excerpt.
Q. Audit Schedule.
R. Audit Plan.
S. Audit Checklist.
T. Audit Report.
U. Gap Analysis/Audit Checklist.

Appendix A

Work Breakdown Structure

A Work Breakdown Structure (WBS) provides a foundation for defining the actual work that needs to be accomplished. It helps further define the cost estimates, schedule estimates, risk management, resource allocation, role definition, assigned responsibilities, and any make/buy/reuse decisions that must be made on any project.

The WBS organizes the activities defined for the project in a hierarchical structure. The method used to organize the activities will be dependent upon the specific reporting needs of the organization and the method selected to report activity status. Some of the methods typically used include:

- *Time phased*—when tasks are accomplished
- *Geographic*—geographic locations (i.e. where work is to be accomplished or used which can include a remote location or a department or project within the same location)
- *Product/system*—specific products or systems (most commonly used method of organization for Process Improvement—this can be the Process Areas and/or Practices within the Process Areas)
- *Functional department*—functional department (i.e. software, system engineering, hardware, . . .)
- *Combination*—combination of one or more (i.e. functional department at the higher levels and then products/systems at the lower levels).

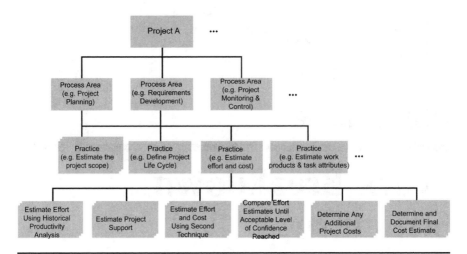

Figure A-1   Typical Hierarchical WBS

The lowest level of the WBS represents a Work Package which can be used to represent the tasks and activities required to meet that requirement. These work packages work well for authorizations and assignment of responsibilities. They can also be used to measure progress of the Process Improvement effort.

The WBS should be developed at the start of the Process Improvement effort and then be used throughout the effort to further refine the tasks and activities as further information is derived. This is not a tool to just put on the shelf, this is an iterative tool that should be used throughout the effort. It should be used by the managers and staff to assign, reassign, replan, reallocate, and reapportion.

The Process Improvement effort can be decomposed in many ways. Figure A-1 illustrates a typical hierarchical WBS and Table A-1 illustrates it in textual form. Figure A-2 illustrates the method of decomposition. Decomposition should be performed until all tasks and deliverables are defined in sufficient detail to support project statusing, budgeting, scheduling, resource management, risk management, and measurement. The level of detail to include in a WBS will be dependent upon the goals for its use.

A WBS Dictionary can be a powerful tool to provide descriptions of activities and tasks, estimated costs per task, resource assignments, duration, and any associated risks. The WBS Dictionary is built from the lowest level tasks and deliverables, typically called a Work Package.

Table A-1   Hierarchical WBS

Level 2	AAB	Project Planning
Level 3	AAB1	Establish Estimates
Level 4	AAB11	Estimate the scope of the project
Level 5	AAB11n	...
Level 4	AAB12	Establish estimates of work products and task attributes
Level 5	AAB12n	...
Level 4	AAB13	Determine estimates of effort and cost
Level 5	AAB131	Estimate Effort Using Historical Productivity Analysis
	AAB132	Estimate Project Support
	AAB133	Estimate Effort and Cost Using Second Technique
	AAB134	Compare Effort Estimates Until Acceptable Level of Confidence Reached
	AAB135	Determine Any Additional Project Costs
	AAB136	Determine and Document Final Cost Estimate
Level 3	AAB2	Establish Estimates
Level 4	AAB21	Estimate the scope of the project
Level 5	AAB21n	...
Level 4	AAB22	Establish estimates of work products and task attributes
Level 5	AAB22n	...
Level 4	AAB23	Determine estimates of effort and cost
Level 5	AAB23n	...
Level 3	AAB3	Develop a Project Plan
Level 4	AAB31	Establish the budget and schedule
Level 5	AAB31n	...
Level 4	AAB32	Identify project risks
Level 5	AAB32n	...
Level 4	AAB33	Plan for data management
Level 5	AAB33n	...
Level 4	AAB34	Plan for needed knowledge and skills
Level 5	AAB34n	...
Level 4	AAB35	Plan stakeholder involvement
Level 5	AAB35n	...
Level 4	AAB36	Establish the project plan
Level 5	AAB36n	...

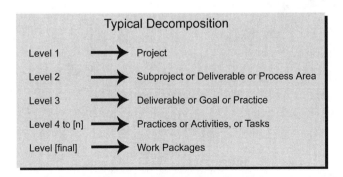

Typical Decomposition

Level 1	➜	Project
Level 2	➜	Subproject or Deliverable or Process Area
Level 3	➜	Deliverable or Goal or Practice
Level 4 to [n]	➜	Practices or Activities, or Tasks
Level [final]	➜	Work Packages

Figure A-2   Method of Decomposition

Appendix B

Wideband Delphi Estimating Method

1. Select four to six experts depending on availability and size of effort (appropriate experience required)
2. Brief experts regarding components, . . . and provide appropriate materials for review
3. Experts provide three estimates (optimistic (E1), pessimistic (E2), and probable (E3)) for each component (should be independent and anonymous)
4. Determine expected sizes by:
5. $E = ((E1 + E2 + (4E3))/6)/\#experts$
6. Repeat steps 3 and 4 until an appropriate level of confidence is met.

Appendix C

Schedule Checklist

Check	Schedule Substantiation	Comments
	Were all critical success factors taken into consideration? Favorable? Adverse?	
	Was overtime allowed?	
	Were holidays and weekends considered?	
	Were task dependencies determined and considered?	
	Does the schedule contain enough detail to facilitate monitoring?	
	Was the schedule based on estimates from previous planning steps? WBS?	
	Is each scheduled task/activity clearly detailed and defined?	
	If used, is the critical path reasonable?	
	Has there been a major rescheduling effort? Any impacts to other items? Any impact to Critical Path?	

Appendix D

Budget Checklist

Check	Budget Substantiation	Comments
	Was budget allocated prior to kickoff of Process Improvement Effort?	
	If yes, by who? When? How much?	
	When will budget be available?	
	How will budget be available?	
	Is budget amount adequate?	
	Were all direct costs considered? Labor? Materials? ODC?	
	Were all indirect costs considered? Administrative? Supplies? Facilities? Other non-attributable costs?	
	Was Management Reserve taken into consideration? What Portion of budget?	
	Were all risk factors considered?	

Appendix E

Initial Executive Management Kickoff Meeting Agenda

[meeting title] Meeting Agenda
[date] – [time]
[location]

Meeting Agenda

1. Vision/Measure Of Success Statement (short description of successful end condition(s))
2. Primary Objectives
3. Teams (including roles and responsibilities)
4. Budget
5. Schedule (include discussion of critical success factors)
6. Risks
7. Concerns
8. Issues
9. Action Items (use this section when an earlier executive meeting was held prior to actual kickoff)

AI #	Description	Assign To	Assign Date	Due Date	Status/Comments

Next Meeting Scheduled: [date] [time]

Appendix F

Initial Executive Management Kickoff Meeting Minutes

[meeting title] Meeting Minutes
[date] – [time]
[location]

Attendees: [name of each attended, . . .]

General Discussions:

1. Vision/Measure Of Success Statement

    - [general description of discussion, any comments or concerns, any changes, any decisions]
    - . . .

2. Primary Objectives

    - [general description of discussion, any comments or concerns, any changes, any decisions]
    - . . .

3. Teams (including roles and responsibilities)
   - [general description of discussion, any comments or concerns, any changes, any decisions]
   - . . .

4. Budget
   - [general description of discussion, any comments or concerns, any changes, any decisions]
   - . . .

5. Schedule (include discussion of critical success factors)
   - [general description of discussion, any comments or concerns, any changes, any decisions]
   - . . .

6. Risks
   - [general description of discussion, any comments or concerns, any changes, any decisions]
   - . . .

7. Concerns
   - [general description of discussion, any comments or concerns, any changes, any decisions]
   - . . .

8. Issues
   - [general description of discussion, any comments or concerns, any changes, any decisions]
   - . . .

Other Discussions:

1.
2.

Action Items

AI #	Description	Assign To	Assign Date	Due Date	Status/Comments

Next Meeting Scheduled: [date] [time]

Appendix G

The Goose Story

The Goose Story

The

next time

you see Geese

heading South for

the Winter, flying along

in V formation, you might

consider what science has dis-

covered as to why they fly that way:

as each bird flaps its wings, it creates an

uplift for the bird immediately following. By

flying in V formation the whole flock adds at least

71% greater flying range than if each bird flew on its own.

People who share a common direction and sense of community

can get where they are going more quickly and easily

because they are traveling on the thrust of one another.

When

a goose falls

out of formation,

it suddenly feels the drag

and resistance of trying to go it alone

and quickly gets back into formation to take

advantage of the lifting power of the bird in front.

If we have as much sense as a goose,

we will stay in formation

with those who are headed the same way we are.

When

the Head Goose

gets tired, it rotates back

in the wing and another goose flies point.

It is sensible to take turns doing demanding jobs

with people or with geese flying South.

Geese

honk from behind to

encourage those up front to keep up their speed.

What do we say when we honk from behind?

Finally,

and this is important,

when a goose gets sick, or is

wounded by gunshots and falls out

of formation, two other geese fall out with that

goose and follow it down to lend help and protection.

They stay with the fallen goose until it is able to fly, or until

it dies. Only then do they launch out on their own, or with another formation

to catch up with their group.

IF WE HAVE THE SENSE OF A GOOSE,

WE WILL STAND BY EACH OTHER

LIKE THAT.

—Source Unknown

Appendix H

Overall Process Improvement Action Plan

[ORGANIZATION]

PROCESS GROUP

HANDBOOK

As of: [date]

"There is nothing more difficult to plan, more doubtful of success, nor more dangerous to manage than the creation of a new order of thing."
—Niccolo Machiavelli

Table of Contents

1. Introduction

This plan provides a roadmap for the process improvement initiative at [organization]. It describes the infrastructure to manage the initiative, and defines an approach for identifying and addressing the process improvement issues throughout the organization and on applicable projects.

[organization] has selected the Capability Maturity Model-Integrated (CMMI) as the methodology that will be used for the process improvement initiative. This plan will integrate all process improvement activities within the organization. A process group has been formed in order to address these efforts and ensure that the efforts continue, are coordinated, and issues resolved. This group will be discussed in detail later in this plan.

The goals, motivation for improving, the commitment required by various parties, the assumptions that are being made, and the overall process to be applied in managing this initiative, and the infrastructure required to facilitate the initiative are some of the critical areas that will be discussed.

In summary, this plan will address the following questions:

- What are our goals for the SPI program?
- What is our motivation to improve?
- What assumptions are we making?
- Who are the players?
- How will we measure successes?
- How will we continue to improve?

This document serves as the project plan for the process improvement initiative, indicating an overall agenda, roles and responsibilities, assumptions and risks, key tasks, success criteria, key milestones, and how this initiative will evolve over multiple iterations of the continuous improvement cycle. A separate detailed schedule will be maintained in order to manage the process improvement initiative.

2. Objectives

The primary objective for any process improvement effort is to create a smooth, efficient working environment for all organization stakeholders and to facilitate new technology introduction. [organization] understands that, by adopting the CMMI model, it helps projects and the organization as a whole avoid common problems, making them more predictable and, hence, more successful. One of our major goals will be to build a process-oriented culture at [organization].

This section will discuss the guiding principles of the process improvement initiative. It will document the key elements that are needed to make the effort successful.

- The process improvement initiative is intended to address business, technical, project management, and quality issues that are deemed worth improving. The organization should be able to explain to stakeholders why a proposed activity or deliverable is important.
- Process-oriented work products must be concise, must add value, and must be usable. There is no intent to produce reams of documentation. The Process Group will always strive to make work products useable by keeping them as simple as possible.
- Process work oriented work products will be developed in a method that allows a reasonable amount of freedom of development and facilitates improvements over time.

- The Process Group will work closely with all projects rather than "throwing things over the fence." This will enable projects to come up to speed process-wise quicker and less painfully.
- The appropriate mindset for process change is to understand "what's in it for us?" as a project team, an organization, or a company and its customers, not just what's in it for any individual.
- The initiative will emphasize the importance of leveraging existing examples and templates. The organization must avoid the "not invented here" syndrome, choosing instead to borrow, buy, or adapt appropriate artifacts that already exist.
- The process improvement initiative will be implemented in the same way as any other project.
  1. A schedule will be developed and maintained with clear milestones and deliverables.
  2. Resources have been allocated to accomplish the work necessary.
  3. The process improvement initiative has clear expectations from higher management.

3. Goals

The main goal of the process improvement initiative is to develop a culture that fully embraces an environment of continuous process improvement. Not only will the organization be developing superior quality work products faster, better, and cheaper than our competitors, but it will also be monitoring the processes currently being used, looking for ways to further improve them.

3.1. Short-Term Goals

The following table lists the short-term (6–12 months) goals that have been identified for the process improvement effort.

Name	Brief Description	Success Measure
Process group training	The Process Group will be trained on the CMMI, process improvement, and the expectations of Process Group members.	All Process Group Team members have undergone training.
Organizational process training	The organization will accomplish process training at varying levels based on the employee's level and position.	All employees have undergone training based on their level and position.
PAT formation	Process Action Teams (PAT) will be formed in order to tackle specific issues as determined and prioritized by the Process Group.	PATs formed and functioning. Results will vary based on actions assigned.

(continued)

Name	Brief Description	Success Measure
Target projects	Target Projects will be selected to start using/tailoring processes as they are developed in order to smooth them out for the organization.	Target projects selected.
Mini-Assessments	Mini-Assessments (initial and progress) will be accomplished on all applicable projects to get an understanding of where they are and where they need to go.	Mini-Assessment Report and recommendations briefed to appropriate higher management and project management teams.
PL rework	The Process Library (PL) will be developed/reworked to make it consistent with the CMMI and to smooth out some issues and take advantage of lessons learned by those that have implemented it in the past.	PL in reasonable shape to be deployed for use on projects.
Repository implementation	Several repositories will be set up to provide historical data, sample items, etc. as required by the CMMI and as needed for the organization.	Repositories set up and populated.
Training organization	A training group will be set up to ensure that the organization's training needs are met both for business and process improvement purposes.	Training needs are being met and documented in an orderly way. Organizational Training Plan developed.

3.2. Long-Term Goals

The following table lists the long-term (>1–3 years) goals that have been identified to facilitate process improvement and organizational success.

Name	Brief Description	Success Measure
CMMI level 3 attainment	[organization] strives to make the organization a CMMI Level 3 organization.	Formal Appraisal of a CMMI Level 3.
PL rework	The ultimate goal for the PL is to make a useable tool to all projects and organizationally by making it available on-line.	A useable PL available to all employees on-line with ongoing improvement efforts to take advantage of emerging technologies.
PAT formation	Process Action Teams will continue to be formed in order to tackle specific issues as determined and prioritized by the Process Group.	Continuing PAT formations to attack issues as they arise.

(*continued*)

Name	Brief Description	Success Measure
Projects process roll-out	Processes will be rolled out and tailored for all applicable projects.	All projects functioning using processes tailored from the organizational processes.
Progress mini-assessments	Progress mini-assessments accomplished periodically to assess current state of processes for projects and organization.	Mini-assessment Report and Recommendations briefed to appropriate higher management and project management teams.
Repositories functioning & used	All repositories fully functional and being used to accomplish estimates, planning, etc.	Repositories fully functional & being used

As the goals are accomplished and change, this plan will continuously be updated to reflect the current plans.

4. Risks, Barriers, Assumptions

This section addresses assumptions underlying the motivations for process improvement, the way process improvement will be pursued, and the existence of elements necessary for success. It also discusses barriers to being successful over the long term with process improvement and risks inherent in the plan.

4.1. Assumptions and Barriers

The following initial assumptions and barriers to success of the process improvement initiative have been identified at this time:

- Process Group members will actively participate in the process improvement initiative in order to make it successful.
- Projects will work with the Process Group members in improving their processes and making them consistent with the organizational processes.
- Higher management will continue to be committed to the process improvement initiative and realize that there are barriers that must be overcome to make it successful.
- Higher management will empower the Process Group with enough authority to make the process improvement initiative successful with minimal paperwork approvals.
- Resource will continue to be available throughout the process improvement effort and a contingent will be in place to maintain the changes made.
- Efforts made by individuals and process improvement teams and subteams will be duly recognized and rewarded based on the impact and merits of the change(s).

- Rewards and recognition will be given to those in the organization that exhibit the desired process improvement-related behaviors as opposed to the fire-fighting behavior of less-mature organizations.
- All employees and subcontractors will tailor and use the organizational processes.
- The Process Group members will take advantage of the varied expertise and experiences of all employees.
- Process Group members will be selected based on what they can contribute to the team as a whole and not simply because they want to be part of the team.
- Process Group members will be retained based on their contributions to team and their ability to act synergistically with the rest of the team.
- All Process Group members will promote the process culture throughout the organization and the idea that "we are all in this together."

4.2. Risks

The major risks facing the success of this initiative are listed in the following table:

ID	Risk Item	P	L	E	Mitigation Approaches
	[identify the risk]	#	#	#	[identify how risk will be mitigated]
	[identify the risk]	#	#	#	[identify how risk will be mitigated]
	[identify the risk]	#	#	#	[identify how risk will be mitigated]

POO = probability of occurrence (0 to 1)
SOI = relative loss factor (0 to 10)
Magnitude = risk exposure = POO × SOI

5. Organization for Process Improvement

The process improvement stakeholders consist of anyone associated with the process improvement effort. This section will discuss the primary stakeholders associated with making process improvement happen in the organization. Figure H-1 depicts the current Process Group. Process Group membership may change over time; this handbook will be updated to reflect changes.

5.1. Senior Management Steering Committee

Executive/senior managers are key to setting the direction for continuing process improvement. The Management Steering Committee consists of [members].

The Management Steering Committee meets periodically to discuss status and set the overall direction of the process improvement initiative. They are responsible for approving plans, reviewing results, monitoring the progress of the Process

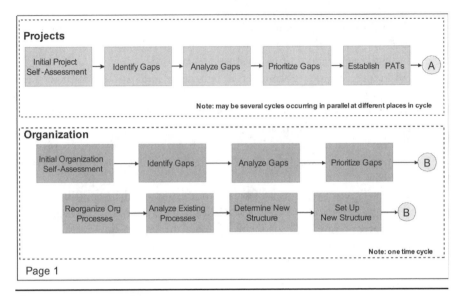

Figure H-1   Process Group

Group, obtaining the required resources to make the effort successful, and resolving issues that have been elevated to that level. They also will act as a process improvement sponsor to the rest of the organization so that the entire organization realizes the importance of the effort.

5.2.   Process Improvement Project Manager

The Process Improvement Project Manager will be responsible for the overall management of the Process Group. The specific responsibilities of the Process Improvement Project Manager include:

- Documenting and implementing the organization's overall process improvement plan.
- Tracking progress against the plan.
- Creating and maintaining a schedule identifying activities, resources, and effort.
- Reviewing and approving PATs action plans.
- Collecting status Process Action Teams and reviewing results.
- Summarizing and reporting status monthly to the Steering Committee.
- Suggesting corrective action to the Steering Committee when actual progress deviates too far from the plans.
- Acquiring and coordinating resources for training and project consulting.
- Ensuring continued enthusiasm by the Process Group and the organization.
- Generating the newsletter on a monthly basis initially and quarterly later in the effort.

- Resolving issues elevated from PATs.
- Accomplishing assigned tasks for process improvement as all other members of the Process Group, sometimes as part of a PAT.

5.3. Process Group

The Process Group is the focal point for the organization's process improvement effort. The Software Capability Maturity Model (SW-CMM) was the precursor to the CMMI. It defined a Process Group that is responsible for accomplishing the process improvement efforts. The CMMI does not specifically define this group but still recommends its use.

Since this team is critical to the process improvement effort, [organization] chose that method for accomplishing the process improvement effort. The Process Group spans the entire lifecycle so the software engineering part of it has been removed.

The SW-CMM defined the EPG as follows: "The software engineering process group is the focal point for process improvement. Composed of line practitioners who have varied skills, the group is at the center of the collaborative effort of everyone in the organization who is involved with software engineering process improvement."

The overall Process Group responsibilities include:

- Establish process standards
- Develop improvement plans
- Form Process Action Teams
- Launch improvement activities
- Manage all the improvement projects
- Work with projects on project processes and tailoring activities
- Report progress and issues to steering group
- Maintain process databases
- Serve as the focal point for technology transition
- Provide project consultation
- Make periodic assessments and status reports for senior management
- Provide process training organization and projects.

5.4. Process Action Teams (PAT)

Process Action Teams (PAT) will be formed from the Process Group in order to tackle issues or process improvement tasks defined by the Process Group. These groups will have the appropriate skills to tackle the specific issue or process improvement task. The following describes the responsibilities of the PATs:

- Determine cause of assigned problem or issue
- Develop plan for tackling the problem

- Analyze the nature of the problem
- Report status and any issues to Process Group
- Propose a solution to the problem
- Pilot test the solution
- Roll out the solution to the rest of the organization
- Follow the plan to accomplish tasking as developed by the approved and Process Group
- Leverage of work previously accomplished and method currently used, as applicable, before creating new methods.

5.5. Project Staff

Projects and the project's staff are key to the success of the process improvement initiative. They are the ones that need to buy-into the processes developed. The Process Group will work closely with the project staff and may include them on the PATs as needed based on their expertise. The Process Group will work closely with the project staff in piloting and rolling out processes. Process training will be provided to the project staff so that they both understand and concur with the processes developed for their use.

6. Process Improvement Roadmap

The roadmap created for the organization's process improvement initiative will be the focus for this section. The strategy that will be used is discussed along with a starting plan. As the plan matures, specific threads will be identified and linked that lead to satisfying the specific goals set forth in this plan. The thread will be based on assessment results, brainstorming, and other methods used to identify issues and problems to tackle. An initial schedule is given that gives the team a starting point. The schedule will be maintained to provide a good map for where we are, where we need to go, who is going, and when we need to get there.

6.1. Process Development Life Cycle

Figure H-2 (Process Development Life Cycle) illustrates the initial life cycle that will be followed to develop processes for both the projects and the organization.

The Process Development Life Cycle takes a dual approach to process development. The organizational processes and process organization will be accomplished in parallel with the project-specific activities. Project-specific activities will be started as needed. Two or more project-specific activities may

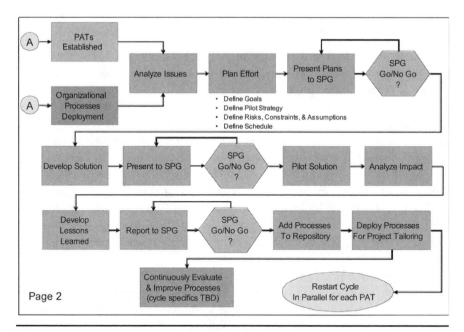

Figure H-2   Process Development Life Cycle

be accomplished concurrently and may be at varying points in the lifecycle at any given time. The following subparagraphs describe each activity.

6.1.1.   Self-Assessment

The projects and the organization will conduct a self-assessment to determine the specific issues that need to be addressed based on the CMMI. Each group will use the established assessment table to determine where they stand concerning CMMI.

6.1.2.   Identify Gaps

The project self-assessment will be used to identify the gaps that exist on their project and organizationally. The resulting gaps will be reported to the Process Group for analysis.

6.1.3.   Analyze Gaps

The Process Group will discuss and analyze each identified gap to determine exactly what the gap is, how extensive it is throughout [organization], potential existing solutions that could fill the gap, impact of the gap if not filled, and other related issues that could be combined with the gaps.

6.1.4. Prioritize Gaps

A triage-based method will be used in order to address the appropriate gaps. Prioritization will be based on potential impact, justified need, and scope of work needed to develop viable processes.

Triage is a method of determining where to concentrate your effort. In medicine triage is a method of sorting patients and allocating their treatment, especially battle or disaster victims, in order to maximize the number of survivors; the usual division is into three groups: those too severely hurt to survive, those who would recover without treatment, and those who would survive only with immediate help; the third group is given priority treatment. The triage approach has been used successfully in several business-related areas, such as by financial planners to manage requests and electronic mail, by Toyota to speed up and manage car repairs, and for Y2K efforts to determine what needs to be fixed and in what order.

In order to maximize the work accomplished and get the most out of the process improvement effort as soon as possible, the Process Group will use the triage method to determine the order in which to accomplish the process improvement tasks. Prioritization will be determined as follows:

Order	Determining Factors
1. Processes getting immediate attention 2. Processes that will be addressed later 3. Processes that will not be addressed until continuous improvement stage of effort	• Meet CMMI requirements? • Meet project needs? • Meet organizational needs? • How much effort needed? • Impact on projects? • Impact on organization?

6.1.5. Establish PATs

For project-related efforts a Process Action Team will be assigned to each selected Process Improvement effort. The PATs will function as shown in the illustration and described in this handbook.

6.1.6. Analyze Issues

The PATs and organizational designee(s) will analyze the assigned issues to determine the best approach to correcting the gap identified. Several methods may be used as determined appropriate for the group and issues at hand. Some useful methods are discussed under the Tools for Success section of this Handbook.

6.1.7. Analyze Issues

Based on the analysis, the PAT or organizational designee(s) will develop a plan for accomplishing the effort. The plan will include, as a minimum:

Planning Content	Brief Description
Goals	Clear, concise goals that define what the task is and the expected results from the effort.
Pilot strategy	A strategy for rolling the process(s) out to a pilot project, define the proposed pilot project, and what is expected of the project.
Risk, constraints, and assumptions	Constraints to the success of the effort, assumptions that are made that could impact the success of the effort such as personnel or information availability, etc.; and risks of events, information, etc., that could adversely impact the effort. Also, include a mitigation plan for each identified risk (short plan).
Schedule	Tasks and timeline for achieving the defined goals.
Other data as needed	Any other information that would assist in implementation of the effort.

6.1.8. Present Plans to Process Group

Each PAT and organizational designee will present the plans to Process Group. The Process Group will then vote on whether or not to continue pursuing the issue or if more information is needed in order to start implementation.

The Process Group will fully discuss any negative votes to determine if the concern is justified. Any controversial or final decision will be made by the Process Improvement Project Manager. Issues concerning that decision will be brought to the Senior Management Steering Committee.

Based on the decision, the PAT or organizational designee will revisit the issue, continue to the next activity in process, or disband.

6.1.9. Develop Solution

Each PAT or organizational designee will develop the appropriate solution to the task and issues as needed. Various methods can be used for accomplishing this activity based on the task or issues to be resolved. In developing processes, the PAT or organizational designee will use the Process Group approved method for projects and organizationally.

6.1.10. Present Solution to Process Group

Using the same method as for the planning, each PAT and organizational designee will present the solution to the Process Group. The Process Group will again vote on whether or not the solution is ready for piloting. Based on the decision, the PAT or organizational designee will revisit the issue, continue to the next activity in process, or disband.

6.1.11. Pilot Solution

Using the pilot strategy defined in the PAT plans, the PAT will pilot the solution to the appropriate project(s) or organizationally.

6.1.12. Analyze Impact and Develop Lessons Learned

The PAT will analyze the impact of the piloted solution and develop lessons learned. They will use various methods for accomplishing the analysis based upon the task/issue.

6.1.13. Present Analysis to Process Group

Using the same method as for the planning and the solution, each PAT and organizational designee will present the solution to the Process Group. The Process Group will again vote on whether or not the solution is ready for piloting. Based on the decision, the PAT or organizational designee will revisit the issue, continue to next activity in process, or disband.

6.1.14. Add Processes to Organizational Repository

The Process Improvement Project Manager or designee will add the new/updated process(es) to the organizational repository and update the project tailoring work products to include the new/updated process(es).

6.1.15. Deploy Processes to All Projects

The new/updated processes will be deployed to the projects as appropriate. If a project is fully CMMI compliant they may obtain a grandfathering-type waiver. These situations will be determined as we get to that point in the process.

6.1.16. Reorganize Organizational Processes

The Process Improvement Project Manager or designee will work on the reorganization of the organizational processes in coordination with the Process Group. The following steps will be followed in order to accomplish this task:

- Analyze Existing Processes
- Determine New Structure
- Set up New Structure.

6.1.17. Continuously Evaluate & Improve Processes

Once the organization has accomplished successful progress mini-assessments to determine that the organization/projects are CMMI-compliant, a new process will be developed based on lessons learned and where we need to go at the time. The handbook will be updated with the new process.

6.2. Tracking and Reporting Process

The Process Improvement Project Manager will report status to the Management Steering Committee on a monthly basis or more often as deemed necessary. A schedule will be developed and maintained with all current process improvement activities. This schedule will be used to track progress for each activity. It will also be used to measure status of overall and individual process improvement activities.

Each PAT will report to the Process Group to report their progress against the established timeline. The Process Group will make decisions as illustrated on the life-cycle diagrams to determine whether a PAT is ready to move to the next phase of the life cycle.

6.3. High Level Schedule

Reference separate MSProject schedule.

6.4. Measures for Success

The typical organizational measures will be used for statusing progress including Schedule Performance Index and Cost Performance Index. Additionally, the progress mini-assessments will be a major measure for success of the Process Improvement Effort. A Stop Light Chart will be provided to executive management and all projects to indicate their progress with each targeted practice.

6.5. Tools for Success

The following tools will be used to accomplish the actions assigned to PATs:

- Mini-Assessments—these can be used very effectively for determining the status of the process improvement effort. Initial Mini-Assessments will be accomplished to baseline the organization and project's weaknesses and Progress Mini-Assessments will be accomplished to track progress and determine residual and perhaps new weaknesses.
- Stop Light Charts/Assessment Index—the baseline results from a mini-assessment will be maintained through use of stop light charts that depict the status of each project and the organization for each process

improvement requirement. These will be updated following each progress mini-assessment and used for reporting to the Senior Management Steering Committee.

- Process Notebook/Implementation Matrix—used for each project and organizationally to ensure that process improvement element requirements are being met. This allows a mapping of each process area to the organizational processes and procedures thus ensuring that goals are met. This tool will be used during a mini-assessment to identify strengths and weaknesses.
- Brainstorming—this is usually a meeting where ideas are offered freely. A key is to avoid any criticism of ideas, no matter how outrageous. Typically discussions are held until all ideas are on the table. They can be very useful in uncovering all possible ideas and approaches. These sessions are sometimes called Cerebral Popcorn.
- Criteria Grid—can be used effectively for many different purposes such as peer reviews, decision making, idea rating, or anything that has criteria to be evaluated.
- FishBone—also called a Cause and Effect Diagram or Ishikawa Diagram, this useful issue/problem resolution tool was developed by Kaoru Ishikawa in Japan at the Kawasaki shipyards. It examines the potential or real causes that result in a single effect. The lines coming from the main horizontal line are the main causes and the lines coming from those are the subcauses. The causes are drawn according to their importance. This helps identify the root causes or areas where problems exist. It also compares the importance of relationships with various factors influencing issue or problem.
- Force Field Analysis—a tool that analyzes opposing forces involved in change initiatives to facilitate decision making. It is based on the premise that change is a result of a struggle between forces of resistance and driving forces.

forces impeding change → ← forces favoring change

- This method helps to identify the best method to implement. The resisting forces are listed on one side and the driving forces are listed on the other. Either a score can be assigned to each or a decision can be made based on having the most or least forces. This method was developed by Kurt Lewin who viewed organizations as systems where each situation is a balance of forces that act against change.
- Nominal Group Process—a method for structuring groups to allow individual judgments to be pooled. These judgments are used when there is uncertainty or disagreement about the nature of the problem and possible solutions. It helps in identification of problems, exploration of solutions,

and establishment of priorities. It ensures a balanced participation of group participants. The process steps typically are:

1. Silent idea generation
2. Round-robin-style sharing of ideas
3. Feedback to group from lead
4. Group discussions
5. Individual reassessment
6. Ideas are ranked by each participant
7. Number added and ideas prioritized from highest to lowest.

- SWOT (Strengths/Weaknesses/Opportunities/Threats)—focuses on the internal and external environments, examining strengths and weaknesses in the internal environment and opportunities and threats in the external environment. This tool is used in industry extensively to analyze their strategies but it can be used effectively for a Process Group with the external environment being the rest of the organization.
- The rule of 7 Plus or Minus 2—based on the premise that individuals have limited processing capabilities and limited storing capacities. It says that individuals can store approximately seven pieces of information in their brain at any given time. It is the basis for "chunking," which is a method of grouping elements such as chunks of information on a page, number of items on a list, number of items on a web page menu, or number of controls. This theory was developed by George A. Miller, a Princeton University psychologist in 1956, based on research he conducted to test short-term/working memory. This method will be used when developing processes, web pages, or plans.

6.6. Training

The level of training will vary based upon the staff position. The Executive Management team requires high-level training to understand the basic concepts of process improvements. Mid-level management should have a lower level of training to fully understand what their project must accomplish and continue to accomplish. The rest of the organizational staff will require only enough training to ensure that they understand the impact of process improvement and how to do their job. The Process Group will require in-depth training to accomplish the process improvement goals.

- Executive Management High Level Training
- Mid-Management Training
- Staff Kickoff Training.

Appendix I

Major Activity
Action Plan

Monitoring & Control (Organizational) Action Plan

Program Management Office Establishment
Problem Definition/Objectives/Purpose:

A consistent, repeatable method is needed for monitoring projects. The purpose of this task is to develop the processes, templates, and guidelines for management of all projects.

Team Members:

Rod Simpson
Jane Smith
John Jackman.

Piloting Strategy:

Piloting will be accomplished by using the selected projects to accomplish the processes developed and improving with lessons learned as we go along. The PLID project has been selected to try the process out due to their current maturity level and availability. They will try it once or twice, and then the rest of the selected piloting projects will attempt to follow the process. The processes will be tweaked along the way to make it work best for each project as well as give the management team the information they need to monitor projects.

Desired Results:

The key expected result is development of a Program Management Office with processes and templates that allow executive management to monitor projects. It also provides an opportunity to manage issues before they become issues for the customer.

Issues & Risks:

Executive Management buy-in
Executive Management using process for statusing projects.

Timeline/Actions:

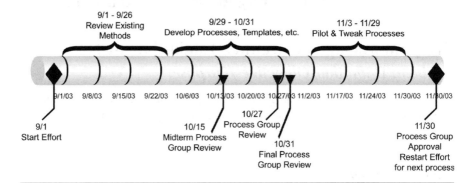

Figure I-1   Timeline/Actions

Deliverables:

Flow Charts (high level and detailed)
Processes
Templates
Specifics to be determined.

Appendix J

Process Template

PROCESS DESCRIPTION

3.2.1—[process name] Process

Purpose: To define the . . .

Entry Criteria:	**Inputs:**
•	•

General Description:

Roles:

In general, the participants in the process may include: [participant roles]. The following describes roles and responsibilities for this process:

[role 1]:	• [responsibility 1]
	• [responsibility n]
[role n]:	• [responsibility 1]
	• [responsibility n]

Activities:

General Flow Diagram

Outputs:	**Exit Criteria:**
•	•

Interfaces and References:

305

Appendix K

CMMI® Process Stop Light Charts

ASSESSMENT INDEX

CMMI Level 2 Process Areas

	Project A	Project B	Project C	Project D	Organizational
RM					
PP					
PMC					
SAM					
M&A					
PPQA					
CM					

CMMI Level 3 Process Areas

	Project A	Project B	Project C	Project D	Organizational
RD					
TS					
PI					
VAL					
VER					
OPF					

(continued)

CMMI Level 3 Process Areas Continued

	Project A	Project B	Project C	Project D	Organizational
OPD					
OT					
IPM					
RKM					
IT					
ISM					
DA&R					
OEI					

Note: All areas start as RED and work up to Green and Blue

Legend

Horizontal		Excellent—ready for assessment
Vertical		Satisfactory—ready for assessment
Diagonal		Partially compliant—not ready for assessment
Grid		Not compliant—not ready for assessment
Dark Gray		Not applicable to project—won't be included in assessment for project

Process Areas
  Maturity Level 2: Managed
    RM = Requirements Management
    PP = Project Planning
    PMC = Project Monitoring and Control
    SAM = Supplier Agreement Management
    M&A = Measurement and Analysis
    PPQA = Process and Product Quality Assurance
    CM = Configuration Management
  Maturity Level 3: Defined
    RD = Requirements Development
    TS = Technical Solution
    PI = Product Integration
    VER = Verification
    VAL = Validation
    OPF = Organizational Process Focus
    OPD = Organizational Process Definition
    OT = Organizational Training
    IPM = Integrated Project Management for IPPD (half goals for IPPD organizations)
    RKM = Risk Management
    IT = Integrated Teaming (for IPPD organizations)
    ISM = Integrated Supplier Management
    DA&R = Decision Analysis and Resolution
    OEI = Organizational Environment for Integration (for IPPD organizations)

Appendix L

Process Group Meeting Agenda

PROCESS GROUP

Meeting Agenda

[date] [time]

1. Updated Master Schedule
   a. Mini-Assessments Updated
2. Tasking Status

Process Group Taskings:

Task	Team Member	Projected Start Date	Projected Due Date	Comments/update

3. PAT Status

Process Action Team Taskings

PAT Name	Lead Team Member	Phase (Planning, Implementation, Piloting, Finalization, Ready for PL)	Projected Due Date	Comments/Update

4. Round Table Discussions

Upcoming Events of Interest:

Date/Time	Event	Location
Jan 19	Martin Luther King Day	
Jan 23	All-Hands/Kick-off Meeting	Main Conference Room

Process Group TDY Schedule:

Team Member	Where	Dates

Next Meeting Scheduled: [date] [time]

Appendix M

Process Group Meeting Minutes

PROCESS GROUP

Meeting Minutes

[date] [time]

Attendees: [attendee names]

General Discussions:

1. Tasking Review and Update

Taskings:

Task	Team Member	Projected Start Date	Projected Due Date

2. Discussion Item [n]

-

Upcoming Events of Interest:

Date/Time	Event	Location
Dec 25	Christmas Holiday	
Jan 1	New Years Day Holiday	

Process Group Holiday Vacation Schedules:

Team Member	Dates

Action Items:

#	Action	Assignee(s)	Due	Status
1				
2				
3				
4				
5				
6				

Next Meeting Scheduled: [date] [time]

Appendix N

Executive Steering Committee Review Meeting Agenda

Executive Steering Committee Review Meeting Agenda

[date] – [time]

[location]

Meeting Agenda

1. Status Summaries
2. Stop Light Charts
3. Schedule (include discussion of critical path)
4. Budget
5. Risks and Risk Mitigation Plans
6. Resources
7. Metrics
8. Issues, Concerns, Problems, Setbacks (Unresolvable—all issues should be resolved at the lowest possible level if possible)
9. Accomplishments

10. Recognition of Individuals
11. Action Items

AI #	Description	Assign To	Assign Date	Due Date	Status/Comments

12. Round Table Discussions

Next Meeting Scheduled: [date] [time]

Appendix O

Executive Steering Committee Review Meeting Minutes

Executive Steering Committee Review Meeting Minutes

[date] – [time]

[location]

Attendees: [name of each attended, . . .]

General Discussions:

1. Status Summaries

   - [general description of discussion, any comments or concerns, any changes, any decisions]
   - . . .

2. Stop Light Charts

   - [general description of discussion, any comments or concerns, any changes, any decisions]
   - . . .

3. Schedule

   • [general description of discussion, any comments or concerns, any changes, any decisions]
   • ...

4. Budget

   • [general description of discussion, any comments or concerns, any changes, any decisions]
   • ...

5. Risks and Risk Mitigation Plans

   • [general description of discussion, any comments or concerns, any changes, any decisions]
   • ...

6. Resources

   • [general description of discussion, any comments or concerns, any changes, any decisions]
   • ...

7. Metrics

   • [general description of discussion, any comments or concerns, any changes, any decisions]
   • ...

8. Issues, Concerns, Problems, Setbacks

   • [general description of discussion, any comments or concerns, any changes, any decisions]
   • ...

9. Accomplishments

   • [general description of discussion, any comments or concerns, any changes, any decisions]
   • ...

10. Recognitions of Individuals

   • [general description of discussion, any comments or concerns, any changes, any decisions]
   • ...

Other Discussions:

1.
2.

Action Items

AI #	Description	Assign To	Assign Date	Due Date	Status/Comments

Next Meeting Scheduled: [date] [time]

Appendix P

Process Notebook Excerpt

This Process Notebook is based on use of the CMMI®. The Process Notebook excerpts include:

1. By Project/Organization (shown is the one for Requirement Management) Process Area
2. Summary (All Process Areas and all Projects and Organization)

Requirements Management (RM) [CMMI Level 2]

CMMI		Practice/ Procedure	Actual Physical Evidence and Notes
Goal			
SG1	Manage Requirements Requirements are managed and inconsistencies with project plans and work products are identified.		
Practices			
SP 1.1	Obtain an Understanding of Requirements Develop an understanding with the requirements providers on the meaning of the requirements.		
. . .			
Goal			
GG 2	Institutionalize a *Managed* Process		
Practices			
GP 2.1	Establish an Organizational Policy Establish and maintain an organizational policy for planning and performing the requirements management process.		
. . .			

[organization] EVIDENCE SUMMARY

CMMI	Practice/ Procedure	Physical Evidence			
		Project A	Project B	Project C	Organizational
Requirements Management (RM) [CMMI Level 2] **Goals**					
SG1	Manage Requirements				
Practices					
SP 1.1	Obtain an Understanding of Requirements	SSDD RVM RTTM Directory Listing of Document under CM Control SDP	RVM with allocation to software Directory Listing of Documents under CM control SDP	RTM with allocation to software Directory Listing of Document under CM Control Tailored Processes IMP	Project Responsibility
. . .					

Appendix Q

Audit Schedule

INTERNAL AUDIT SCHEDULE

FOR

[year]

ID	Target Area	Associated Process(s)	Audit Team	Scheduled Month
1	Process Group			May
2	Training Program			May
3	Management Representative			September
4	Engineering			June
5	Contracts			July
6	Quality Assurance			July
7	Project Management			September
8	Business Operations			August
9	Business Development			October
10	Security			January
11	Procurement			March
12	Human Relations			September
13	Data Management			June
14	Configuration Management			August

Appendix R

Audit Plan

Configuration Management Audit Plan

Date: Target Area/ID:

Scope and Purpose

Criteria

Evaluation Plans and Procedures

Evaluators

Specific Requirements/Planned Contacts

Appendix S

Audit Checklist

Audit Checklist				
Date:			Target Area/ID:	
Scope and Purpose				
ID #	Done	(O)pen (C)losed	Work Product of Process	Comments

Appendix T

Audit Report

Configuration Management Audit Report

Date: Target Area/ID:

Scope and Purpose

Criteria

Evaluation Plans and Procedures

Evaluators

Contacts

Summary of Findings (reference checklist for specifics)

Audit Report

Appendix U

Gap Analysis/Audit Checklist

ISO Section to Quality Record Requirement(s) Mapping

ISO	Section	Quality Record Requirement(s)	How Requirement(s) are Met
9001	4.1.2.1	Identify and record any problems relating to the product, process, and quality system.	
9001	4.1.3	Records of management reviews shall be maintained.	
9001	4.2.3.h	The supplier shall give consideration, as appropriate, to the identification and preparation of quality records.	
9001	4.3.4	Records of contract reviews shall be maintained.	
9001	4.4.6	Records of design reviews shall be maintained.	
9001	4.4.7	The design-verification measures shall be recorded.	
9001	4.6.2.b	Quality records of the previously demonstrated capability and performance of subcontractors shall be maintained.	

(continued)

329

ISO	Section	Quality Record Requirement(s)	How Requirement(s) are Met
9001	4.6.2.c	Establish and maintain quality records of acceptable subcontractors.	
9001	4.7	Any such product that is lost, damaged, or is otherwise unsuitable for use shall be recorded and reported to the customer.	
9001	4.8	Product identification and traceability shall be recorded.	
9001	4.9	Records of process control shall be maintained for qualified processes, equipment, and personnel, as appropriate.	
9001	4.10.2.3	Where incoming product is released for urgent production purposes prior to verification, it shall be positively identified and recorded in order to permit immediate recall and replacement in the event of nonconformity to specified requirements.	
9001	4.10.5	The supplier shall establish and maintain records which provide evidence that the product has been inspected and/or tested. These records shall show clearly whether the product has passed or failed the inspections and/or tests according to defined acceptance criteria. Records shall identify the inspection authority responsible for the release of the product.	
9001	4.11.1	Where test software or comparative references such as test hardware are used as suitable forms of inspection, they shall be checked to prove that they are capable of verifying the acceptability of product, prior to release for use during production, installation, or servicing, and shall be rechecked at prescribed intervals. The supplier shall establish the extent and frequency of such checks and maintain records as evidence of control.	
9001	4.11.2.e	The supplier shall maintain calibration records for inspection, measuring, and test equipment.	
9001	4.13.2	The description of the nonconformity that has been accepted and of repairs, shall be recorded to denote the actual condition.	
9001	4.14.1	The supplier shall implement and record any changes to the documented procedures resulting from corrective and preventative action.	
9001	4.14.2.b	The procedures for corrective action shall include investigation of the cause of nonconformities relating to product, process, and quality system, and recording the results of the investigation.	

(continued)

ISO	Section	Quality Record Requirement(s)	How Requirement(s) are Met
9001	4.14.3.a	The procedures for preventative action shall include the use of appropriate sources of information such as processes and work operations which affect product quality, concessions, audit results, quality records, service reports, and customer complaints to detect, service reports, and customer complaints to detect, analyze, and eliminate potential causes of nonconformities.	
9001	4.16	CONTROL OF QUALITY RECORDS The supplier shall establish and maintain documented procedures for identification, collection, indexing, access, filing, storage, maintenance, and disposition of quality records. Quality records shall be maintained to demonstrate conformance to specified requirements and the effective operation of the quality system. Pertinent quality records from the subcontractor shall be an element of these data. All quality records shall be legible and shall be stored and retained in such a way that they are readily retrievable in facilities that provide a suitable environment to prevent damage or deterioration and to prevent loss. Retention times of quality records shall be established and recorded. Where agreed contractually, quality records shall be made available for evaluation by the customer's representative for an agreed period. NOTE 19 Records may be in the form of any type of media, such as hard copy or electronic media.	
9001	4.17	The results of audits shall be recorded. Follow-up audit activities shall verify and record the implementation and effectiveness of the corrective action taken.	
9001	4.18	Appropriate records of training shall be kept.	
9000-3	4.1.1.2.1.b	Identify and record any product quality problems.	
9000-3	4.1.1.3	Records of management reviews shall be maintained.	
9000-3	4.3	The results of internal quality system audits shall be documented and brought to the attention of the personnel having responsibility in the area audited.	
9000-3	5.3.1	The purchaser's requirements specification records functional requirements.	

(continued)

ISO	Section	Quality Record Requirement(s)	How Requirement(s) are Met
9000-3	5.4.3	Progress reviews should be planned, held, and documented to ensure that outstanding resource issues are resolved and to ensure effective execution of development plans.	
9000-3	5.6.4	Records of design and implementation reviews should be maintained.	
9000-3	5.7.3.a	The test results should be recorded as defined in the relevant specification.	
9000-3	5.7.3.b	Any discovered problems and their possible impacts to any other parts of the software should be noted and those responsible notified so the problems can be tracked until they are solved.	
9000-3	5.8.1	The method of handling problems detected during the acceptance procedure and their disposition should be agreed between the purchaser and supplier and should be documented.	
9000-3	5.10.5	All changes made during software maintenance should be documented in accordance with the procedures for document control and configuration management.	
9000-3	5.10.6	All maintenance activities should be recorded in predefined formats and maintained. Rules for the submission of maintenance reports should be established and agreed upon by the supplier and purchaser. Maintenance records should include the following items for each software item being maintained: a. list of requests for assistance or problem reports that have been received and the current status of each b. organization responsible for responding to requests for assistance or implementing the appropriate corrective actions c. priorities that have been assigned to the corrective actions d. results of the corrective actions e. statistical data on failure occurrences and maintenance activities. The record of the maintenance activities may be used for evaluation and enhancement of the software product and for improvement of the quality system itself.	
9000-3	5.10.7.e	Release procedures should include requirements for records indicating which changes have been implemented and at what locations, for multiple products and sites.	

(continued)

ISO	*Section*	*Quality Record Requirement(s)*	*How Requirement(s) are Met*
9000-3	6.1.3.3	The supplier should establish and maintain procedures to record, manage, and report on the status of software items, of change requests, and of the implementation of approved changes.	
9000-3	6.3	The supplier shall establish and maintain procedures for identification, collection, indexing, filing, storage, maintenance, and disposition of quality records. Quality records shall be maintained to demonstrate achievement of the required quality and the effective operation of the quality system. Pertinent subcontractor quality records shall be an element of these data. All quality records shall be legible and identifiable to the product involved. Quality records shall be stored and maintained in such a way that they are readily retrievable in facilities that provide a suitable environment to minimize deterioration or damage and prevent loss. Retention times of quality records shall be established and recorded. When agreed contractually, quality records shall be made available for evaluation by the purchaser or his representative for an agreed period.	
9000-3	6.7.2	The supplier shall establish and maintain records of acceptable subcontractors, including records of subcontractors' previously demonstrated capability and performance.	

Appendix V

Sample Criteria Grids

Sample Criteria Grid 1:

Weak	Satisfactory	Strong	Criteria	Reviewer's Comments
			Assertion: clarity, importance	
			Evidence: relevance, strength, credibility	
			Organization: arrangement of ideas	
			Mechanics: spelling, grammar, punctuation	
			Overall effectiveness	

Sample Criteria Grid 2:

Criteria	Weak	Fair	Strong	Comments
Layout/Organization				
Table of contents/page numbers?				
Structure (organization into sections, subsections, appendices)?				
Figures and tables (clearly labeled and professional)?				
Clearly stated purpose and objective(s)?				
Accomplished its purpose?				
Good overall structure? Ideas ordered effectively?				

(continued)

Sample Criteria Grid 2: Continued

Criteria	Weak	Fair	Strong	Comments
Transitions used?				
Introduction & conclusion focus clearly on the main point?				
Paragraphs right length?				
Development & Support				
Major ideas/topics well developed?				
Supporting material persuasive?				
Adequate references and resource materials?				
Unnecessary repetition avoided?				
Style				
Topic and level of formality?				
Sentences and words varied?				
Wordiness?				
Grammar and Mechanics				
Grammar?				
Spelling?				
Punctuation?				
Recommend three specific changes:				
1.				
2.				
3.				

Sample Criteria Grid 3:

Criteria	1	2	3	4	5	Rating
Implementation	Extremely difficult	Very difficult	Moderately difficult	Somewhat easy	Easy	
Timing	Long term	Lengthy	Moderate	Reasonably quick	Very quick	
Cost	None	Some	Moderate	Significant	Large	
ROI	Extensively below limit	Somewhat below limit	Meets limit	Somewhat above limit	Extensively above limit	
Understandability	Extensive training needed	A lot of training needed	Some training needed	Little training needed	No training needed	
Fits organizational strategy	No	Minimally	Moderately	Well	Very well	
Resource requirements	Extensive	Significant	Some	Little	None	
Compatibility	No	Significant changes needed	Moderate changes needed	Minor changes needed	Yes	
Fits organizational culture	No	Some	Moderately	Very	Yes	

Appendix W

APIM Checklist

APIM CHECKLIST

Complete	Step	Objectives
Pre Maturity		
	Launch	• Executive Approvals
	Launch	• Set Process Improvement Goals
	Launch	• Task Authorization
	Launch	• Executive Steering Committee
	Launch	• Initial resources/Appointments
	Launch	• Budget
	Planning	• Kickoff Meeting(s)
	Planning	• Develop Brief Action Plan
	Planning	• Communications Planning
	Planning	• Data Management Planning
	Planning	• Issue Resolution Planning
	Planning	• Process Peer Review Planning
	Planning	• Process Format Planning
	Planning	• Quality Assurance Liaison Planning
	Planning	• Risk Management Planning
	Planning	• Tool Planning: databases, techniques, methods, and models
	Planning	• Detail Master Schedule
	Planning	• Develop metrics and measures

(continued)

Complete	Step	Objectives
	Planning	• Select projects
	Planning	• PAT Action planning
	Planning	• Establish regular status meetings and reports
	Planning	• Process Group meeting planning
	Planning	• Executive Steering Committee
	Planning	• Plan and conduct training: organizational and Process Group
Maturity Cycle		
	Awareness	• Conduct mini-assessment to identify strengths and weaknesses— initial and progress
	Awareness	• Select mini-assessment methodology
	Awareness	• Compose mini-assessment team
	Awareness	• Conduct Pre mini-assessment activities
	Awareness	• Conduct mini-assessment activities
	Awareness	• Conduct Post mini-assessment activities
	Awareness	• Baseline mini-assessment results
	Triage	• Prioritize actions using triage approach
	Triage	• Develop key selection criteria
	Triage	• Conduct Process Group Meeting to prioritize
	Triage	• Manage actions
	Resolution	• Establish Process Action Teams
	Resolution	• Develop action plan
	Resolution	• Resolve process action or issue as assigned — Develop processes (remember KISS) • Process flows • Policies • Procedures • Forms • Templates
	Resolution	• Conduct Peer Reviews
	Resolution	• Report status and any issues
	Resolution	• Propose a solution to the problem
	Resolution	• Train staff involved in pilot
	Resolution	• Pilot test the solution mentoring staff throughout
	Resolution	• Manage actions
	Training	• Determine methods to be used for training
	Training	• Prepare training materials
	Training	• Conduct training
	Training	• Accomplish post training assessment
	Deployment	• Pilot processes to selected project
	Deployment	• Tweak processes, as needed
	Deployment	• Mentor pilot project(s)
	Trial	• Assess effectiveness of processes
	Trial	• Determine outcome
	Trial	• Deploy processes
	Trial	• Collect & analyze lessons learned

(continued)

Complete	Step	Objectives
Post Maturity		
	Appraise	• Determine maturity level
	Appraise	• Identify strengths and weakness for future improvement
	Improve	• Keep the momentum going
	Improve	• Develop Continuing Process Improvement Plan
		— Improvement measures
		— Audit Plans
		— Audit Reports
		— Periodic Progress Assessments
		— Updated Risks
		— Updated Budget
		— Updated Action Plan
		— Task completion criteria
	Improve	• Audit Processes
	Improve	• Conduct training assessment

Appendix X

Acronyms

ACM	Association of Computing Machinery
ACWP	Actual Cost of Work Performance
APIM	Accelerated Process Improvement Methodology
BCWP	Budgeted Cost of Work Performance
BCWP	Budgets Cost of Work Performance
BCWS	Budgets Cost of Work Scheduled
BMS	Business Management System
BPM	Business Process Management
BPR	Business Process Reengineering
CAR	Causal Analysis and Resolution
CBA IPI	CMM-Based Appraisal for Internal Process Improvement
CEO	Chief Executive Officer
CM	Configuration Management
CMM®	Capability Maturity Models
CMMI®	CMM Integration
COBIT	Control Objectives for Information and related Technology
CPI	Cost Performance Index
CV	Cost Variance
DAR	Decision Analysis and Resolution
DFD	Data Flow Diagram
EIA/IS	Electronic Industries Alliance/Interim Standard
ESSI	European Systems and Software Initiative
ETVX	Entry-Task-Validation-Exit
ETXM	Entry-Task-eXit-Measure
ICAM	Integrated Computer-Aided Manufacturing

IDEAL	Initiating, Diagnosing, Establishing, Acting, and Leveraging
IDEF	Integrated Computer-Aided Manufacturing (ICAM) Definition
IEEE	Institute of Electrical and Electronics Engineers
IPM	Integrated Project Management
ISM	Integrated Supplier Management
ISO	International Organization for Standardization
IT	Information Technology
KISS	Keep It Short and Simple
LOC	lines of code
MA	Measurement and Analysis
MOF	Microsoft® Operations Framework
ODC	Other Direct Cost
OEI	Organizational Environment for Integration
OID	Organizational Innovation and Deployment
OPD	Organizational Process Definition
OPF	Organizational Process Focus
OPIAP	Overall Process Improvement Action Plan
OPP	Organizational Process Performance
OT	Organizational Training
PAT	Process Action Team
P-CMM®	People CMM
PDCA	The Plan-Do-Check-Act
PDSA	The Plan-Do-Study-Act
PI	Process Improvement
PMBOK®	Project Management Body of Knowledge
PMC	Project Monitoring and Control
PMI	Project Management Institute
PMP®	Project Management Professionals
POO	Probability of Occurrence
PP	Project Planning
PPQA	Process and Product Quality Assurance
PSP^{SM}	Personal Software Process
QPM	Quantitative Project Management
RD	Requirements Development
REQM	Requirements Management
RSKM	Risk Management
SADT	Structured Analysis and Design Technique
SAM	Supplier Agreement Management
SAVI	Somatic, auditory, visual, intellectual
SCAMPI^{SM}	Standard CMMI® Appraisal Method for Process Improvement
SECM	System Engineering Capability Model
SEI	Software Engineering Institutes
SEPG	Software Engineering Process Group
SOI	Severity of Impact
SPI	Schedule Performance Index
SPICE	Software Process Improvement and Capability dEtermination
SPIRE	Software Process Improvement in Regions of Europe
SV	Schedule Variance
SWAG	Scientific Wild Anatomical Guess
SW-CMM®	Software Capability Maturity Model
SWOT	Strengths/Weakness/Opportunities/Threats

TQM	Total Quality Management
TS	Technical Solution
TSP^{SM}	Team Software Process
VAL	Validation
VER	Verification
WBS	Work Breakdown Structure
XP	eXtreme Programming

Appendix Y

Glossary of Key Terms

Accelerated Process Improvement Methodology (APIM)	The APIM takes an agile approach with simplicity and common sense the magic words. Many times organizations tend to over-process with multiple forms, plans, and procedures that end up being meaningless. The APIM has three phases: Pre Maturity, Maturity, and Post Maturity. Each phase consists of various steps required to develop an organization's maturity.
Process Maturity	Process Maturity means constant change and evolution in a new direction in terms of an organization's way of accomplishing their business. Along with Process Maturity comes a new adjustment to the way things are done.
Process Improvement	Process Improvement puts the focus on the process in order to make the product better. It gives project staff and organizational staff members a consistent method of getting the same work done in the same general way, not technically but administratively thus not reinventing the wheel each time a new effort is started and utilizing the valuable lessons learned from previous efforts.
Process	The method in which organizations accomplish business whether it's manual or automated. It is a means of documenting, organizing, and controlling the ways organizations accomplish business.

Plan-Do-Check (Study)-Act Cycle (aka PDSA Cycle or PDCA Cycle or Shewhart Cycle or Deming Cycle)	The PDSA Cycle indicates an uphill progression of never-ending improvement; when you complete one cycle another is started on its heels. The PDSA Cycle is a four-step process: Planning, Doing, Studying, and Acting.
IDEAL^{SM} Model	The IDEAL^{SM} Model that was developed by the SEI for process improvement. This model defines five basic stages: Initiating, Diagnosing, Establishing, Acting, and Leveraging.
Structured Analysis and Design Technique (SADT)	The SADT was developed in the early 1970s by Doug Ross, Softech/MIT. It is used extensively in modeling systems. The diagrams are arranged in a hierarchy to show increasingly more detail at lower levels.
Integrated Computer Aided Manufacturing (ICAM) Definition (IDEF)	The IDEF is based on the SADT modeling technique. It is a family of methods that supports modeling of an enterprise and business area. It was originally developed for systems engineering but has been evolved to support other areas of modeling.
Data Flow Diagrams (DFD)	DFDs identify the functional components and indicate the data that flows between the function components. They are used primarily for data discovery. These diagrams provide a useful tool for developing process diagrams as well to show how data flows through the process.
Role Activity Diagrams (RAD)	The RAD is a Role-Based Model that groups activities into roles. It is a flowchart-type notation that depicts a business in terms of roles and their interactions.
Petri Net	The Petri Net is a Role-Based Model that groups activities into roles. A key feature of this method is the depiction of concurrently occurring events.
Entry-Task-Validation-eXit (ETVX)	The ETVX is a popular process model that is expressed as a set of interconnected activities with attributes of entry, task, validation, and exit. In this task-based model, every cell is oriented around a task. The combined cells are combined to create processes.
Entry-Task-eXit-Measure (ETXM)	The ETXM takes the ETXV a step further by adding measures. It is used extensively for Process Improvement.
Flowcharting	Flowcharting has been used effectively for many years to visualize software but it is equally as effective in visualizing a process for process improvement. The method provides a graphical representation of a process, depicting inputs, outputs, decision points, and units of activity where the steps are represented in boxes and each arrow represents the sequence of steps. It can be used with whatever level of detail is needed, allowing for analysis and optimization as needed.
Chunking	Chunking is a method used to organize and arrange information so that it is easier to read, understand, access, and retrieve. It is a method of subdividing and organizing into short "chunks" of information in a uniform format.
Information Mapping®	Information Mapping® provides a method of organizing information in such a way as to make it more visual and thus more understandable. This method has evolved over time, providing a structured method of visualizing information based on how the human brain reads, processes, remembers, and retrieves information.

Organizational Process Library	The organizational process library is typically where processes are stored. It typically includes all process-related artifacts such as guidelines, templates, checklists, diagrams, tools, etc.
Agile Programming Methodologies	A grouping of new methodologies for developing software. Agile Programming Methodologies have been receiving more and more attention since the early 1990s. Several agile methodologies have evolved during the last several years. There are several recurring themes in the agile methodologies. These include short iterations, close collaboration both with customers and within development team, open communications, frequent deliveries, tight teaming, simplicity, refactoring, continuous testing, and proactive plan management.
Refactoring	Refactoring is the process of reworking any written material to improve its readability or structure while keeping the meaning or behavior intact.
PMBOK®	PMBOK® is the PMI's standards document. It "includes proven, traditional practices which are widely applied, as well as innovative and advanced ones which have seen more limited use."
International Organization for Standardization (ISO) 9001	ISO 9001 is part of the ISO 9000 family of international quality management standards and guidelines. It provides the requirements for certification by ISO as being a developer of quality products which refers to "services, processed material, hardware and software intended for, or required by, your customer."
Software Capability Maturity Model® (SW-CMM®)	The SW-CMM® is based on the "vision" of Watts Humphrey. It is based upon what the SEI found were best practices of many successful organizations, as well as process management concepts of well-known software engineering and management gurus like Walter Shewart, Philip Crosby, W. Edwards Deming, and Joseph Juran. It provides a framework for generating and maturing software processes for organizations.
Capability Maturity Model® Integration (CMMI®)	CMMI® integrated the SW-CMMI® with several other models, making it applicable to system development as opposed to just software development. The biggest difference is that the CMMI® takes a systems-level approach rather than a software-specific approach to processes needed to make projects successful.
Software Engineering Institute's (SEI) Personal Software Process (PSP^{SM})	The PSP^{SM} is a methodology for engineers based upon the practices set forth in the CMMI®. It helps engineers make more accurate and realistic estimates and develop products with the needed quality, within budget, while meeting all customer commitments.
Software Engineering Institute's (SEI) Team Software Process (TSP^{SM})	The TSP^{SM} methodology is based on the practices set forth by the CMMI® but it is intended for use by teams. Team members must be PSP^{SM}-trained engineers prior to being part of a TSP^{SM} since TSP^{SM} is built upon the foundation of the CMM® and PSP^{SM}. The TSP^{SM} acts as "a guide in forming and managing high-performance integrated product teams." It is intended for software teams of three to twenty engineers with the proper training in PSP^{SM} and TSP^{SM}.

People Capability Maturity Model® (P-CMM®)	The P-CMM® concentrates on the people side of Process Improvement. It focuses on "improving the management and development of human assets." This includes knowledge development, skill development, and staff motivation.
Software Process Improvement and Capability dEtermination (SPICE)	SPICE is a major initiative to support institution of an international standard to be used to assess a software process.
Total Quality Management (TQM)	TQM is a process for managing quality as well as a philosophy of perpetual improvement. It was a very popular philosophy in the 1980s.
Software Process Improvement in Regions of Europe (SPIRE)	The SPIRE project concentrates on Process Improvement projects for small software developers.
Microsoft® Operations Framework (MOF)	The MOF is a set of processes developed by Microsoft® for management of distributed IT systems.
Control OBjectives for Information and related Technology (COBIT)	COBIT provides a Management Guideline and Maturity Model that identifies critical success factors, key goal indicators, key performance indicators, and a maturity model for governing IT projects.
Business Process Reengineering (BPR) and Business Process Management (BPM)	In an effort to improve the way a company does business, BPR/BPM was adapted by many companies in the 1990s. BPR/BPM is a key methodology for restructuring business operations to give them that needed competitive advantage.
System Engineering Capability Model (SECM) also called Electronic Industries Association/ Interim Standard (EIA/IS) 731	The SECM, sometimes called the SE-CMM®, is a model for improving and appraising systems engineering processes. It was a major model used in the CMMI® project. It provides the systems engineering aspect to the CMMI® with focus on "plateaus of performance" that organizations must achieve to improve their system engineering processes.
Six Sigma	Six Sigma is a quality improvement methodology focused on reduction of product and services failure rate.
Knowledge Management	Harnessing information within an organization for use when it's needed, by whom it's needed, and where it's needed, is the primary purpose of knowledge management. It focuses on making good use of data collected and investments in data by organizations.
Keep It Short and Simple (KISS)	The KISS principle can be used effectively in a number of ways. For example: • To put easy to use, succinct processes in place • To put useable "living" plans in place for Process Improvement • To put many basic elements in place quickly to kick things off thus building a foundation for continued improvement.
Key success criteria	APIM defines nine key success criteria that are important for an organization to possess or attain prior to undertaking a Process Improvement effort.

CMMI® Continuous Model	CMMI® Continuous Model allows organizations to choose a Process Area to concentrate upon. It is composed of Capability Levels where each Capability Level is composed of a set of practices relating to a single Process Area.
CMMI® Staged Model	The CMMI® Staged Model has staged levels much like a staircase which allows organizations to climb their way to success. Each Maturity Level is composed of various Process Areas which contain the practice's key for success of organizations and associated projects.
Maturity Levels	These levels show where an organization is in developing processes based on the best practices defined by the CMMI®. Each level is a layer in the foundation to a mature organization. The five levels are initial, managed, defined, quantitatively managed, and optimizing.
Process Areas	The process areas define the activities that must be performed in order to meet that maturity level. These are all based on best industry practices.
Specific Goals	The goals provide a summary of the practices with the specific goals related to the specific practices. Each of these specific goals is considered key to enhancing process capability.
Generic Goals	The goals provide a summary of the practices with the generic goals related to the generic practices. Each of these generic goals is considered key to enhancing process capability. The same generic goals are included in multiple process areas.
Specific Practices	These practices are the activities designated as important to achieving the associated goals. They describe processes that organizations will typically implement.
Generic Practices	These practices are the activities that ensure the processes developed to meet the specific process areas will be effective, repeatable, and lasting.
Commitment to Perform	One of the common features used to indicate whether the implementation and institutionalization of a Process Area is effective, repeatable, and lasting. Commitment to Perform is the organizational expectations for processes. The key is organizational direction from senior management.
Ability to Perform	One of the common features used to indicate whether the implementation and institutionalization of a Process Area is effective, repeatable, and lasting. Ability to Perform is what is needed to perform the process and achieve established objectives. The key is the plan, resources, assigned responsibility, training, process definition.
Directing Implementation	One of the common features used to indicate whether the implementation and institutionalization of a Process Area is effective, repeatable, and lasting. Directing Implementation is the establishment of product integrity. The key is managing products through configuration, stakeholder involvement, process monitor and control, and measures.

Verifying Implementation	One of the common features used to indicate whether the implementation and institutionalization of a Process Area is effective, repeatable, and lasting. Verifying Implementation is the credible assurance that the established processes are being followed. The key is to evaluate adherence and management review.
CMMI® Categories	The CMMI® process areas can be separated into four areas or categories: Project Management, Process Management, Engineering, and Support.
CMMI® Process Areas	The process areas separate the practices into succinct areas for concentration. Each Maturity Level is composed of Process Areas that define the activities needed to meet the needs to the success of attaining a particular level.
CMMI® Goals	The goals are absolute, they are what needs to be done for implementation of that Process Area. The specific and generic goals are required to meet the requirements of the associated Maturity Level. These are what are used during appraisals to determine where an organization falls in terms of process maturity.
CMMI® Practices	Specific practices are for implementation to satisfy the goals where the generic practices provide for institutionalization to satisfy the goals.
Pre Maturity Phase	The Pre Maturity Phase consists of steps that need to be accomplished in preparation for the Process Improvement effort. This phase will set the stage for later phases. It is the key to getting early buy-in from key managers and the resources needed to get the effort off to a good start.
Maturity Phase	The Maturity Phase is iterative. It is repeated until an organization is ready for a more formal appraisal or for continued Process Improvement. This is the most critical phase in the process because this is where most of the real work is accomplished.
Post Maturity Phase	The Post Maturity Phase consists of steps that should be accomplished when the organization decides it is ready to move away from the APIM and into a formal appraisal or continuous improvement.
Wideband Delphi	The Wideband Delphi method is the most popular method used for estimating, especially when little or no historical data is available. It helps to filter out some of the more extreme early estimates and disregards politics that may impact the estimates.
Earned Value Management	Earned Value Management is based on the work that is accomplished; the value of that work is "earned".
PERT Chart	The PERT Chart is used in scheduling to depict the schedule as a flowchart that shows all tasks and task dependencies. The tasks are represented by boxes and task dependencies are represented by lines connecting the boxes.
Gantt Chart	The Gantt Chart is used in scheduling to depict the schedule as a graphical representation with horizontal bars. The activities are listed down one side and the other side provides the dates across the top with the horizontal bars showing the duration.

Work Breakdown Structure (WBS)	A Work Breakdown Structure (WBS) provides a foundation for defining the actual work that needs to be accomplished. It helps further define the cost estimates, schedule estimates, risk management, resource allocation, role definition, assigned responsibilities, and any make/buy/reuse decisions that must be made on any project. The WBS organizes the activities defined for the project in a hierarchical structure. The method used to organize the activities will be dependent upon the specific reporting needs of the organization and the method selected to report activity status.
Master Schedule	The Master Schedule provides a calendarization of the project plan. A schedule can serve many purposes, including documenting the baseline schedule, documenting actual work completed performance dates, documenting forecasted dates for work not yet begun, and tracking completed work as planned.
Action Plan	The Action Plan provides the detailed activities that are required to help an organization meet their Process Improvement goals.
Probability of Occurrence (POO)	POO is used in Risk Management to calculate Magnitude of a risk. It is the likelihood of the risk occurring.
Severity of Impact (SOI)	SOI is used in Risk Management to calculate Magnitude of a risk. It is the effect that the risk will have if it does occur.
Magnitude	Magnitude is used in Risk Management. It is calculated by POO × SOI = Magnitude.
Stop Light Charts/ Assessment Index	Stop Light Charts/Assessment Index indicate the baseline results from a mini-assessment. They depict the status of each project and the organization for each Process Improvement requirement.
Mini-assessments	Mini-assessments can be used very effectively for determining the status of the Process Improvement effort.
Process Notebook/ Implementation Matrix	Process Notebook/Implementation Matrix can be used for each project and organizationally to ensure that Process Improvement elements requirements are being met. They allow a mapping of each process area to the organizational processes and procedures thus ensuring that goals are met.
Brainstorming	Brainstorming is usually a meeting where ideas are offered freely. A key is to avoid any criticism of ideas no matter how outrageous. Typically discussions are held until all ideas are on the table. They can be very useful in uncovering all possible ideas and approaches. These sessions are sometimes called Cerebral Popcorn.
Criteria Grid	Criteria Grid can be used effectively for many different purposes such as peer reviews, decision-making, idea rating, or anything that has criteria to be evaluated.
FishBone	FishBone is also called a Cause and Effect Diagram or Ishikawa Diagram. It examines the potential or real causes that result in a single effect. The lines coming from the main horizontal line are the main causes and the lines coming from those are the subcauses. The causes are drawn according to their importance. This can help identify the root causes or areas where problems exist. It also compares the importance of relationships with various factors influencing issue or problem.

Force Field Analysis	Force Field Analysis is a tool that analyzes opposing forces involved in change initiatives to facilitate decision making. It is based on the premise that change is a result of a struggle between forces of resistance and driving forces:

forces impeding change → ← forces favoring change

	This method helps to identify the best method to implement. The resisting forces are listed on one side and the driving forces are listed on the other. Either a score can be assigned to each or a decision can be made based on having the most or least forces.
Nominal Group Process	Nominal Group Process is a method for structuring groups to allow individual judgments to be pooled. These judgments are used when there is uncertainty or disagreement about the nature of the problem and possible solutions. It helps in identification of problems, exploration of solutions, and establishment of priorities. It ensures a balanced participation of group participants.
SWOT (Strengths/ Weaknesses/ Opportunities/Threats)	SWOT focuses on the internal and external environments, examining strengths and weaknesses in the internal environment and opportunities and threats in the external environment. This tool is used in industry extensively to analyze their strategies but it can be used effectively for a Process Group with the external environment being the rest of the organization.
The rule of 7 Plus or Minus 2	The rule of 7 Plus or Minus 2 is based on the premise that individuals have limited processing capabilities and limited storing capacities. It says that individuals can store approximately seven pieces of information in their brain at any given time.
Critical path	A critical path can be identified on a schedule once the tasks have been defined. This path represents the sequence of activities which take the longest total time to ensure that the entire project finishes on time. Each task on the critical path becomes a critical task.
Initial Mini-Assessment	The initial mini-assessment will set the baseline for progress mini-assessments.
Progress mini-assessments	Progress mini-assessments are accomplished for each iteration of the maturity phase as illustrated in the APIM diagram or on an event-driven basis. The initial mini-assessment baseline is used as a yardstick and the areas that were identified as weak concentrated upon.
Triage	Triage is from an old French word, *trier*, which means "to sort". It has been used in the treatment of patients, especially battle and disaster victims, according to a system of priorities designed to maximize the number of survivors. It can be effectively used in Process Improvement to prioritize actions needed to improve the organization's processes.
Pair Programming	In eXtreme programming and other agile methodologies, the code is developed by two people who work together at one computer. It is recommended that they slide the keyboard and mouse back and forth, allowing each one the opportunity to contribute either physically or tactically. The one not at the keyboard thinks through the problem to solve it, while the other one accomplishes the physical inputs of information. They take turns doing and thinking. It is important that both members are able to see the monitor most of the time or it isn't true pair programming.

SAVI	Many training organizations are using an accelerated learning technique called SAVI which applies basic brain principles to learning. These brain principles are: somatic (S), auditory (A), visual (V), and intellectual (I). These principles are related to learning in order to provide the optimal learning experience.
Standard Capability Maturity Models Integration (CMMI®) Assessment Method for Process Improvement (SCAMPI^{SM})	SCAMPI^{SM} is a series of assessments with the purpose of providing "benchmark quality ratings." It comes in three different versions, each developed for various purposes. The three version are: SCAMPI^{SM} Class C → approach, SCAMPI^{SM} Class B → deployment, and SCAMPI^{SM} Class A → implementation.
Process Improvement Manager	The Process Improvement Manager spearheads the Process Improvement effort.
Process Group	All Process Improvement revolves around this group. They are responsible for planning and implementing the Process Improvement effort. They are typically composed of a group of organizational staff with diverse skills spanning all areas associated with the Process Improvement goals.
Process Action Team (PAT)	A PAT is established to tackle the actions for the Process Improvement effort. They are typically selected based on their knowledge and experience with a specific area as well as their availability.
Executive Steer Committee	This important committee will set the direction and goals for the Process Improvement effort. They will ensure that the appropriate resources are available for the process group. They are typically formed prior to the Process Improvement effort to accomplish the early planning efforts and kick the project off. Once the Process Improvement effort has started they will act as the in between for the Process Group and Executive Management.
Chaos Theory	The Chaos Theory is about finding the underlying order in apparently random data. It comes from the fact that the systems that the theory describes are apparently disordered but having an underlying order. This theory of chaos is directly related to managing organizational change. You can't always predict what a system will do next but you can put things in motion in smaller ways to perpetuate changes on a large scale. How a pattern eventually looks is very dependent upon the initial conditions that are set up.
Open Systems Organizations	Open Systems helps define organizational structures. The use of the term open systems for defining organizations comes from the comparison to the human body or our biological cells, as well as our solar system, in that they are all engaged in active transactions with their environment. Dr. Uhlfelder states that "An open system has certain characteristics that need to be understood if one is going to work in and change it."
Everett Roger's Adoption Curve	Everett Roger's Adoption Curve is a theory concerned with how new ideas are disseminated and accepted by groups of people.
Deductive Marketing	Deductive Marketing is where the marketer presumes what the customer wants based on their needs.

Inductive Marketing	Inductive Marketing in essence tells the customer what they want or induces products onto the market.
The Perspective Factor	The Perspective Factor basically tells us that what you see is relative to where you're standing. When dealing with others' realities, we have to see things from their perspective and make it relative to them. How you see something depends on what vantage point you're coming from. We all look at things differently based on our background, education, experience, and simply from where we are standing at the moment.
Information Portals	Information Portals provide an open environment for managing and delivering knowledge, applications, and services. It provides a single integration point in order to provide a multitude of varied information to diverse users. There are many types of portals defined, but the portal discussed here refers to the enterprise or intranet portal for organizations to manage applications and information, or also called business to employees (B2E) portals.
Business Intelligence (BI)	Business Intelligence (BI) software can virtually provide users with information on demand. This technology provides timely access to relevant data from a variety of data sources.
Stakeholders	Stakeholders include anyone that is affected by the project and the resulting products, such as managers, including executive, mid-level, and project managers; all staff members; all customers and end-users. In other words nearly everyone.

Appendix Z

Useful Web Sites

http://www.sei.cmu.edu/
http://www.pmi.org/
http://www.standishgroup.com/
http://www.standishgroup.com/quarterly_reports/
http://www.iso.org/
http://www.sqi.gu.edu.au/
http://www.cse.dcu.ie/spire/
http://www.whomovedmycheese.com/
http://www.stsc.hill.af.mil/
http://www.stsc.hill.af.mil/crosstalk/
http://www.dci.com/si/
http://www.portalsmag.com/
http://www.portalscommunity.com/
http://www.extremeprogramming.org/
http://agilemanifesto.org/
http://www.agilealliance.com/
http://www.gantthead.com/
http://www.kpmg.ca/en/
http://www.informationweek.com/
http://www.around.com/
http://www.forrester.com/

References

1. Appraisal Requirements for CMMI^{SM}, Version 1.1 (ARC, V1.1) *Technical Report*, CMU/SEI-2001-TR-034, December 2001.

2. Brooks, Frederick P. *The Mythical Man-Month: Essays on Software Engineering, 20th Anniversary Edition*, Addison-Wesley Publishing Company, Reading, Massachusetts; 1st edition, August 2, 1995.

3. Capability Maturity Model® Integration (CMMI^{SM}), Version 1.1 CMMI^{SM} for Software Engineering (CMMI-SW, V1.1) Continuous Representation CMU/SEI-2002-TR-028 ESC-TR-2002-028, March 2002.

4. Capability Maturity Model® Integration (CMMI^{SM}), Version 1.1 CMMI^{SM} for Software Engineering (CMMI-SW, V1.1) Staged Representation CMU/SEI-2002-TR-029 ESC-TR-2002-029, March 2002.

5. Capability Maturity Model^{SM} for Software, Version 1.1 Technical Report CMU/SEI-93-TR-024 ESC-TR-93-177, February 1993.

6. Carnegie Mellon University. *CMMI^{SM} for Systems Engineering/Software Engineering, Version 1.1, Staged Representation*, CMU/SEI-2002-TR-002. Pittsburg, Pennsylvania: Carnegie Mellon University, December 2001.

7. Carnegie Mellon University. *IDEAL^{SM}: A Users Guide for Software process Improvement*. CMU/SEI-96-HB-001. Pittsburg, Pennsylvania: Carnegie Mellon University, February 1996.

8. Carroll, Lewis. *Alice's Adventures in Wonderland and Through the Looking Glass*, Signet Classics; Reissue edition, Penguin Putnam Inc, New York, New York, December 1, 2000.

9. *CHAOS: A Recipe For Success*, 1998, Standish Group, published 1999.

10. *CHAOS Reports*, www.standishgroup.com.

11. Chiocchi Roger. *Inductive vs. Deductive Marketing: The Paradigm Shift*, Journal of Integrated Marketing Communications, Northwestern University, 1999–2000.

12. CMM^SM-Based Appraisal for Internal Process Improvement (CBA IPI): Method Description Technical Report CMU/SEI-96-TR-007 ESC-TR-96-007, April 1996.

13. Deming, W. Edwards. *Out of the Crisis*, The MIT Press, Cambridge, Massachusetts, 1st edition, August 11, 2000.

14. Desmond, Michael. *Portal Potential*, Portals Magazine, October 2002.

15. Drucker, Peter F. *The Essential Drucker : The Best of Sixty Years of Peter Drucker's Essential Writings on Management*, HarperBusiness, July 2003.

16. Frederick R. Bernard, *Printers' Ink*, March 1927.

17. Gleick, James. *Chaos: Making a New Science*, Penguin (Non-Classics); Reprint edition, December 1, 1988.

18. Humphrey, Watts. *A Discipline for Software Engineering*. Reading, Massachusetts: Addison-Wesley, 1995.

19. Humphrey, Watts. *Managing the Software Process*. Reading, Massachusetts: Addison-Wesley, 1990.

20. Johnson, Spencer. *The Present, The Secret to Enjoying Your Work and Life, Now!*, Doubleday, September 23, 2003.

21. Johnson, Spencer. *Who Moved My Cheese? An Amazing Way to Deal with Change in Your Work and in Your Life*, Putnam Pub Group, September 1, 1998.

22. Jones, Caper. Programming Productivity (McGraw-Hill Series in Software Engineering and Technology), McGraw-Hill Companies, January 1, 1986.

23. Key Practices of the Capability Maturity Model^SM, Version 1.1 Technical Report CMU/SEI-93-TR-025 ESC-TR-93-178, February 1993.

24. Ould, M.A., C. Roberts. *Modelling iteration in the software process*, Proceedings of the Third International Software Process Workshop, Breckenridge, Colorado, USA, 17–19 November 1986, IEEE Computer Society Press.

25. McConnell, Steve. *Software Project Survival Guide*, Microsoft Press, Redmond, Washington, November 14, 1997.

26. Paulk, M. C., C. A. Weber, B. Curtis, and M. B. Chrissis. *The Capability Maturity Model: Guidelines for Improving the Software Process*. Reading, Massachusetts: Addison-Wesley, 1995.

27. People Capability Maturity Model® (P.CMM®) Version 2.0 CMU/SEI-2001-MM-01, July 2001.

28. People CMM®-Based Assessment Method Description Version 1.0, August 1998.

29. Pike, Robert W. *Creative Training Techniques Handbook: Tips, Tactics, and How-To's for Delivering Effective Training*, Human Resource Development Press; 3rd edition, January 1, 2003.

30. Project Management Institute. *A Guide To The Project Management Body Of Knowledge: PMBOK Guide*. Project Management Institute; 3rd edition, October 31, 2004.

31. Rogers, Everett. *Diffusion of Innovations*, 5th Edition, Free Press; 5th edition, August 16, 2003.

32. Standard CMMI® Appraisal Method for Process Improvement (SCAMPI^SM), Version 1.1: Method Implementation Guidance for Government Source Selection and Contract Process Monitoring HANDBOOK CMU/SEI-2002-HB-002.

33. *The Standish Group Report—CHAOS* 1994, The Standish Group, Boston, published 1995.

34. Tim Olsen, QIC, Inc., Software Engineering Process Group Conference, Atlanta, GA, March 8–11, 1999, *Defining Software Processes In Expert Mode.*

35. Tolkien, J.R.R. *The Lord of the Rings*, Houghton Mufflin Company, Boston, Collector's Edition, November 1974.

36. Uhlfelder, Helene F. and Lawrence M. Miller. *Change Management: Creating the Dynamic Organization Through Whole System Architecture*, Miller Howard Publications, Atlanta, GA, December, 1997.

37. Wheatley, Margaret J. *Leadership and the New Science: Discovering Order in a Chaotic World*, Revised, Berrett-Koehler Publishers; San Francisco, CA; 1st edition, January 15, 2001.

38. Yourdon, Edward. *Death March—The Complete Software Developer's Guide to Surviving "Mission Impossible"*, Projects, Prentice Hall, Upper Saddle River, New Jersey, 1999.

39. Frederick W. Taylor. *The Principles of Scientific Management*, Harpers & Row Publishers, New York, 1911.

40. Blaise Pascal. *Pense'es and Other Writings*, A new translation by Honor Levi, Oxford University Press, Great Clarendon Street, Oxford, 1999.

41. Herzberg, Frederick. *Herzberg On Motivation*, Penton Media Inc, New York, New York, December 1, 1991.

Index

Auditing